CHILD DAY CARE

CHILD DAY CARE

EDITED BY
BRUCE HERSHFIELD
AND
KAREN SELMAN

Transaction Publishers
NEW BRUNSWICK (U.S.A.) AND LONDON (U.K.)

Copyright © 1997 by the Child Welfare League of America, Inc. Originally published as *Child Welfare*, vol. 74, no. 6, © 1995 Child Welfare League of America, Inc.

This book is printed on acid-free paper that meets the American National Standard for Permanence of Paper for Printed Library Materials.

Library of Congress Catalog Number: 96-17935
ISBN: 1-56000-910-1
Printed in the United States of America

Library of Congress Cataloging-in-Publication Data

Child day care / edited by Bruce Hershfield and Karen Selman.
    p. cm.
Includes bibliographical references.
ISBN 1-56000-910-1 (paper : alk. paper)
1. Child care services—United States. 2. Child welfare—United States. I. Hershfield, Bruce. II. Selman, Karen.
HQ778.63.C55 1996
362.7'12—dc20   96-17935
                                              CIP

CONTENTS

INTRODUCTION

With more parents in the workforce today than ever before, child day care has become an essential element of family life. In 1993, over 60% of mothers with children of preschool age were in the workforce; 66% of employed mothers with children under the age of six worked full-time; over 20% of mothers in the workforce were their family's sole wager earner; and over one million single fathers had children under the age of 18 [Poersch et al. 1994: 1]. More than half of all children under age six have parents in the workforce, and the mothers of 54% of these children are in the workforce [Poersch et al. 1994: 2].

Comprehensive child day care services[1] are not only important to our nation's economic well-being, but are also a vital part of the continuum of child welfare services. According to the Child Welfare League of America's *Standards of Excellence for Child Day Care Services,* "The purpose of child day care is to supplement and enhance the care, the attention to developmental needs, and the protection that children receive from their parents" [Child Welfare League of America 1991: 6]. The *Standards* define developmental child day care as supplying "a nurturing environment that cultivates the physical, emotional, intellectual, social, and cultural potential of the child as it helps all family members pursue their own individual and collective goals" [Child Welfare League of America 1991: 6].

Child day care services incorporate child development, nutrition, health, and family services; play a significant role as a preventive, remedial, and therapeutic service; and are used

---

1. Much variation exists in the field over the nomenclature of the services discussed in these articles. For clarity, this book uses the term *child day care* in referring to the broad range of programs known variously as child care, day care, early care and education, and early childhood education. Child day care may encompass center-based and family-based care, part-time or full-time care, and care that is licensed or regulated as well as care that is exempt. The term *family child care* is used in reference to care provided in a home other than the child's own. Family child care is one form of child day care.

to strengthen and support at-risk families. Comprehensive quality child day care, designed and provided as a child development and a child welfare service, promotes and supports families' own resources by supplementing—not replacing—the ability of families to meet their responsibilities.

- Stable, nurturing child day care environments make parents feel secure about their children's well-being. Although child day care services are often promoted and offered for purposes in which the interests of the child may appear to be a secondary consideration (such as enabling both parents or a single head-of-household parent to work or complete schooling or training), or as part of a support service to assist abusive parents or at-risk families, good quality child day care is also designed as a developmental and formative service for children.

- In some cases, child day care may serve a *remedial or therapeutic* function, responding to the psychological harm caused by abuse or neglect, deprivation, family instability, substance abuse, violence, or stress in the home; or to the consequences of congenital anomalies and developmental delays. Comprehensive, quality child day care has become an important component of a community's response to the growing problem of child abuse and neglect. A growing number of state and local public agencies are using child day care as part of their intervention and treatment programs. Research indicates that child day care provided in a location other than the child's own home can be extremely helpful to children who have been physically or sexually abused. Child day care also provides abused and neglected children with carefully structured assistance to maximize their development and their ability to engage constructively with caregivers and peers.

- Child day care serves a *preventive* function—it can help ameliorate the social, emotional, or health problems that may affect children and parents. It can help parents learn how to handle problems of child-rearing and family stress. Child day care strengthens and supports at-risk families by providing a safe and caring place for children while parents learn to cope with their difficulties and to alter their child-rearing behaviors.

The availability of child day care services also assists in the recruitment of foster parents who may work outside of the home and would otherwise be unavailable to provide care.

Although the goals of child day care are high, all too often the quality of the services provided are not. Studies indicate that a large portion of child day care is of mediocre to poor quality regardless of setting or governing auspices [Cost, Quality and Child Outcomes in Child Care Centers 1995:2, 8]. These studies, however, do identify indicators that can be helpful in raising the quality of child day care.

In family child care and care by relatives, a major predictor of quality is the desire of the provider or the relative to work with children. This "intentionality," described in the 1994 Families and Work Institute study on family child care and relative care, can be seen in the provider's involvement with others in the field, operation as a business, obtaining of continuing education and training, and license or regulatory status [Galinsky et al. 1994]. These characteristics demonstrate a professional commitment to the care of young children.

For center-based programs, several studies have also identified components of quality. The most important of these is the employment of a well-trained, experienced teaching staff. To recruit and retain such a staff, however, better wages and benefits are required than are currently available in most child day care centers. Teachers should have a college education and have specialized training in child development. Low child-to-staff ratios and small class sizes have also been found to be predictive of high quality care. The 1995 study *Cost, Quality, and Child Outcomes in Child Care Centers* found that states that had more demanding licensing standards had fewer poor-quality centers than those with relatively relaxed standards [Cost, Quality and Child Outcomes in Child Care Centers 1995: 4]. Other indicators of quality as determined by that study were the presence of experienced administrators, and a reliance on and access to sources of income other than parent fees.

This book encompasses these and other vital matters. Chapters linking child day care and child welfare; child day care, poverty, and welfare reform; and training and quality are presented because they are timely and critical if child day care is to continue to be a viable service to support and strengthen families. The effectiveness of specifically designed child day care programs for specialized populations and purposes is discussed in several of the chapters. The international overview of toddler day care and family support presented in one chapter (including implications for policy, program development, and practice) provides much food for thought for policymakers in this country. Finally, several chapters examine current thought and the innovations and collaborations that may change the future of child day care services.

Although child day care and family child care services have many roles—and the need for high quality services is acute—many questions must be considered and resolved if child day care is to maintain its place in the continuum of child welfare services. We hope this book will stimulate discussion and a search for solutions.

Bruce Hershfield
Director, CWLA Child Day Care Services

Karen Selman
Regional Director
Children's Home and Aid Society of Illinois

References

Cost, quality, and child outcomes in child care centers. (1995). Denver, CO: University of Colorado at Denver, Economics Department.

Child Welfare League of America. (1991). *Standards of excellence for child day care services.* Washington, DC: Author.

Galinsky, E., Howes, C., Kontos, S., & Shinn, M. (1994). *Study of children in family child care and relative care.* New York: Families and Work Institute.

Poersch, N., Adams, G., & Sandfort, J. (1994). *Child care and development.* Washington, DC: Children's Defense Fund.

1

Child Day Care: A Key Building Block of Family Support and Family Preservation Programs

Martha G. Roditti

With all of the stresses on families in the 1990s, child day care has become a necessity of life. While child day care services have always been a part of child welfare, they have sometimes taken a back seat to the crises that arise in protective services. As child welfare services are reframed to emphasize family support, strengths, and resiliencies, an enhanced role for child day care services is emerging. Using the Pyramid of Services model, this article organizes the complexity of child day care systems and delineates their place in the framework of family preservation and support services.

Martha G. Roditti, M.S.W., is Faculty Member, School of Social Work; Training Coordinator, Graduate Title IV-E Child Welfare Training Project; and Director, Undergraduate Family Preservation and Support Child Welfare Training Project, San Francisco State University, San Francisco, CA.

Child day care is one of the most frequently used and most cross-cultural and cross-class family service in the United States. With the unprecedented number of women in the work force, and the unrelenting stresses on family functioning, child day care can be an essential family support, family maintenance, and family preservation service. Without the support of child day care, many families are vulnerable to losing their struggle to stay healthy and are at increasing risk of becoming part of the child welfare system.

On the one hand, many social service practitioners have a parent-focused, utilitarian view of child day care, perceiving it chiefly as a service for parents who work or are in school, a place to keep children safe, or a place where children can learn. They often do not have a broad understanding of the variety of child day care choices, the components of quality in child day care, and the potential of child day care to link families with other services. On the other hand, quality child day care providers in centers and in family child care homes strive to deliver child-focused and developmentally appropriate services, but often miss the opportunity to involve and strengthen families. They undervalue their potential contribution to parents as role models and their ability to teach positive parent-child interactions.

This article offers a framework for viewing the relationship between child day care and social services. It utilizes family support and family preservation concepts and demonstrates the place of child day care in a pyramid of services. To understand these programs, it is important to first explore the background of the 1993 family support and family preservation legislation.

Family Support and Family Preservation: Reframing Social Services for Families

Family support services and family preservation services have been used by communities throughout the country for the past 20 years. Both services operate on the premise that the earlier services are provided to families, the better the chance of preventing problems. The family support and family preservation legislation passed as part of the Omnibus Budget Reconciliation Act of 1993 (P.L. 103–66) was designed to create a family-focused national system adapted to the needs of individual states. The services are directed toward "enhancing parents' ability to create stable, nurturing home environments that promote healthy child development; assisting children and families to resolve crises, connect with necessary and appropriate services, and to remain safely together in their homes; and avoiding unnecessary out-of-home placement of children, and helping children already in out-of-home care to be returned to and be maintained with their families or in another planned, permanent living arrangement" [Children's Bureau 1994].

The Congressional intent was to have each state plan in an inclusive and collaborative fashion. "Because the multiple needs of vulnerable children and families cannot be addressed adequately through categorical programs and fragmented service delivery systems, we encourage states to use the new program as a catalyst for establishing a continuum of coordinated and integrated, culturally relevant, family-focused services for children and families" [Children's Bureau 1994].

Family Support Services

Family support services are core services that should be accessible to all families. Such services are preventive, universally available, voluntary, and have no eligibility requirements. Their goals are to keep families strong, healthy, and intact by providing or linking them with a range of services that increase parents' confidence and competence in their parenting abilities, provide children with supportive and stable family environments, and enhance child development [Allen 1993].

Family support services have their origins in the 1960s and 1970s [Weissbourd 1994], when programs began providing the various types of supports that many nostalgically remember as once available in close-knit families and communities. The early programs tended to be child care programs such as Head Start, child care co-ops, and child care collectives that put heavy emphasis on parent participation. Many of the leaders in the child day care and parent support movements learned about family-focused care by actively involving themselves in their children's day care setting. Some of these leaders developed the early family resource centers, child care resource and referral lines, parenting hot lines or warm lines, and parent education programs.

The federal legislation defines family support services as "primarily community-based, preventive activities designed to alleviate stress and promote parental competencies and behaviors that increase the ability of families to successfully nurture their children; enable families to use other resources and opportunities available in the community; and create supportive networks to enhance child-rearing abilities of parents and help compensate for the increased social isolation and vulnerability of families" [Children's Bureau 1994].

Family Preservation Services

Family preservation services are family-focused, community-based services that are designed to help families cope with significant stresses or problems that interfere with the parents' ability to nurture their children, or to maintain the safety of their children within the family. They assist families in obtaining services and other supports in a manner that respects cultural and community differences [CDF 1994]. The more narrowly defined intensive family preservation services are designed for families in impending crisis or those already in crisis, particularly those at risk of having their children placed in out-of-home care. They are designed to be short-term, placement-preventive services, and are usually (but not always) accessed through referral to public child welfare programs [Allen 1993].

Family preservation services grew out of disillusionment with traditional child welfare services and a reaction to an out-of-home care system where children stayed longer than necessary, often in multiple placements, while families' priorities were ignored. The innovators in family preservation came from social work and child welfare services and designed programs that have provided alternatives to out-of-home care. Such alternatives are a significant part of Public Law 96–272 [Pecora et al. 1992; Beggs 1993]. Family preservation services depend on an infrastructure of family support services to provide ongoing basic support. They were "designed to help families alleviate crises that might lead to out-of-home placement of children; maintain the safety of children in their own homes; support families preparing to reunify or adopt; assist families in obtaining services and other supports necessary to address their multiple needs in a culturally sensitive manner. (If a child cannot be protected from harm without placement or the family does not have adequate strengths on which to build, family preservation services are not appropriate)" [Children's Bureau 1994].

Guiding Principles for Family Support and Family Preservation Services

The guiding principles for family support and family preservation, as articulated by the Children's Bureau, are based on a strengths perspective, are family-focused, and fit with the philosophy of quality child day care and development programs. They represent a paradigm shift from previous deficit and pathological models.

- The welfare and safety of children and of all family members must be maintained while strengthening and preserving the family whenever possible. Supporting families is the best way of promoting children's healthy development.
- Services focus on the family as a whole, looking toward identifying, enhancing, and respecting family strengths as opposed to focusing on family deficits or dysfunctions. Service providers work with families as partners

in identifying and meeting individual and family needs.

- Services are easily accessible (often delivered in the home or in community-based settings, using schedules convenient to parents) and are delivered in a manner that respects cultural and community differences.
- Services are flexible and responsive to real family needs. Linkages to a wide variety of supports and services outside the child welfare system (e.g., housing, substance abuse treatment, mental health, health, job training, child care) are generally crucial to meeting families' and children's needs.
- Services are community-based and involve community organizations and residents (including parents) in their design and delivery.
- Services are intensive enough to meet family needs and keep children safe. The level of intensity necessary to achieve these goals may vary greatly between preventive (family support) and crisis services [Children's Bureau 1994: 11].

The Place of Child Day Care in Family Support and Family Preservation Services

Child day care programs generally follow the above principles of family support and family preservation. Child day care program services are invaluable for teaching parents about child development, consistency, parenting, parent-child relations, boundary-setting, and the skills necessary to raise healthy children. Using child day care gives the family in stressful circumstances the breathing room needed to cope with vital survival and therapeutic issues. Over the past ten years, the population of people with the fastest growing need for services consists of parents with children under age five [Report of the Carnegie Task Force on Meeting the Needs of Young Children 1994]. Their children are the most vulnerable to abuse and neglect and the most in need of protection. "Child day care offers opportunities for reaching children early in life, and for giving support to families in times of strain and crisis, thus strengthening families and preventing difficulties. Many advocate that child day care should be a publicly supported service or social utility that any parent would be entitled to use by choice, and that would offer enriching developmental experiences to benefit all children. Programs such as these, born out of necessity, are common in developed counties all over the world" [Child Welfare League of America 1992: 14].

The Pyramid of Services and Its Relation to Child Care, Family Support, and Family Preservation

The Pyramid of Services (figure 1) model is a visualization of children's services that incorporates the values of family support and family preservation. "When communities are able to offer a pyramid of assistance that matches the pyramid of family needs, problems are likely to be solved or alleviated at earlier stages, when they are easier and less costly to address. As family needs grow in intensity, so do services to meet those needs" [Children's Defense Fund 1992].

The pyramid's premise is that families who receive appropriate services at any level of the pyramid often have a lessened need for services at the next level. Families can move up and down in their need for services and may use family support and other early intervention programs while they also use intensive family preservation programs. To be most effective, prevention services must intervene at the earliest possible point and must be coordinated so that families' needs can be dealt with comprehensively [Children's Defense Fund 1992]. Other efforts to conceptualize the organization of services for children and families include:

- **Arrays:** The Family Resource Coalition views family support services as an array of services throughout a

FIGURE 1
Building a Pyramid of Services

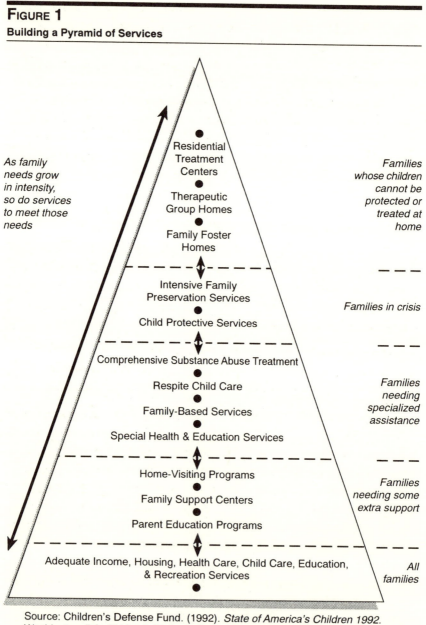

As family
needs grow
in intensity,
so do services
to meet those
needs

● Residential Treatment Centers
● Therapeutic Group Homes
● Family Foster Homes

Families whose children cannot be protected or treated at home

● Intensive Family Preservation Services
● Child Protective Services

Families in crisis

Comprehensive Substance Abuse Treatment
● Respite Child Care
● Family-Based Services
● Special Health & Education Services

Families needing specialized assistance

● Home-Visiting Programs
● Family Support Centers
● Parent Education Programs

Families needing some extra support

Adequate Income, Housing, Health Care, Child Care, Education, & Recreation Services
●

All families

Source: Children's Defense Fund. (1992). *State of America's Children 1992*.
Washington, DC: Chidren's Defense Fund. Used with permission.

community that serve the needs of all families [Allen 1993]. The arrays can be visualized as intersecting circles.

- **Matrix:** Los Angeles County conceives of services as a neighborhood-based central hub with services attached to one central service. The county has a family services system that includes a matrix of family support, family preservation, and alternative family services [Community Plan for Family Preservation in Los Angeles County 1992].
- **Continuum:** Some communities conceive of services in a linear fashion, as a continuum from least restrictive to most restrictive programs.

The following analysis of the various forms of child day care demonstrates how each fits into the Pyramid of Services at each level of the model.

Level 1: All Families

What services do all families need and how do they get them? All families need adequate income, food, clothing, housing, child care, education, and recreational services [CDF 1992].

Not all families are in trouble . . . yet. Many American families of all income levels function quite well and have fairly well-adjusted children. Those whose income is high enough can afford to purchase the basics of life and even some low-income families are able to access acceptable services. Unfortunately, the *availability* of these services is being eroded by underfinancing. Well-functioning families, regardless of income, may soon be facing significant losses in family resources.

Families need child care in order to work. Child care is increasingly essential for families where both parents work outside the home. Many parents believe it to be fundamental as well for reasons of their children's social and educational readiness. Although a large percentage of working parents of all income levels continue to use relatives for child day care, families are increasingly looking to child day care centers and family child care homes to provide their children with a secure and loving environment and the social and educational readiness they need for entry into elementary school. Personal preferences, family values, and cost are important parts of the process of choosing. The popular press has attempted to educate families about the various forms of child day care. An increasingly common form of support service, the child care resource and referral program, is particularly effective in linking parents with child day care services.

Low-income parents have more limited choices of child day care than do upper-income parents. Low-income families pay a disproportionate amount of their income for child day care. The U.S. General Accounting Office reports that such families pay more than one-fourth of the family's monthly income for child day care. Non-poor families pay about 7% of their income for such services [Child Care Law Center 1995].

Some quality state and federally subsidized child care programs have been available to low income-working parents and low-income parents in training programs. The availability of these subsidies is diminishing and federal budget cuts are threatening their future. In a time of growing poverty, "child care problems keep poor parents out of the work force" [(Child Care Law Center 1995]. Government-subsidized child day care programs enable families who are on the edge of poverty to work, prevent them from falling into welfare dependency, and provide social support. They enable families on AFDC to be trained and to become self-sufficient. They offer children a developmentally supportive and protective environment. Federally funded child day care programs include the Child Care and Development Block Grant, the At-Risk Child Care Program, and child care entitlements currently available to AFDC recipients who are in job training or who are making the transition to work. The federal government funds Head Start, a part-time, part-year social service and child development program. Many states offer subsidized child care programs using state funds. In California, for example, the state's comprehensive child day care program funds full day care and part day care for children of high-risk parents, low-income parents, and parents in training programs, as well as care for migrant children, disabled children, and children of teen parents. California also funds child care resource and referral programs in every county to link parents with the full range of public and private child care. Local cities and counties and United Way and foundations fund basic as well as innovative child care programs.

Families need child care programs during normal life transitions. With the growing number of single-parent families and the reduced availability of extended family and community supports, parents are increasingly relying on child day care personnel as experts who can understand them and educate them during the normal crises of child-rearing, such as toilet training of their children and teaching socialization skills. Some parents look to child day care programs, staff members, and other parents for support during the increasingly common crises of divorce and separations, as well as other conditions of living formerly handled by the extended family. Many quality programs have been able to build in social work services, mental health consultation programs, or referrals to services to help families through difficult times.

Families need to have reasonable access to child day care. Families in which the parents work rely heavily on child day care, but how do they find it? Parents in all kinds of families find child day care by asking friends, other parents, relatives, looking on bulletin boards, reading the paper, checking the phone book, and/or using their local child care resource and referral agency [Powell & Eisenstadt 1982]. Some families find child day care through their local public welfare department. Although child day care is a basic program, it is also a complex system to access. Parents need to know what they want and what they can afford before they choose. The child care resource and referral service is a "community-based service that offers parents consultation and assistance in their search for quality child care; offers children enhanced resources for safe and developmentally appropriate care, offers providers consultation, including technical assistance, training and support . . . ; and offers the community data, planning, policy analysis, education, and advocacy on child care needs and supply" [Child Welfare League of America 1992: 121]. In every state, child care resource and referral agencies are support services that deal with the supply and demand aspects of child day care. Resource and referral counselors help parents through the maze of the local public and private child care system; help them clarify affordability, accessibility, and availability; help them find subsidized child care if eligible; and provide an entry into the wide array of parenting services.

Parents who access child day care services need to find providers with the flexibility to adapt to parental work schedules. Most working parents need child care programs that open early and close late. With the reduction of jobs due to changes in the economy, a growing number of parents are forced to work evening shifts, necessitating alternative evening child care. Since this form of child day care is almost nonexistent, many children are left alone while their parents work at night. In addition, working parents need child care programs to care for sick children. Staying home with a sick child could mean loss of wages and possibly loss of a job to the parent. For most people, the live-in or reasonably available relative is no longer a child day care option.

What Happens if Families Don't Have Child Day Care?

The lack of child day care in any of its forms can deprive a child of the continuity of close friends, a loving caregiver, and developmental support. The loss of child day care can result in the parents' loss of a job and the loss of a significant support system of caregivers and peers. Child day care may be the one factor that keeps a single parent economically independent, or that gives a child structure, intellectual stimulation, and predictability. The loss of care can add enormous stress on families that are already fragile, pushing them into level 2 of the pyramid.

Level 2: Families Needing Extra Support

What services do families access when they need more than the basics?

The concept of family resource and support has gained popularity in the past ten years. Family resource and support programs are designed to be universally available to all families and to "provide emotional, informational, and instrumental assistance to young and older families, particularly to families isolated by poverty, joblessness, poor health, or other factors" [Kagan & Weissbourd 1994]. The programs offer families easy access to a range of useful services and are helpful for the family that has many basic strengths, but needs extra support because of life stresses. The programs are responsive to parents' needs and make available a range of services, including hot lines, warm lines, drop-in groups, respite care, counseling, and parenting classes.

Family resource and support centers. Child day care plays a significant role in social support networks for families [Long 1983; Powell 1987]. Since child day care programs exist in virtually every neighborhood in America, they could be enhanced to act as family support centers. Some quality child day care programs already provide services to families and are considered by many as the least stigmatizing form of support for those who need extra help. Indeed, the original Head Start model was designed to offer parents extra social services and parent education for themselves and their children within the developmental and educational services of child day care.

Rather than develop isolated family support services and family resource centers, efforts should be intensified to layer these services into already existing programs. With adequate funding, quality child day care programs can act as a base for family support programs. Garbarino and colleagues [1993], in *Children in Danger*, see child day care programs as an important source of support for young children and their families. The authors believe that child day care can foster resiliency and act as a protective factor for children who live in troubled and often violent environments, and that the strong and continued relationships with mature adults, the predictable environment, and the opportunities to enhance self-esteem are all part of a child care culture that can change a child's life.

This is not a novel idea. The Child Welfare League of America [1989] recommended that all family support centers have child day care programs attached to them or work closely with a neighborhood child day care program. Traditionally, neighborhood houses or settlement houses have always had a child day care program as part of their services to parents. This service connection worked well in times past and should be revisited.

Parenting programs. While many social service programs develop their own parenting programs for their clients, they may be unaware that they are duplicating activities already in place. Child day care programs see parents twice a day and have ongoing opportunities to observe the growth and development of children and their relationship with their parents. They often offer parents support groups, education programs, and conferences with teachers. The well-trained staff of child day care programs can be the first line of support for a family undergoing stress and can increase parents' confidence in their abilities.

Child development. "Developmental child care supplies a nurturing environment that cultivates the physical, emotional, intellectual, social, and cultural potential of the child" [Child Welfare League of America 1992]. Full-day child day care programs, both family child care and center-based care, have encouraged strong child development components. Part-day programs such as Head Start were designed to provide developmental programming for children while involving their parents. Co-ops have been traditionally used by parents for child development and social support. These programs depend on well-trained and educated staff members to provide the consistency and quality demanded by children and parents.

Respite care. Unlike previous generations, many parents in the 1990s do not have grandparents or relatives easily accessible for evening and weekend support or the occasional time out. The families that need some informal form of respite child care are often those who are least able to afford it or access it. Babysitting cooperatives and exchanges can meet this need. They are available through child care resource and referral programs and could be developed in child care programs and family resource centers.

What Happens if Families Don't Have Child Day Care?

Child day care may be only one of a variety of services families use, but it may be the link that enables parents to attend training or counseling, or go to a parenting class and receive the information and coping skills that could prevent a crisis at a later time. Children benefit from the stable interpersonal attachments and grow psychologically and socially. When parents have marginal support systems and are isolated, they may be psychologically vulnerable and may make unwise life choices that are risky for their children. The family on the edge may move to Level 3.

Level 3: Families Needing Specialized Assistance

Some families need special programs such as comprehensive substance abuse treatment, respite child care, family-based services, and special health and education services.

Family support programs may not be enough for some families who are having problems coping. These families may need a form of family-focused casework service that is intended to aid in keeping the family together and to prevent the escalation of a crisis. Families often move up and down in levels of need depending on the level of crisis in their life, sometimes needing particularly focused services, sometimes needing particularly flexible services. Child day care has important roles to play on this level of service. "For the child who has been deprived of experiences that stimulate intellectual, social, and emotional development, the child day care program has an even greater opportunity to supply the developmental learning and socialization experiences a child in our society requires" [Child Welfare League of America 1992].

Family-focused services. Social work services located in child day care programs can be effective in providing family-focused early intervention [Child Welfare League of America 1992]. Well-trained social workers and child development experts make a powerful intervention and support team. They can build on the trust developed in the child day care center to help a family through a crisis. They can evaluate the need and enable parents to use other services, including substance abuse treatment programs, mental health services, and special-needs services, when appropriate [Seitz et al. 1985). These services are first-line interventions in child abuse and neglect situations. Some visionary child day care programs have continued to seek funds for social work services to meet the increasing needs of parents. Professional social work services, however, are minimally available to child day care programs and are rarely found in family child care homes and small centers [Kadushin & Martin 1988]. This is due, in part, to the emphasis by most child day care programs on the child as the focus of attention and not on the needs of the child as a part of a family system; in part, to the lack of social workers trained to work in a child day care setting; and, in part, to the cost of these services.

Substance abuse treatment and on-site child day care. With the avalanche of crack-addicted young mothers with very young children, substance abuse treatment programs have had to adjust their male-oriented model of services to one more oriented to women and families [Nelson-Zlupko et al. 1994]. While a dearth of programs for substance-abusing women continues, the few innovative programs are involving children in their service constellation. Without child day care, the woman cannot complete her inpatient or outpatient program and may either leave or relapse. The alternative to serving the children of the addicted women in residential settings is almost always removal of the children from the mother's care and placement in out-of-home care. Providing on-site child day care is an important component of residential treatment, outpatient, and day treatment programs. When child day care programs are added to substance abuse treatment programs, however, planners should carefully think through the quality of the child day care program and its significant potential for long-lasting value in terms of the child's development and socialization and the enhancement of parent-child relationships. When viewed as an integral part of a family-focused substance abuse program instead of as an afterthought, child day care becomes an essential component of the therapeutic program that a substance abusing parent receives.

Child day care for teen parents. If we really wished to reduce school dropout rates for young parents, we would provide quality, available, affordable child day care for them. Young parents cannot attend school without child day care and most cannot afford infant care. The grandmothers and aunts who used to care for these children a generation ago cannot afford to stay home; they are now working.

While educators agree that child day care is important for teen parents, the expense is a barrier to the provision of services. Experience in teen parenting programs has demonstrated that

social services, child development, education and training, and
child day care are essential in reducing adolescent school dropout rates and repeat pregnancies, and in enhancing parenting
skills. The mentoring provided by well-trained child day care
providers, the positive environment, the well-supervised counseling, and a nurturing parenting program can help keep adolescents girls in school [Sipe & Batten 1994; Loomis 1987].

Respite care and crisis nurseries. "Respite, temporary relief for
caregivers and families, is a service in which care is provided to
children with disabilities, chronic or terminal illnesses, and/or
children at risk of abuse and neglect. Respite can occur in out-of-
home settings for any length of time depending on the needs of
the family and available resources. Crisis nurseries are a type of
respite that focuses on children at risk of abuse and neglect. As a
vital part of the continuum of services for families, respite helps
prevent out-of-home placement and possible abuse and neglect
situations, preserves the family unit, and supports family stability" [ARCH 1994].

Respite services, while highly effective, are poorly funded
and very limited. They are available as separate services or
through family support programs, family preservation programs, some limited child care resource and referral programs,
and public child welfare programs. There are many models of
respite: (1) center-based models in a licensed child day care
facility designed as a crisis nursery to provide around the clock,
full-year services; (2) center-based models that have contracted
with an existing child day care facility for emergency services
during regular center times of operation; (3) crisis shelters working with existing programs for families; (4) family child care
homes with foster care licenses caring for children on a crisis
basis 24 hours a day; (5) crisis nurseries—in home models providing child care services within a parent's home [Broughton
1992]; and (6) subsidized vendor voucher models providing

short-term crisis child care using a choice of trained family child care homes and centers.

Therapeutic nurseries and special health and education services. Child day care is essential for parents who have children with special mental health, health, and educational needs. Therapeutic nurseries are the most difficult services to find for children with special needs and are among the most expensive. The availability of child day care for ill children or children with special needs would reduce greatly the stress on any family faced with a challenging child; child day care is a service that can also help the children cope.

Children prenatally exposed to drugs and/or alcohol can benefit greatly from the assistance of sensitive child day care providers. Well-informed providers can offer intelligent support to families whose infants have these risk factors. The prognosis for the children's development can be positive when well-trained child day care providers use a strengths and protective factors model instead of a deficit model to provide consistent, specialized services to troubled children [Myers & Kaltenbach 1992].

What Happens If Families Don't Have Child Day Care?

The Pyramid of Services is cumulative. If parents do not have the foundation of social support, they will lack the resiliency to cope with stress, will be susceptible to major and minor crises, and will possibly be at risk of abusing and neglecting their children. Child day care as a concrete service that provides emotional support should be a part of any coordinated system of services for high-risk parents. Without the full complement of full-day, part-day, and emergency child day care for infants and toddlers, pre-schoolers, and school-age children in centers and in family child care homes, troubled parents cannot take advantage of services available to them, and children may not have the advantages of cognitive, developmental, and social supports that will advance their healthy growth. The family that remains isolated may find its needs escalating into level 4.

Level 4: Families in Crisis

Families who are at risk of breaking down and are strong candidates for child welfare system intervention are in need of this level of service. Timely intervention, intensive services, and an emphasis on family strengths and empowerment may prevent out-of-home placement.

Intensive family preservation services. The strategies used in many models of intensive family preservation are home-based and include a full use of community resources. Families referred to these programs are in crisis and have children at immediate risk of out-of-home placement. Most programs stipulate that the family must have sufficient strengths available to them and must voluntarily work with the family preservation service. In addition, the family's situation must be of such intensity that other less comprehensive services would not be sufficient to solve the problem.

For families with young children, child day care must be a core referral service in the family-focused plan. The range of child day care services—from infant care to after school—should be part of the effort used by a well-trained family preservation worker to intervene with and stabilize the family. Using the services of child care resource and referral agencies can help the worker navigate the various child day care programs and their requirements. Though limited, there are some options. Since the families involved are at risk of abusing and or neglecting their children, they are the priority for many subsidized child day care programs, respite care programs, crisis nurseries, and therapeutic child care services. Special education programs in school districts are sometimes available, but workers will need to be advocates to demonstrate the child's need. Social workers who are able to assemble innovative "wraparound child day care," creating full-day, emergency care or 24-hour care using scarce child day care resources can help families avoid out-of-home placement of their children when emergencies occur. These arrangements all require close cooperation and coordination with child day care and social service family-oriented agencies.

Child protective services. Child day care is often the safest place for children who have just entered the child welfare system and are still living with their parents. This includes children who are in home situations that are not so dire as to require the child's removal, but who have significant familial problems and need voluntary child protective services. It also includes children who are court dependents living at home who need the protection of child day care while their parents are attempting to fulfill time-limited court requirements. These are often the children and families who are at risk of being separated by placement and who can best benefit from family preservation services.

A strong, respectful partnership between child welfare workers and child day care programs can strengthen case planning, facilitate family maintenance, and sensitize decision-making. If a child is in child day care, child welfare workers have the opportunity to utilize the child development knowledge of child day care staff members when the workers formulate their assessments of family interactions, strengths, and child risk. When child welfare workers view the child day care agency as a partner, they begin to comprehend the importance of the attachments the child has to the people in the program. For some children, removal from their home *and* their child day care arrangement is a double separation that may prove devastating to the child's sense of self. The relationship the child has with his or her child day care provider may be the most trusting and consistent relationship in his or her life. Continuity of child day care after out-of-home placement may be a stabilizing factor for the child.

Child day care and mental health consultation. While child day care is an excellent resource for families experiencing stress, child care workers are often unprepared for the serious problems these families present. Ongoing training and support from specialists in social work, child development, and child and family mental health can aid child day care program staff in their efforts to serve troubled families. Since few child day care programs have on-site social workers and mental health specialists, many use specialized child day care mental health consultation services available from family service agencies, hospitals, child care resource and referral agencies, and mental health centers.

What happens if families don't have child day care?

For troubled families, child day care is an essential thread in a strand of services that allows the family to remain unified. Sometimes, however, child day care and other supportive services are not enough. Some parents are unable to mobilize themselves to use child day care when it is made available to them, or conditions at home are so unsafe for their children that child day care personnel or other individuals report the parents for child abuse or neglect. Some vulnerable families are so overwhelmed that they enter level 5 and the child welfare system.

Level 5: Families Whose Children Cannot Be Protected or Treated at Home

"The number of children in foster care rose by 68% between 1982 and 1992. An estimated 442,000 children were in foster care in June 1992" [Children's Defense Fund 1994]. When the foundation for the pyramid erodes, the rest of the services disintegrate as well. As the basic social support infrastructure programs a family has and the help it receives in small emergencies diminishes, other crises begin to occur. When parents are unable to fulfill their roles, their children are placed in out-of-home care, relative care, or institutions. Child day care, however, continues to have a role for children in such placements.

Residential treatment centers and therapeutic group homes. Some residential treatment centers are diversifying and developing therapeutic child day care programs for younger children, using the center's professional staff members as additional sources of support. Programs serving teen mothers in residential settings, such as Florence Crittenton homes, often provide infant care and parenting services on-site for their young parents [Mayden 1994].

Foster family homes. Foster parents are reflecting the trend of all Americans: they are becoming working parents in order to survive financially. As such, they need child day care for their foster children while they work. Concurrently, the children in family foster care are more troubled than those in previous generations [Pasztor & Wynne 1995]. While foster parents are committed to their role, some of the children for whom they care present unusual challenges that require additional services. Many children demonstrate significant emotional problems, are in need of special stimulation, or have unusual physical problems such as HIV/AIDS. Therapeutic child day care and respite care are essential to support foster parents' efforts in parenting, to relieve stress, and to ensure the stability of placement and the retention of the foster parent. Child care providers can be essential allies to foster parents in their work with children [Barney et al. 1994].

Relative care or kinship care. The number of relatives who care for children in the child welfare system has increased in the past 10 years [Children's Defense Fund 1994]. Relatives are often grandparents and parents' siblings. While relatives offer their hearts and homes to children they, like foster parents, often need to work to support their families. Child day care is essential to their ability to stay employed. Respite care and therapeutic child day care are also necessary as the children for whom relatives care often present emotional and physical challenges.

Conclusion

This article has attempted to show the linkages between family support programs, family preservation programs, and child day care, using the Pyramid of Services model. The relationships among these programs are complex. When used wisely, however, the programs can have a beneficial effect on all families, typical and vulnerable.

Family preservation and family support programs have re-framed our view of family services. Gone are the narrow clinical programs that served a few families who knew where to find them. Community and family-friendly models have emerged that have the capacity to solve service delivery dilemmas and reach families in need before they collapse. Child day care can no longer be seen as separate from the mainstream of family services; it is a viable service in a new construct of programs.

Child day care programs can be found in every small town, city, county, and state. They are the backbone of services for all families. Parents discover them anew every year with every new child. Children grow and develop as a result of the care of nurturing providers. The family focus of family preservation and family support can utilize the unique elements of child day care as a vehicle for family empowerment. All parents—healthy, troubled, young, and old, of all cultures and classes—use the vast array of child care services in all levels of need. ◆

References

Allen, M. (1993). *Definitions for family programs.* Chicago: National Resource Center on Family Based Services.

ARCH. (1994). *Respite: Prevention, preservation and family support.* Chapel Hill, NC: Access to Respite Care and Help, ARCH National Resource Center for Crisis Nurseries and Respite Care Services.

Barney, M., Levin, J., & Smith, N. (1994). Respite for foster parents. *ARCH fact sheet number 32*. Chapel Hill, NC: Access to Respite Care and Help, ARCH National Resource Center for Crisis Nurseries and Respite Care Services.

Beggs, M. (1993). *Family preservation programs: State's successful new strategy to keep children at home*. San Francisco: Zellerbach Family Fund.

Broughton, B. (1992). Crisis nursery care: Respite for children at risk of abuse and/or neglect. *ARCH fact sheet number 1* (revised 1994). Chapel Hill, NC: Access to Respite Care and Help, ARCH National Resource Center for Crisis Nurseries and Respite Care Services.

Child Care Law Center. (1995). Child care as welfare prevention. In *Working for change*. San Francisco: Author.

Child Welfare League of America. (1989). *Standards for services to strengthen and preserve families with children*, Washington, DC: Author.

Child Welfare League of America. (1992). *Standards of excellence for child day care services*, Washington, DC: Author.

Children's Bureau. (1994). *Program instructions log no. ACYF-PI-94–01* (pp. 5–15). Washington, DC: U.S. Department of Health and Human Services, Administration on Children, Youth and Families.

Children's Defense Fund. (1992). *State of America's children 1992* (pp. 65–70). Washington, DC: Author.

Children's Defense Fund. (1994). *State of America's children 1994*. Washington, DC: Author.

Community plan for family preservation in Los Angeles County. (1992). Los Angeles: Commission for Children's Services, Family Preservation Services.

Garbarino, J., Dubrow, N., Kostelny, K., & Pardo, C. (1993). *Children in danger: Coping with the consequences of community violence* (pp. 134–172). San Francisco: Jossey-Bass Publishers.

Kadushin, A., & Martin J. (1988). *Child welfare* (4th ed.). New York: Macmillan Publishing Company.

Kagan, S. L., & Weissbourd, B. (1994). *Putting families first: America's family support movement and the challenge of change*. San Francisco: Jossey-Bass Publishers.

Long, F. (1983). Social support networks in day care and early child development. In J. Whittaker & J. Garbarino (Eds.), *Social support networks: Informal helping in the human services*. New York: Aldine Publishing Company.

Loomis, A. (1987). *A public-private partnership for school dropout prevention of pregnant and parenting teens*. San Francisco: The Teenage Pregnancy and Parenting Project, Family Service Agency of San Francisco.

Mayden, B. (1994). Florence Crittenton Homes: The 20th century. *Children's Voice, 4*(1), 12–13.

Myers, B. J., & Kaltenbach, K. (1992). Cocaine-exposed infants: Myths and misunderstandings. *Zero to Three, 13*.

Nelson-Zlupko, L., Kauffman, E., & Dore, M. M. (1994). Gender differences in drug addiction and treatment: Implications for social work intervention with substance-abusing women. *Social Work, 72*, 45–54.

Pasztor, E. M., & Wynne, S. F., (1995). *Foster parent retention and recruitment: The state of the art in practice and policy*. Washington, DC: Child Welfare League of America.

Pecora P. J., Whittaker, J. K., & Maluccio, A. N. (1992). *The child welfare challenge: Policy, practice and research*. New York: Aldine De Gruyter.

Powell, D. R., & Eisenstadt, J. R. (1982). Parents' searches for child care and the design of information services. *Children and Youth Services Review, 4*, 239–253.

Powell, D. R. (1987). Day care as family support system. In S. L. Kagan, D. R. Powell, B. Weissbourd, & E. F. Ziegler (Eds.), *America's family support programs*. New Haven, CT: Yale University Press.

The Report of the Carnegie Task Force on Meeting the Needs of Young Children. (1994). *Starting points: Meeting the needs of our youngest children*. New York: Carnegie Corporation of New York.

Seitz, V., Rosenbaum, L. K., & Apfel, N. H. (1985). Effects of family support intervention: A ten-year follow up. *Child Development, 56*, 376–391.

Sipe, C. L., & Batten, S. T. (1994). *School-based programs for adolescent parents and their young children: Overcoming barriers and challenges to implementing comprehensive school-based services*. Bala Cynwyd, PA: Center for Assessment and Policy Development.

Weissbourd, B. (1994). The evolution of the family resource movement. In S. L. Kagan & B. Weissbourd (Eds.), *Putting families first: America's family support movement and the challenge of change* (pp. 28–47). San Francisco: Jossey-Bass Publishers.

2

Child Day Care in Welfare Reform: Are We Targeting Too Narrowly?

Marcia K. Meyers

Welfare reform efforts at both the state and federal levels are emphasizing work and economic self-sufficiency for participants in Aid to Families with Dependent Children (AFDC), the primary welfare program for families. Although child day care assistance for welfare recipients has expanded substantially in recent years, coverage remains extremely limited and narrowly targeted by parents' activity status. In a study reported in this article, data from interviews with AFDC recipients suggest that efforts to increase target efficiency in public child day care subsidies by narrowly restricting eligibility may be reducing effectiveness on related policy goals by reducing access for those in need.

Marcia K. Meyers, Ph.D., is Assistant Professor, Department of Public Administration, Maxwell School of Citizenship and Public Affairs, Syracuse University, Syracuse, NY.

Welfare reform efforts at both the state and federal levels emphasize work and economic self-sufficiency for participants in Aid to Families with Dependent Children (AFDC), the primary welfare program for families. The emphasis on moving parents of young children into the labor force has elevated child day care from a peripheral to a central concern in welfare policy.

Background

Affordable child day care is important to working parents. A large and still growing majority of women with young children are in the workforce, and most rely on nonmaternal care during their working hours [Hofferth et al. 1991]. Consistent with an intuitive understanding of the role of child day care in work decisions, researchers have demonstrated that high child day care costs discourage women's entry into paid labor [Ribar 1992; Blau & Robins 1988, 1991].

The cost and availability of child day care may be especially important for low-income families and for families trying to make the transition from welfare to self-sufficiency. One-quarter of young, unemployed mothers report that they are out of the labor force because of child day care problems; the fraction of poor mothers citing child day care problems is even greater (34%) [Cattan 1991]. When asked directly about how the availability of child day care affects their employment decisions, substantial fractions of unemployed low-income and AFDC recipient parents report that they would seek work if satisfactory and affordable child day care were available [Presser & Baldwin 1980; Kisker et al. 1989; Seigel & Loman 1991]. The U.S. General Accounting Office [1994b] estimates that fully subsidizing child day care could increase the proportion of poor mothers in paid employment from 29% to 44%. Kimmel [1994] estimates that child day care subsidies would increase the probability of labor force participation among single parent welfare recipients from its current level of 12% to as much as 38%.

As the focus of welfare reform efforts shifted during the 1980s to emphasize work and economic self-sufficiency, federal and state policymakers created several new child day care subsidies to assist the population of low-income families expected to achieve economic self-sufficiency outside the welfare system. Child day care subsidies created through JOBS, Title IV-A of the Social Security Act, the Child Care Development Block Grant, and other federal and state sources specifically and narrowly targeted benefits for parents who were using, exiting, or at risk of entering the welfare system.

Despite this substantial increase in federal child day care funding, coverage for the at-risk population remained extremely limited in the early 1990s. In 1992, for example, four new federal child day care programs provided over $2 billion in new child day care funds to reduce welfare dependency. Even after this expansion, only 5% to 6% of the AFDC caseload received AFDC child day care subsidies, and less than 30% of JOBS program participants received child day care assistance from *any* funding source [U.S. General Accounting Office 1994a].

As federal and state policymakers continue efforts to reform welfare, it is critically important to understand why categorical child day care subsidies failed to assist such a large fraction of the potentially eligible target populations.

Inadequate funding is the first and most obvious explanation for limited assistance. Although both child day care tax credits and direct federal funding for child day care expanded substantially in the last decade, child day care funding still fell far short of need. A 1992 Children's Defense Fund study reported that half of all states spent less than $25 per child per year on child day care [Adams & Sandfort 1992]. Waiting lists for subsidized care remained long; Texas, for example, estimated that at least 40,000 children were waiting for services and an estimated 255,000 children were on waiting lists in California [U.S. General Accounting Office 1994a].

Inadequate federal funding was exacerbated by financing mechanisms that created incentives for states to ration assistance and underutilize those funds that were available. For example, few states drew down all the matching funds available under the JOBS, Transitional Child Care, and At-Risk programs [U.S. House of Representatives 1994]. Because these funds required a substantial state match, financially strapped states rationed services, shifted resources from other groups such as the working poor to meet AFDC child day care obligations, and substituted nonmatching funds (e.g., from the Child Care and Development Block Grant) for those that required a state match [Hagen & Lurie 1992; Ebb 1994]. The loss of assistance was substantial. As of August 1993, states had failed to use 21% of fiscal year 1992 federal funds under the Title IV-A At Risk child day care program for the working poor [Ebb 1994].

Narrow categorical targeting of benefits created a third obstacle to adequate assistance. As federal and state funding expanded, so too did the number of categorical programs and the complexity of eligibility, application, and benefit rules. Even before the expansion of child day care subsidies between 1988 and 1990, there were at least 46 separate federal child day care programs [U.S. General Accounting Office 1989]. Most tied eligibility for assistance to quite specific characteristics of parents, including income, employment and welfare status, and created program-specific eligibility criteria, benefit ceilings, and regulatory standards. As the U.S. General Accounting Office [1994a] noted, "despite similarities among families in all programs, the patchwork of child day care funding makes fine distinctions among categories of families" [p. 8]. Highly targeted, categorical assistance created gaps in service, breaks in eligibility, and extremely complex and often time-consuming application procedures.

Many states have taken steps to integrate the growing number of child day care programs, but few have succeeded in creating truly seamless services [U.S. General Accounting Office 1994a; U.S. Advisory Commission on Intergovernmental Relations 1994]. Ross and Kerachsky [1995] have described the coordination of child day care subsidies in a sample of 23 cities along a continuum from integrated to mixed systems. In the relatively more integrated systems, at least a portion of public child day care subsidies are administered by a single administrative entity, program rules are harmonized, and single points of entry are created for accessing assistance and making transitions between programs. Even these integrated systems, however, typically exclude some forms of assistance (e.g., Head Start), have limited success in facilitating parents' transitions between programs (e.g., between welfare-based assistance and Transitional Child Care), and perpetuate significant categorical barriers (e.g., by locating services in local welfare offices). In cities with relatively less integrated—or mixed systems—parents are able to apply for help through multiple points of entry, but have little assurance that they will receive complete information or access to a full range of benefits at any entry point.

Study Questions

Although policymakers in Washington, D.C., and the states have expanded child day care assistance for low-income families, the resulting patchwork of highly targeted, categorical subsidies may have created substantial obstacles for the very clients who were in need of help. Public child day care policies need to strike a balance between many competing policy goals, including equity, accessibility, cost, quality, and administrative and target efficiency [Meyers 1990; Hofferth & Phillips 1991; Ross & Kerachsky 1995]. The narrow categorical eligibility criteria that were adopted in the 1980s and 1990s were well suited to increasing the target efficiency of child day care subsidies because they limited access, including only clients with the greatest identified need. Effectiveness on this dimension has to be weighed, however, against success in achieving other policy goals, including equity, accessibility, and coordination on related policy goals such as promoting economic self-sufficiency.

The analysis reported in this article uses data from California to examine the effectiveness of categorical child day care subsidies in providing assistance to targeted groups of welfare recipients in 1993. Three criteria are considered: (1) Were potential recipients aware that they were entitled to benefits?; (2) Were benefits limited to target groups?; and (3) Were members of target groups receiving benefits?

Six different child day care subsidies were studied, representing variations in the scope and target of categorical restrictions adopted by 1990. The first, GAIN* child day care, targeted AFDC recipients in school, training, or job search activities designed to increase self-sufficiency. AFDC recipients with children under age 13 were entitled to benefits if they were participating in approved education and training programs and if local resources permitted.

Two of the six programs studied were designed to help AFDC recipients make the transition from welfare to work. The Transitional Child Care (TCC) program provided up to 12 months of child day care assistance to AFDC recipients who left welfare through work. The AFDC disregard allowed current AFDC recipients who were working to disregard a portion of their employment income that was spent on child day care.

Two additional programs were categorically restricted by children's ages, but not necessarily by parents' activities. Head Start was a means-tested federally funded preschool program for children ages three to five. Free or reduced cost after-school care (funded by a mixture of state and federal funds) was available to a portion of income-eligible families with older children in most California communities. Head Start and after-school programs were not tied to parents' activities, but because funds were limited, local programs may have given priority to employed parents or those in school.

---

*The California JOBS program authorized by the Family Support Act.

Finally, the Child and Dependent Care Income Tax Credit was a nonrefundable tax credit that could be used to reduce tax liability for a portion of income that was spent on private child day care. Benefits were restricted to parents with employment earnings and with children under age 14.

Methods

Sample

This study used data from a stratified random sample of AFDC recipients in California to analyze recipients' knowledge and use of various targeted child day care programs. The sample for the analysis is a subset of a sample created by the California Department of Social Services and University of California Berkeley [Survey Research Center 1994]. The original sampling frame for the study included all AFDC cases open in four California counties (Los Angeles, San Bernardino, San Joaquin, and Alameda) as of December 1, 1992. A random sample of 15,000 cases was drawn from this frame using state Medicaid records. The sample was stratified by county (to include 6,000 cases from Los Angeles and 3,000 each from the remaining counties) and case type (to oversample two-parent AFDC cases). All 15,000 cases were later assigned to "experimental" or "control" status and subjected to differing AFDC benefits and program rules.

Telephone interviews were conducted with a randomly selected subsample of approximately 15% of all families headed by an adult who spoke English or Spanish. Surveys were conducted in 1994 by the Survey Research Center at the University of California, Berkeley. A total of 2,214 household heads were successfully interviewed.

This study used a subset of the survey by limiting analysis to cases headed by a single mother (AFDC-FG cases) with at least one child under the age of 14. A total of 1,343 cases were available for analysis. The sample was weighted to represent the cases in the four counties, and should be generalized to larger populations of AFDC recipients with caution. Because none of the elements of the state demonstration concerned child day care, cases subject to both "experimental" and "control" conditions were included in this analysis. Statistical tests revealed no significant interaction between experimental status and any of the analysis in this paper.

Measures

The structured telephone interview included questions about family and household characteristics, labor market and educational activities, household and individual income, and welfare receipt. Each respondent with at least one child under age 14 was asked to describe current child day care and payment arrangements for their youngest child. Respondents' knowledge of child day care subsidies was measured by a series of questions about nine differently targeted child day care programs. Interviewers asked whether the respondent had used or applied for help through the program, or whether they had ever heard of the services.

Different child care programs were described by both program name (e.g., "Transitional Child Care") and in terms of the type of assistance available (e.g., "child day care for people who are going off welfare") (see figure 1). For those respondents who had any experience with each of the programs, interviewers probed for their subsequent receipt of aid.

Limitations

The sample used in this analysis was well suited to describing characteristics of current AFDC recipients, but it had some important features that limit generalization. Most obviously, it is a sample of cases from four counties in a single state and may not reflect the experiences of AFDC recipients in other regions. California exemplifies a mixed and minimally integrated system for managing child day care subsidies. At the time of the survey, California was relatively more generous than other states in both

FIGURE 1

Child Day Care Knowledge and Use Survey Questions

Asked of all single-parent AFDC recipients with child under age 14

- How about GAIN child care? In the last 12 months, have you used or applied for that kind of help or haven't you ever heard of child care services provided by GAIN?

- How about NET child care or non-GAIN education and training child care, which you get through the AFDC office while you go to school? In the last 12 months, have you used or applied for that kind of help or haven't you ever heard of this program?

- How about TCC or transition or "at-risk" child care for people who are going off welfare? In the last 12 months, have you used or applied for that kind of help or haven't you ever heard of this program?

Asked of all single-parent AFDC recipients with child under age 6

- How about Head Start or other public preschool or child development programs? In the last 12 months, have you used or applied for that kind of program?

Asked of all single-parent AFDC recipients with child between 6 and 13

- How about free or reduced cost after-school care? In the last 12 months, have you used or applied for this kind of care or aren't you aware of any of this programs?

Asked of all single-parent AFDC recipients with child under age 14

- How about the Dependent Care Income Tax Credit (Dep Car)? In the last 12 months, have you used or applied for this or aren't you aware of this program?

- How about the AFDC child care disregard, which reduces the amount taken out of your AFDC check when you work? In the last 12 months, have you used or applied for that or aren't you aware of this program?

the availability of, and subsidy levels for, state and federally funded child day care. In terms of coordination, California employed a mixed system with substantial decentralization of responsibility. Administration of major federal and state programs was shared at the state level between the Departments of Education and Social Services; this administrative split was reproduced at the county level. The state took some steps to reduce fragmentation at the local level by supporting an extensive system of Child Care Resource and Referral (CCRR) agencies. Because the management of these services was also decentralized, the role of the CCRRs in local child day care and welfare programs varied substantially among localities.

The sample is also limited in the AFDC families represented. Two groups of families, those headed by an adult who did not speak English or Spanish and those headed by two parents, are not included in the present analysis. A second caution is raised by the sampling methodology. The sample represents the AFDC caseload at a point in time. A substantial literature on welfare dynamics has demonstrated that because the majority of AFDC recipients receive aid for two years or less, such point-in-time samples overrepresent long-term cases. Any conclusions from this analysis, therefore, are likely to overemphasize the experiences of long-term and relatively more disadvantaged AFDC recipients.

Despite these limitations, some generalization is warranted by the fact that the four study counties represent over half of the total AFDC caseload for the state of California, and the state itself had 17% of all AFDC cases in the United States in 1993 [U.S. House of Representatives 1994].

Findings

Awareness among Potential Recipients

The first questions concerned respondents knowledge of the targeted child day care subsidies for which they were potentially eligible (see figure 1). The majority of single-parent AFDC recipients with children under age 14 were unaware of many child day care benefits for which they might have been eligible (see table 1). Head Start and other public preschool programs were the most important exception to this finding. Among potentially eligible individuals (those with at least one child under age six) only 7% indicated that they were unaware of public preschool programs, whether or not they had used these services in the previous year. Knowledge of GAIN child day care benefits, the single largest source of child day care assistance for AFDC recipients in school or training programs, was also relatively high, with only one-third (33%) of respondents lacking any awareness of the program.

Knowledge of other child day care assistance was extremely limited. Nearly two-thirds (61%) of current AFDC recipients said they were unaware of the AFDC disregard that would allow them to deduct their child day care expenses if they went to work. Seventy percent of those with school-aged children indicated that they were not aware of free or reduced cost after-school child day care. Fully 85% of all respondents were not familiar with the child day care subsidies designed explicitly to assist working parents: Transitional Child Care for parents who leave welfare for work, and the Child and Dependent Care Income Tax Credit.

Restriction of Benefits to Target Groups

On the questions of target efficiency, or restriction of benefits to target groups, results were more consistent with policy goals. Although knowledge of child day care subsidies was very limited in the group of AFDC families, their use of subsidies and, to a lesser extent, their knowledge of these benefits were consistent with program targets. With the exception of public preschool and some after-school programs, all of the child day care subsidies described in this article are categorically restricted to parents in school or training programs (GAIN) or employment (Transi-

TABLE 1

AFDC Recipients' Knowledge of (and Application for) Categorical Child Day Care Subsidies

Program	Applied for Assistance	Aware of Program but Never Applied	Unaware of Benefit
Child under Age 13			
GAIN (JOBS child day care)	14%	53%	33%
TCC (Transitional Child Care)			
or At-Risk	2%	13%	85%
Child and Dependent Care			
Income Tax Credit	2%	13%	85%
Child under Age Six			
Head Start or other public			
preschool	24%	69%	7%
Currently Receiving AFDC			
AFDC Child Care Disregard	6%	33%	61%
Child Aged Six to 12			
Free/reduced cost after-school			
care	4%	26%	70%

tional Child Care, Dependent and Child Care Tax Credit, AFDC disregard). Figure 2 compares awareness and use of four child day care subsidies by four groups of respondents corresponding to these categorical restrictions: those who had attended school or training programs in the previous 12 months ("school"), those who had worked for pay in any of the three months prior to the interview ("work"), those with both recent school and work experience ("work and school"), and those who had neither recent school nor recent work experience ("home").

Substantial and significant differences ($\chi^2 > 124.16$, $p < .001$) in respondents' use of the three categorically restricted child day care programs suggests that benefits were effectively limited to target groups. Seven percent of all respondents reported using GAIN child day care benefits, between 14% and 23% of those recently in school had been assisted with child day care through GAIN, and another 10% of recent students had applied for benefits but had not received help or were currently on waiting lists.

FIGURE 2

Assistance from Categorical Child Care Programs by Parents' Activity Status

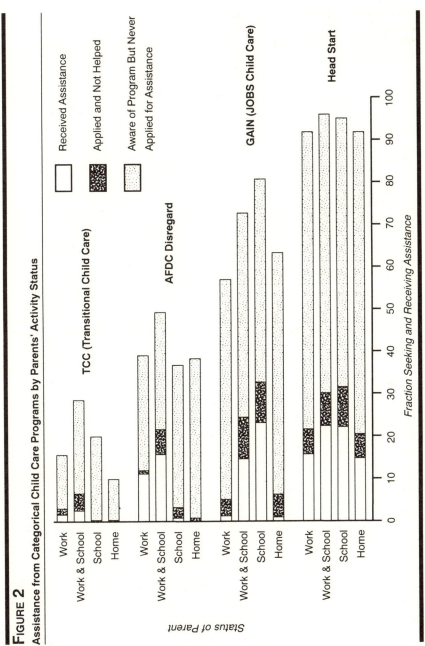

Fraction Seeking and Receiving Assistance

Five percent (5%) of all AFDC recipients reported using the AFDC disregard in the previous year; among those who had worked in the previous quarter, however, from 12% to 16% had used the disregard. Use of Transitional or At-Risk child day care benefits was extremely limited, with fewer than 1% of all respondents indicating that they had benefited from these programs. Although still limited, use was significantly higher for those with recent work experience: from 2% to 3% reported using the programs, and another 2% to 4% had applied for benefits unsuccessfully.

As expected, Head Start and other preschool programs were once again the exception to the rule. Eligibility for these programs is restricted by children's ages but not by parents' activities, and participation rates were both substantial (15% to 22%) and statistically independent of parents' recent work or school status ($\chi^2 = 13.83$, $p = .13$).

Benefit Coverage

The third and final question for this study concerned the extent of benefit coverage for target groups. By this criterion, the performance of categorically restricted child day care programs was disappointing.

A substantial fraction of the single-parent AFDC recipients in this study were actively involved in work or work-preparation activities in the month prior to their interview. Nearly one-quarter (24%) had worked in regular or odd jobs in the previous month, and about one-fifth (19%) were in regular school or in job preparation activities (vocational training, English-language classes, or job club activities). A small subset (4% overall) reported both paid work hours and school in the previous month.

As would be expected, single mothers who were working or in school were more likely to use regular child day care arrangements than other mothers. Though less than half of all respondents (42%) made regular use of child day care, family child care, or babysitters for their youngest child, 69% of those in school or training, 68% of those with work hours, and 77% of those with both work and school hours used one or more of these child day care arrangements regularly.

Table 2 shows child day care payment arrangements by parents' activity status in the previous month. Overall, 10% of the single mothers reported that the child day care they used was fully subsidized and another 3% received a partial subsidy, or used a mixture of care only some of which was subsidized. Fifteen percent used only free care (babysitting by relatives or friends) regularly, and nearly the same fraction (14%) paid the entire cost of their regular child day care arrangements.

Use of free, subsidized, and purchased care was significantly different for parents who were working, in school, or at home ($\chi^2 = 129.00, p < .001$). Parents who did not have regular school or work hours were much less likely to use child day care regularly; when they did, however, it was nearly always free or fully subsidized care. Only 3% of single mothers who were not in school or in paid employment reported paying for child day care regularly.

Slightly more than one-quarter of the single mothers who were enrolled in school, training, or job clubs had partly (6%) or fully (19%) subsidized child day care for their youngest child. Another 18% were able to arrange free care. But nearly one-fifth (19%) of those in school were paying the full cost of child day care themselves.

Single mothers with paid work hours fared the worst in access to subsidized child day care. Respondents who were working or combining work and school were the most likely to report regular day care or babysitting arrangements for their youngest. Only 9% of those who were working had fully subsidized care for these children; another 7% reported partial subsidies or mixed subsidized and purchased care. (Workers who were also in school or job preparation activities were more likely to have subsidized (23%) or partly subsidized (12%) care, perhaps reflecting greater access to subsidies through the GAIN program). Thirty-seven percent (37%) of workers, and over one-

TABLE 2

Payment Arrangements for Child Day Care (Including Babysitting) for Youngest Child, by AFDC Recipients' Activity Status

Mothers' Activity During the Prior Month	Child Day Care Payment Arrangement				
	No Regular Care	Care Was Free	Fully Subsidized	Partially Subsidized	Paid Full Amount
Home	76%	14%	7%	0	3%
School, Training, or Job Club	31%	18%	25%	6%	19%
Working Regularly or Odd Jobs	32%	14%	9%	7%	37%
School and Working	23%	14%	23%	12%	29%

quarter (29%) of those mixing work and school paid the entire cost of their regular child day care arrangements.

Discussion

This analysis suggests that highly targeted, categorical child day care subsidies may be more effective at excluding ineligible clients than at providing benefits to those in need. By the single criterion of target efficiency, categorical child day care programs appear to perform well. Application for and receipt of benefits was significantly higher among those recipients who met the categorical tests of parents' enrollment in school or employment. By the more inclusive criteria of assuring equity, promoting access to services, and assisting families in their efforts to leave welfare, these programs were much less successful.

As would be expected, single-parent AFDC recipients who are not in school or work were unlikely to use child day care regularly and rarely reported paying out-of-pocket when they did. Use of care and receipt of subsidies were much higher for single parents who were attending school or training programs. Although nearly one-quarter of those in school or training had fully subsidized care, however, almost the same fraction paid for all or part of their children's care. Single mothers in paid employment fared the worst. They were most likely to use child day care regularly, and far more likely than the other groups to shoulder the full burden of payment.

Limited use of child day care subsidies may be due, in part, to a pervasive lack of knowledge about targeted child day care programs. The majority of single-parent AFDC recipients in this sample were familiar with the major public preschool program (Project Head Start), and with child day care available through the state JOBS program (GAIN). Less than half, however, were familiar with categorical child day care subsidies for working parents. Awareness dropped as low as 15% for programs such as Transitional Child Care and the Child and Dependent Care Tax Credit, which were created specifically to assist low-income, working parents.

These findings suggest that efforts to narrowly target child day care assistance, and to link that assistance categorically to parents' school and work status, may have produced a system so restrictive that it excludes the very families the policies were designed to serve. Policymakers' efforts to narrowly target child day care assistance may be working at cross-purposes with efforts to move large numbers of AFDC recipients quickly from welfare to work.

These findings have implications for both policy and practice. In the short term, there is a critical and ongoing need to inform low-income parents about the full range of child day care subsidies for which they might be eligible. Aggressive outreach, information, and education efforts are called for to increase parents' knowledge of available programs and to assist them in making strategic choices about child day care arrangements. Because AFDC recipients, and low-income parents more generally, are often in a turbulent phase of life, it important to provide continuing assistance to help them make what may be multiple transitions between school, training, welfare, and work. Other short-term solutions include model efforts, in several parts of the country, to consolidate and simplify application procedures and combine categorical funding streams into "seamless" delivery systems on the local level.

Improved outreach, education, and local integration of services may help eligible parents negotiate a system of narrow, categorical child day care benefits. These strategies do not confront the more fundamental problems of inadequate funding for child day care and narrowly targeted services that link eligibility for the care of children to the activities of parents. These categorical distinctions increase target efficiency, but impose hidden costs by creating gaps and cliffs in eligibility, increasing the costs of information and transaction, and increasing the risk that economically vulnerable families will not receive the assistance necessary for them to achieve stable economic self-sufficiency.

Although there may be a substantial realignment of federal, state, and local responsibility for social and health services by the end of the decade, there is every reason to expect that all levels of government will continue to shoulder some responsibility for financing child day care. As funding is reorganized and expanded, it is critically important to integrate funding streams, broaden eligibility criteria, and refocus eligibility on the needs of *children* rather than on the characteristics and activities of their parents. This simplification of the child day care subsidy system must not be achieved by eliminating child day care guarantees or reducing funding. Little will be gained if, in consolidating and simplifying child day care financing, we force even more families to compete for a place on long child day care waiting lists. Instead, our goal should be to build on and expand child day care entitlements to create a genuinely seamless system of child day care assistance that guarantees every child access to safe, developmentally appropriate child day care and assures all parents who want to work that they can find and afford such care. ♦

References

Adams, G., & Sandfort, J. R. (1992). *State investments in child care and early childhood education*. Washington, DC: Children's Defense Fund.

Blau, D. M., & Robins, P. K. (1988). Child care costs and family labor supply. *The Review of Economics and Statistics, 70*, 374–381.

Blau, D. M., & Robins, P. K. (1991). Child care demand and labor supply of young mothers over time. *Demography, 28*, 333-351.

Cattan, P. (1991, October). Child care problems: An obstacle to work. *Monthly Labor Review*.

Ebb, N. (1994). *Child care tradeoffs: States make painful choices.* Washington, DC: Children's Defense Fund.

Hagen, J. L., & Lurie, I. (1992). *Implementing JOBS: Initial state choices.* Albany, NY: Nelson A. Rockefeller Institute of Government.

Hofferth, S. L., Brayfield, A., Deich, S., & Holcomb, P. (1991). *National child care survey, 1990.* Washington, DC: Urban Institute Press.

Kimmel, J. (1994). The role of child care assistance in welfare reform. *Employment Research, 1*, 1–4.

Kisker, E. E., Maynard, R., Gordon, A., & Strain, M. (1989). *The child care challenge: What parents need and what is available in three metropolitan areas.* Princeton, NJ: Mathematica Policy Research, Inc.

Kisker, E. E., Hofferth, S. L., & Phillips, D. A. (1991). *A profile of child care settings: Early education and care in 1990.* Princeton, NJ: Mathematica Policy Research, Inc.

Meyers, M. K. (1990). The ABCs of child care in a mixed economy: A comparison of public and private sector alternatives. *Social Service Review, 64*, 559–579.

Presser, H. B., & Baldwin, W. (1980). Child care as a constraint on employment: Prevalence, correlates, and bearing on work and fertility nexus. *American Journal of Sociology, 85*, 1202–1213.

Ribar, D. C. (1992). Child care and the labor supply of married women. *Journal of Human Resources, 21*, 134–164.

Ross, C., & Kerachsky, S. (1995). Strategies for program integration. In D. Besharov (Ed.), *Enhancing early childhood programs: Burdens and opportunities.* Washington, DC: Child Welfare League of America.

Seigel, G., & Loman, A. (1991). *Child care and AFDC recipients in Illinois.* Chicago: Illinois Department of Public Aid.

Survey Research Center. (1994). *California work pays demonstration project survey.* Berkeley, CA: University of California.

U.S. Advisory Commission on Intergovernmental Relations. (1994). *Child care: The need for federal-state-local coordination.* Washington, DC: U.S. Advisory Commission on Intergovernmental Relations.

U.S. General Accounting Office. (1994a). *Child care: Working poor and welfare recipients face service gaps.* Washington, DC: Author.

U.S. General Accounting Office. (1994b). *Child care: Child care subsidies increase likelihood that low-income mothers will work.* Washington, DC: Author.

U.S. General Accounting Office. (1989). *Child care: Government funding sources, coordination, and service availability.* Washington, DC: Author.

U.S. House of Representatives. (1993). *1994 green book.* Washington, DC: Committee on Ways and Means, U.S. House of Representatives.

3

Moving from Welfare to Work: A Snapshot Survey of Illinois Families

Elizabeth C. Smith

The role of child day care in enabling parents to leave welfare for employment is a central issue in the current welfare reform debate. Little information is available, however, about parents and children who use child day care after leaving AFDC. Information gathered from 207 parents using the Transitional Child Care subsidy six months after leaving welfare was used to examine their characteristics and demographics and illustrate the life circumstances they face. Findings suggest that income, erratic schedules, and ages of children contribute to the complexities parents face in accessing and using child day care. This information is crucial to discussions of child day care as a tool to help parents on AFDC move toward employment.

Elizabeth C. Smith, M.A., is Public Service Administrator, Illinois Department of Public Aid, Chicago, IL. The author thanks Michele Piel and Mirian Franklin, Illinois Department of Public Aid Child Care and Development Section, for their assistance; Dr. Sumati Dubey and his students Maureen Milkevitch, Lyn Bos, Beth Brown, Rose Kelly, and Linda Shaver of the University of Illinois, Chicago, for mailing the surveys and recording the data; and Susan Drachler, student at the University of Colorado, for compiling the data.

Much of the discussion regarding the reform of America's welfare system concerns families moving between welfare and work. The cycle between welfare and work for parents who are single heads of household often hinges on the availability of affordable, reliable child day care. Policymakers at the state and federal level are responsible for developing programs that will have a profound impact on these families. What information can policymakers use to make the most informed decisions? How can policymakers gather the information they need?

In 1991, the Illinois Department of Public Aid (DPA), wanting to ask consumers of federal child day care subsidies what their needs and experiences regarding child day care were, commissioned an in-depth study of 8,000 parents on AFDC [Siegel & Loman 1991]. Since then, periodic snapshot surveys have been made by DPA staff to keep abreast of the needs of these families.

The Survey Sample

In 1994, DPA staff conducted a snapshot survey of families using time-limited child day care subsidies who moved from welfare to work. With the assistance of graduate students of the University of Illinois, the DPA staff developed a survey instrument asking 14 questions related to child day care and employment. The survey was mailed to 800 randomly selected parents receiving Transitional Child Care (TCC) subsidies in the spring of 1994. Two hundred and seven parents responded. This article examines the demographics and life circumstances of this sample.

TCC is a time-limited child day care program mandated by the federal Family Support Act of 1988 (P.L. 100–485). In Illinois, it provides child day care subsidies to parents for 12 months after their income from employment exceeds the eligibility limits of AFDC. Provision of this subsidy is not guaranteed beyond the time limit established by the federal act. The information provided by responding parents indicates that their earnings and the schedules they work affect their ability to purchase care in the marketplace.

The Impact of Child Day Care Subsidies

The survey found that the average family using TCC was headed by a woman of 28 years of age. She had two children (a pre-schooler and a school-age child) and earned $5.42 per hour working full-time. Assuming that the preschool-age child is three years old and the school-age child is seven, the average family would continue to need child day care for at least 10 years.

Figure 1 shows the family's potential earnings and the impact of child day care subsidies on them over a ten-year period. A family of three on AFDC, with two children of the same ages as our study population, would have a spendable income of $8,052 the first year in cash assistance and food stamps. The families in our study were employed, had hourly earnings of $5.42 per hour, and received a child day care subsidy. Their total income includes food stamps, the Earned Income Tax Credit, the Child and Dependent Care Credit, and adjustments for state and federal taxes. Their spendable income would be $14,579 per year. If their child day care subsidy is time-limited to 12 months, however, in year 2 the family would have a spendable income of only $8,910, notwithstanding the assumption that they would receive a 5% increase in their hourly wages. If, however, the family receives an ongoing subsidy for the cost of care of their school-age child and their preschooler, their spendable income would be $15,045.

Over the ten-year span, it is assumed that the head of household receives a 5% increase in her hourly wages each year. The family with the ongoing subsidy pays a child day care fee that increases every year as the parent's income rises. The income for this family will include food stamps for as long as they are eligible, the federal Earned Income Tax Credit, the Child and Dependent Care Credit, and adjustments for state and federal income taxes. The spendable income for a family with a time-

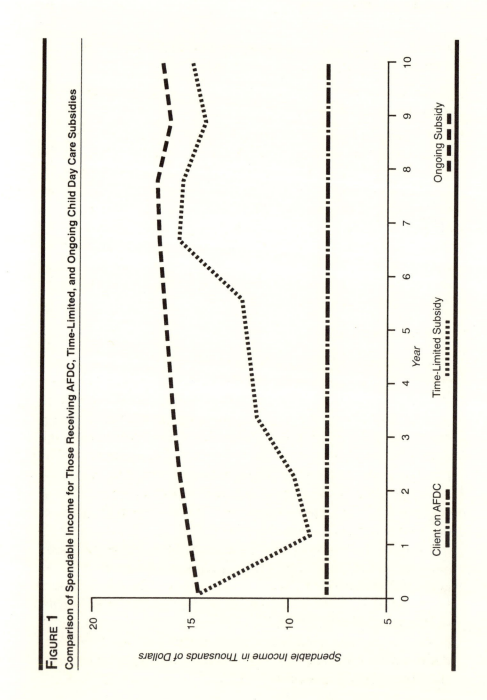

FIGURE 1

Comparison of Spendable Income for Those Receiving AFDC, Time-Limited, and Ongoing Child Day Care Subsidies

limited subsidy remains well below that of the same family receiving an ongoing subsidy.

Results

This example leads us to consider what families making the
transition from welfare to work face if they have only time-
limited child day care subsidies. Responses to the survey
questions provided a wealth of information regarding the circumstances of the families: How old were the children in the
households surveyed? How much money were parents earning?
What were their schedules? Could these factors be influencing
the type of care parents could use? Were these conditions influencing parents' ability to maintain the child day care arrangement after the subsidies ended?

Family Characteristics

Of the 207 respondents, 97% were female. Corroborating the
results of the 1991 departmental study, most (87%) were between
the ages of 21 and 35, with 6% ages 18 to 20, and 6% ages 36 or
above. Only 14% of the respondents in this group reported less
than 12 years of education, 38% had 12 years of education (high
school diploma), and 48% reported some college education. The
average family had two children, with 36% reporting one child,
35% reporting two children, and 21% reporting three or more
children. Eight percent of respondents did not report the number
of children in their household.

Most of the 379 children (91.5%) were below 13 years of age,
and therefore required care while their parents were working. As
in the 1991 departmental study, many children (58.8%) were five
years old and under. Children six to 13 years old represented
32.7% of all children; only 8.5% of the children were over age 13.
Eighty-six percent of the households contained at least one child
under age five, and 42% of the households contained at least one
child between the ages of six and 13.

Employment Characteristics

Since employment was a requirement for eligibility for the TCC program, all of the parents were employed at the time of the study. As figure 2 shows, the job classifications of the respondents varied. Twenty-three percent were employed in paraprofessional jobs (including certified nurse assistant, data specialist, child day care aide). Service jobs (including service representative, prep-cook, bus driver, sales person, mail clerk, waitress) were represented in 19% of the responses. Factory and industrial jobs (including janitorial, factory, construction) accounted for 18% of the responses. Only 2% of respondents reported holding professional jobs (bookkeeper and teacher). The remaining 37% of the respondents reported jobs that did not fit into any of these categories.

Most respondents (69.8%) worked more than 32 hours a week at the time of the survey. Only 23.4% worked 20 to 32 hours a week, and 6.8% worked less than 20 hours. This information suggests that most respondents required full-time care (more than five hours a day) for their children.

The respondents reported average earnings of $5.42 per hour with a range of $0.00 to $11.00 an hour. When computing these figures, the staff assumed that respondents were working 40-hour weeks. Respondents who reported relatively higher wages, however, may have been working more than 40 hours a week. The compilation of the responses showed that 43.0% of respondents earned $5.00 or less per hour, 43.7% earned $5.01 to $8.00 per hour, 11.4% earned $8.01 to $11.00 per hour, and 2.0% earned more than $11.00 per hour.

Type of employment had some connection with the hourly wages reported. The service and paraprofessional jobs clustered in the $5.00 to $8.00 per hour range, factory/industrial jobs were below the $5.00 per hour wage category, and professional jobs concentrated in the $8.00 to $11.00 per hour category.

Figure 2

Employment Categories of Respondents*

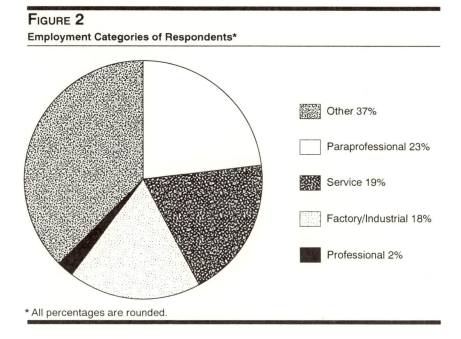

Other 37%

Paraprofessional 23%

Service 19%

Factory/Industrial 18%

Professional 2%

*All percentages are rounded.

Work Schedules

The majority of respondents to the survey (72%) were working irregular (nights and weekend) and/or erratic (not permanently set) schedules (see figure 3). Only 28% of the parents who responded reported working fixed daytime schedules.

Figure 4 breaks down further the types of schedules respondents worked: 31% of the respondents worked weekends; 9% worked nights; 24% had work schedules involving nights and weekends; and 25% reported varied schedules. Finally, 11% of the respondents reported working an arrangement not in one of these categories.

The availability of child day care for nights and weekends is limited. Licensed centers providing care on weekends and evenings are virtually nonexistent. Many parents who work these schedules rely on friends and relatives for the care of their chil-

FIGURE 3

Type of Schedules of Respondents

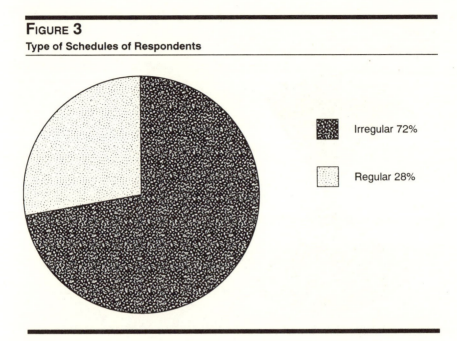

Irregular 72%

Regular 28%

dren. This is especially true for parents who work nights. They may wish to have someone come into their home to care for the children so the children have as little disruption as possible; the parents may prefer not to wake their children or take them on public transportation in the middle of the night.

Since night and weekend care is often unavailable and impractical, the schedules of these parents is significant. Most child day care providers operate during daytime hours, and most child day care resources are therefore directed at daytime care. In addition, another major source of child day care—pre-kindergarten programs and Head Start—is also available only during the day. The parents responding to this study would have little flexibility in changing or otherwise adjusting their child day care arrangements when they lose the TCC subsidy, because the supply of care would not be there to allow them many options.

Figure 5 shows that most respondents are likely to be working irregular schedules no matter how many hours they work.

Figure 4
Schedules of Respondents

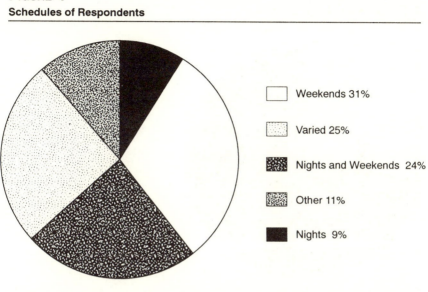

Weekends 31%

Varied 25%

Nights and Weekends 24%

Other 11%

Nights 9%

There is some indication, however, that as hours worked increase, the likelihood of irregular scheduling decreases. Most (91.67%) respondents working less than 20 hours a week had an irregular schedule, but somewhat fewer (69.9%) of those working more than 32 hours a week had irregular schedules. This information leads to a question that requires further study. Is it true that parents working more than 32 hours a week have more stable and traditional schedules, and if so, why? Does length of time in the workforce or type of job change this?

Child Day Care Arrangements

Families reported using various kinds of child day care arrangements. In-home care is provided in the child's home. Center-based care is provided in a child day care center. Family child care is care by a relative or nonrelative provided in a home other than the child's, for a fee. Figure 6 shows that 21.0% of respondents used in-own home care, 21.0% used family child care pro-

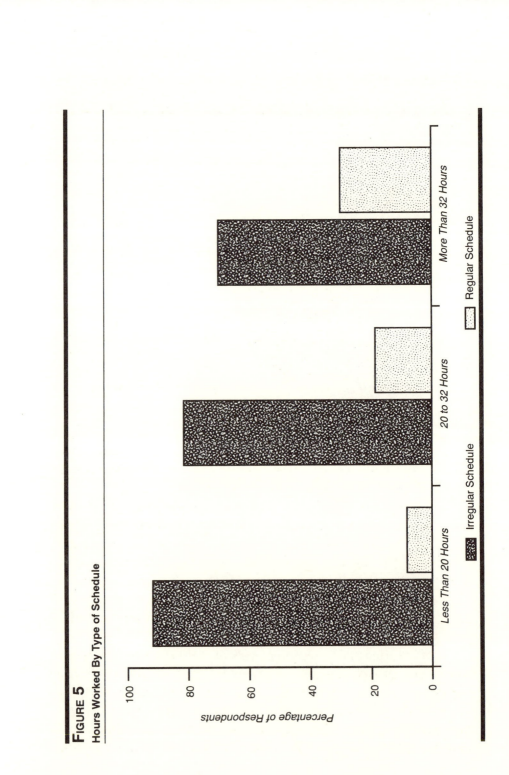

FIGURE 5

Hours Worked By Type of Schedule

FIGURE 6
Type of Child Day Care Used*

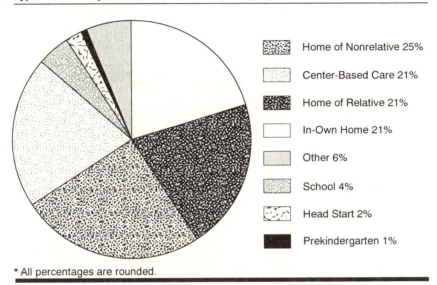

Home of Nonrelative 25%

Center-Based Care 21%

Home of Relative 21%

In-Own Home 21%

Other 6%

School 4%

Head Start 2%

Prekindergarten 1%

* All percentages are rounded.

vided in the home of a relative, 25.0% used family child care provided in the home of a nonrelative, 21.0% used center-based care, and 13.0% used other care arrangements.

As the number of hours worked increases, use of in-own home and in home of relative family child care decreases (figure 7), while the use of nonrelative family child care, center-based care, and other care increases. Most respondents (70.6%) working less than 20 hours a week used in-own home or home of relative family child care, while only 36.0% of parents working more than 32 hours a week used in-own home or home of relative family child care.

This information would suggest that respondents who work more than 32 hours a week use more center-based care and home of nonrelative care than those who work less than 20 hours a week. The question that remains unanswered is why these parents are using these types of care. Are relatives less inclined to care for children as parents work more hours? Or is it that the

FIGURE 7

Type of Care Used By Hours Worked

parents who work more hours have day jobs and can access the full range of options, including center-based care?

Schedule Influence on Type of Care

Because respondents tended to have irregular schedules, it was important to learn if the type of care used varied by the schedules worked. Figure 8 suggests that parents with all categories of schedules made use of home-based child day care, whether in-own home, in home of relative, or in home of nonrelative. Parents working nights and varied schedules, however, were most likely to use care in-own home: this type of care was used by 30.8% of respondents working nights, 32.6% of respondents working varied schedules, 15.1% of respondents working weekends, 19.1% of respondents working both nights and weekends, and 22.2% of respondents working other schedules.

The study found that most parents (72.5%) used only one child day care provider; most of the remaining parents used only two providers. As wages increased, however, respondents used additional providers (see figure 9). It follows that those parents with relatively higher hourly earnings may have required several providers to span the length of time they were working. Parents may also have been working several jobs to increase their hours and earnings, making the use of several providers a necessity.

Use of Child Day Care After Loss of the Subsidy

The study's final set of questions asked respondents how they intended to pay for child day care after they exhausted the 12 months of TCC subsidy. Most parents (74.8%) reported not knowing what they would do when their child day care subsidy ended: 2.5% of respondents reported they were on a waiting list for another subsidy, and 7.4% reported they had other plans (including taking the child to work, leaving the child with the spouse, or quitting their job). Finally, 15.4% reported they would pay for the care themselves.

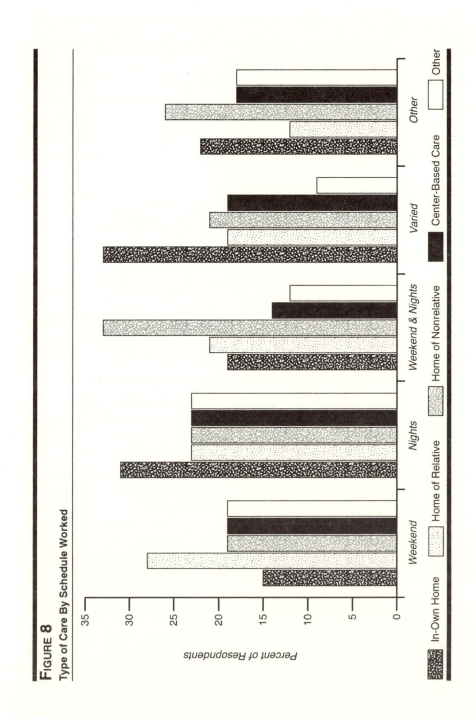

FIGURE 8

Type of Care By Schedule Worked

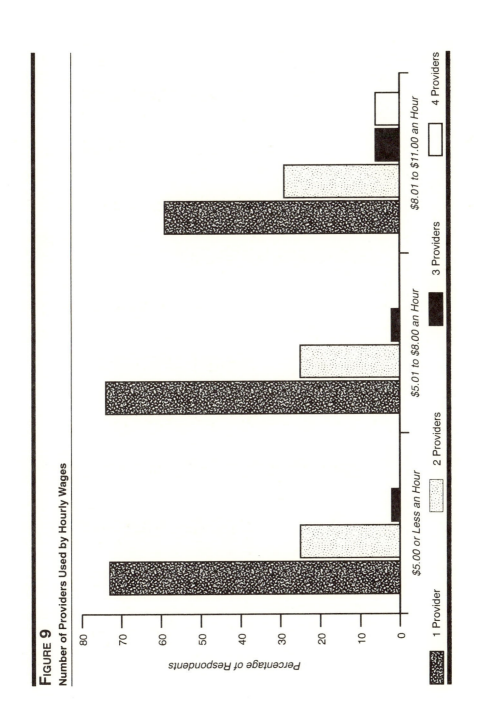

FIGURE 9

Number of Providers Used by Hourly Wages

How realistic is it that parents would be able to afford the cost of care without a subsidy? Information from the Illinois TCC program shows that the average monthly child day care subsidy is $440.00 per month. A parent who works 40 hours per week at $5.00 per hour will gross $800.00 a month. The child day care cost of $440.00 would be 55% of their gross income. These parents clearly cannot afford to pay for child day care without assistance. For someone making $11.00 an hour, the cost of care represents 25% of their gross income. They would be more able to pay for the care than the parent with the lower income, but they may still find it hard to do so for very long.

Conclusion

Information collected through this study indicated that those receiving child day care subsidies were primarily women with young children. These women tended to work more than 32 hours a week and to earn relatively low wages. Their earnings were generally between $5.00 and $8.00 per hour. On average, their child day care costs consumed 25% to 55% of their gross income. This would indicate that these parents are likely to have difficulty paying the full cost of child day care. Most of the respondents were working nights, weekends, or some combination of both. Not only did these respondents earn very little, but because of their schedules, they had few options for alternative care. The care that is available when they need it (weekends and nights) is limited.

Policies restricting the length of time a client can use a subsidy should consider the ability of parents to maintain payments over time. ♦

Reference

Siegel, G. L., & Loman, L. A. (1991). Child day care and AFDC recipients in Illinois: Patterns, problems and needs. St. Louis, MO: Institute for Applied Research.

4

Providing Quality Child Day Care in a Comprehensive Program for Disadvantaged Young Mothers and Their Children

Barbara Fink

This study examined the quality of center-based child day care provided as a part of New Chance, a nationwide program serving teenage mothers on welfare and their children. Assessments of quality were based on researcher's observations and surveys completed by center directors. The data show the feasibility of supplying good quality center-based child day care as a part of a program of this kind. The disparity, however, between the good quality of child day care services found in the New Chance program and the highest level of quality found nationally raises questions about whether the care can actually enhance the development of children seriously at risk.

Barbara Fink, M.P.A., is Research Associate, Manpower Demonstration Research Corporation, New York, NY. The author thanks Marilyn Price for her help in collecting the data for this study and Robert Granger for his overall guidance and support.

69

C hildren from economically disadvantaged backgrounds are at high risk of having behavioral problems and doing poorly in school [Berrueta-Clement et al. 1984] and children of teenage mothers are considered to be particularly at risk. Research has shown that children of adolescent mothers have more cognitive and behavioral problems, both short- and long-term, than do children of adult mothers, and that high-quality, early child day care programs can positively affect school readiness among economically disadvantaged children [Hofferth 1987; Berrueta-Clement et al. 1984].* Consequently, some social scientists argue that a sensible public policy for programs targeting welfare recipients, especially programs for teenage mothers and others with young children, would emphasize high-quality child day care as a compensatory educational strategy for these children [Smith et al. 1992].

The importance of providing high-quality child day care for low-income children prompted the Manpower Demonstration Research Corporation (MDRC), a nonprofit organization that designs and evaluates social programs, to undertake a special study to assess the quality of child day care as part of its ongoing evaluation of the New Chance program. This special study is hereafter referred to as the New Chance Child Care Study.

New Chance, a program designed to help disadvantaged teen mothers (high school dropouts who receive welfare) and their children, ran in 16 sites across the U.S. and is being evaluated at this writing. The program was operated by community-based organizations, schools, a community college, and municipal agencies, and provided services to over 1,250 young

---

*The distinction between custodial child day care and early childhood education programs has blurred in recent years. The current consensus is that programs vary along a common continuum of quality, without regard to the length of care per day or the programs' ostensible purposes. Thus, there are low- and high-quality part- and full-day programs, some of which are primarily considered to be child day care and others that are viewed as preschool centers. This article refers to all centers as "child day care centers," regardless of the educational content or curriculum used.

women. New Chance was designed to help mothers 16 to 20 years old attain economic self-sufficiency and improve their overall well-being and that of their children. The model included a variety of services intended to help these young women gain the skills necessary for employment (e.g., education and career-planning services), and to support them in dealing with personal matters (e.g., health education and case management). Parenting education and child day care services were also offered as a part of the New Chance model.

The central concern of the New Chance Child Care Study is whether it is feasible to offer high-quality child day care as part of a program focused on welfare recipients. This question is particularly important given the trend within welfare reform efforts to mandate the participation of mothers with young children in out-of-home activities as a condition of welfare receipt.

The Welfare Reform Context

Despite some convergence in welfare and child day care policies, recent welfare reform strategies that require parents to engage in activities outside of the home exacerbate concern about the quality of available child day care. Before passage of the Family Support Act (FSA) of 1988, which included the Job Opportunities and Basic Skills training program (JOBS), only welfare recipients with school-age children were expected to participate in employment and training programs.* Since the passage of FSA, states are required to have welfare recipients whose youngest children are three years old or older (one year old or older at state option) participate in services that will help them to enter the labor force.

---

*The Job Opportunities and Basic Skills Training (JOBS) program, created by the Family Support Act of 1988, gives state welfare agencies increased funding for delivering education, vocational skills training, and other employment-related services to welfare recipients. The JOBS legislation includes a financial incentive structure that encourages states to focus on groups at high risk of long-term welfare receipt, including young parents without a high school diploma.

In addition, mothers under age 20 without a high school or equivalency diploma, regardless of the age of their children, may be required to attend educational, job training, and other programs. Current welfare reform proposals would deny welfare benefits to some of these families altogether, resulting in an increased use of nonparental child day care for impoverished children, particularly infants [Pear 1994].

Welfare policy has tended to ignore considerations of child day care *quality*, viewing child day care primarily as a support system for the parent. FSA creates an open-ended entitlement to child day care for parents on welfare who participate in approved JOBS activities, and, to help these parents (usually mothers) cross the bridge to employment, offers a child day care subsidy for up to one year after the parent leaves welfare due to earnings. Nonetheless, it seems that the primary intent of these provisions is to provide affordable and convenient child day care so that parents may participate in educational and training programs, rather than to provide care that will directly enhance the development of children.

Some social scientists have argued that separating the needs of low-income parents from those of their children is short-sighted public policy; they respond with proposals to help welfare recipients together with their children through "two-generational" program models [Smith et al. 1992]. In these proposals, the primary child-focused strategies are providing parenting education and high-quality child day care programs.

New Chance followed this two-generational approach by providing child day care that sought to promote positive development among children while enabling their mothers to participate in 30 hours per week of program activities. MDRC collaborated with child development experts to provide guidelines for high-quality care, but because the focus of New Chance was on services to the parents, little was done to raise the quality of its child day care services.

Study Overview

This article reports findings from the New Chance Child Care Study's assessment of the quality of center-based child day care provided as part of New Chance. The majority (61%) of New Chance participants used center-based care, which was directly provided either by the New Chance sponsor agency (referred to as on-site care) or through arrangements with centers located nearby. Data on the quality of child day care were derived from a survey completed by center directors and from researchers' observation-based ratings of the overall quality of the child day care environment. Quality was measured in two ways: by whether the centers met established standards of quality care, and by comparing the quality of care to that in typical centers accessible to low-income populations. The results document that, for the most part, New Chance child day care centers met the established standards for quality and exceeded the quality of comparable centers. Nonetheless, New Chance centers were discovered to have provided *good* care, but not the *highest* quality care, raising doubts about their ability to enhance the development of the low-income children they serve. In this context, the results are sobering for those trying to use two-generational programming to help young children in welfare families.

It is beyond the scope of this research to explain why the child day care centers associated with the New Chance program were of better quality than those typically used by low-income children. The relatively higher quality could be attributed to the New Chance site selection process, MDRC's recommended guidelines, or many other factors. Regardless, the data do show that New Chance succeeded in providing above-average center-based care for impoverished children. These findings are encouraging for those trying to integrate decent quality child day care with educational and job training services for disadvantaged mothers.

Methodology and Data Sources

The sample of New Chance child day care centers consists of 11
centers in six states, associated with eight of the 16 New Chance
sites, that cared for a substantial number of New Chance children
during their mothers' participation in the program.* The percentage of participants' children enrolled in each center depended on
the number of available openings (or "slots") in different age
groups, on site policy in making slots available for participants,
and on participants' preferences. Several New Chance site administrators who provided sufficient slots strongly encouraged
all participants to use the on-site centers.

Data for measuring the quality of New Chance centers were
derived from a survey completed by center directors and from
researchers' observation-based ratings. The survey focused on
characteristics of the caregivers and the center environment that
presumably increase or decrease caregivers' ability to interact
positively with children. The observational ratings were directly
derived from observations of interactions between staff members
and children. Together, these two data sources provide a more
comprehensive picture of the quality of New Chance child day
care centers than would have been possible with either one alone.
The following sections describe the quality measures captured by
these data sources.

Structural Characteristics and Survey-Based Quality Measures

The surveys completed by center directors provide descriptive
characteristics of each center (e.g., type of sponsor agency, hours
of operation, age range and ethnicity of children served) and
information associated with quality of care (e.g., child-staff ra-

---

*The remaining eight New Chance sites were excluded from this study because they
provided only temporary, drop-in care (two sites); no single child day care center served
a sizable group of New Chance participants' children (four sites); the site suspended its
provision of New Chance services before this study was under way (one site); or staff
members were reluctant to participate in this study (one site).

tios; caregivers' training and education, salary, and benefits; and staff turnover). Most of the questions on the survey were derived from those used by two other recent studies: the Profile of Child Care Settings (PCS) [Kisker et al. 1991], and the National Child Care Staffing Study (NCCSS) [Whitebook et al. 1990]. PCS analyzed the characteristics of a nationally representative sample of 2,089 child day care centers, and NCCSS examined the quality of 227 child day care centers in five U.S. cities.

Child-staff ratios and group size are among the most frequently used measures of child day care quality and are presumed to reflect the style and frequency of caregivers' interactions with children. Research has shown that large child-staff ratios and group sizes appear to have negative effects on development, especially for young children [for a review of the literature see Hayes et al. 1990]. Data from the New Chance survey were used to calculate child-staff ratios and group size for the 11 New Chance centers. For each group of children, directors reported the number of children enrolled and the number of caregivers (teachers, assistant teachers, and aides) scheduled for each group during a typical morning activity period. This information generated the average "enrolled" group size and child-staff ratios for infants (under one year old), toddlers (12 to 35 months old), and preschoolers (three years old and older). Mixed-age classrooms with infants were included with infant classrooms; other mixed-age classrooms were categorized based on the midpoint of the age range. Directors also reported the number of children absent from each group on a typical day. This information was used to calculate average child-staff ratios and group size based on the usual number of children in attendance. As expected, ratios and group size measures based on enrollment exceeded those based on attendance.

As a complement to the survey data, the MDRC staff observed and recorded the number of children and caregivers in the room throughout the day. These data, recorded twice in the morning and twice in the afternoon, were used by researchers to calculate "observed" child-staff ratios and group size for specific classrooms. These ratios and group size measures were even lower than those based on attendance.

Caregiver characteristics, such as receipt of specialized training in early childhood education and level of formal education, are seen as proxies for program quality, though studies differ on the relative importance attributed to each. NCCSS, for example, found that the level of formal education was the strongest predictor of appropriate teacher behavior, in contrast to the National Day Care Study [Ruopp et al. 1979], which found that specialized training was more highly correlated with children's development than was formal education.

Another common measure of the quality of child day care centers is staff stability. Child development research has determined that children must form secure attachments to parents as a precursor to healthy emotional and intellectual development. Extending this finding to nonparental care, children must have stable and secure relationships with caregivers in child day care centers for healthy development; therefore, caregiver stability is also associated with positive child development. Turnover at the New Chance centers was calculated by dividing the number of caregivers employed at the center for less than 12 months (excluding the number of new positions created in the past year and adding any unfilled positions) by the total number of teachers plus unfilled positions. Further research by NCCSS showed that staff stability was influenced by staff wages and benefits (better paid staff were less likely to leave their center), and importantly, that wages were correlated with other quality measures.

Rating Scales

Observational measures of quality can significantly enhance survey-based information regarding program and caregiver characteristics. The primary observational data in the New Chance Child Care Study came from a pair of commonly used and carefully tested scales that yield ratings of multiple areas of quality. The Early Childhood Environment Rating Scale (ECERS) [Harms & Clifford 1980] measured the overall quality of the child day care setting in preschool rooms, and the Infant and Toddler Environment Rating Scale (ITERS) [Harms et al. 1990] was used to obtain quality ratings in infant and toddler classrooms. The ECERS and ITERS rating scales, which measure 37 and 35 items, respectively, provide a comprehensive picture of the quality of care. Each item on both the ECERS and ITERS is rated along a scale of one to seven, with one indicating inadequate care and seven indicating excellent care. Items in both scales are grouped into categories according to different dimensions of care. Categories on ECERS included personal care routines of children (e.g., diapering, meals, nap), furnishings and displays, language-reasoning experiences, fine and gross motor activities, creative activities, social development, and adult needs (such as meeting rooms). ITERS covers the same general areas but also includes age-specific items, such as listening and talking, learning activities, interaction, and program structure (e.g., the daily schedule).

Two MDRC staff members were trained to rate centers using the ECERS and ITERS scales. For the actual New Chance ECERS/ITERS ratings, MDRC staff observed two classrooms associated with each of the 11 sites in the study, one room appropriate for ITERS and one for ECERS. Observations began around the time most of the children arrived in the morning and lasted until they left in the afternoon.

Comparison Strategy

To assess the quality of New Chance child day care, the study compared the child-staff ratios and group size of the centers against criteria set by the National Association for the Education of Young Children (NAEYC) as part of its accreditation system of early childhood programs. These criteria represent established national standards for quality care [Bredekamp 1984].

The second standard against which New Chance centers are measured is a relative one: the average quality found in other centers serving similar populations. Data from the PCS study formed a nationally representative comparison sample of centers serving sizable numbers of low-income children. A subsample of centers, similar to the New Chance centers on certain salient characteristics and selected from the entire PCS sample of 2,089 center-based child day care centers, constitutes this comparison sample. This low-income PCS sample consists of the 84 centers meeting three criteria: they had nonprofit status, they operated full-day programs (seven hours or more a day, five days per week), and they had a client population of which 70% or more of the children were from families receiving public assistance. Various characteristics of the New Chance and low-income PCS centers are compared.

A subgroup of the 227 NCCSS centers serves as a second comparison sample. This low-income NCCSS sample includes the 25 nonprofit child day care centers in the NCCSS with 75% or more children from low-income families (i.e., subsidized children). Unlike the low-income PCS sample, this group of NCCSS centers is not statistically representative of the centers nationwide and may overrepresent higher quality centers.

The ECERS and ITERS ratings supplement these comparisons in two ways. First, the scales themselves are an established standard for measuring quality and provide accepted depictions of excellent, good, minimal, and inadequate care. Second, because the NCCSS used the two scales, the ECERS and ITERS ratings for the low-income NCCSS sample provides another means for comparing New Chance centers with care typically available to low-income populations.

The New Chance Child Day Care Centers

As shown in table 1, several types of nonprofit agencies sponsored New Chance and its child day care centers. The New Chance child day care centers were full-day programs, gener-

TABLE 1
Sponsorship of New Chance Child Day Care Centers*

Type of Sponsor Organization	# Sites
Head Start	2
Social Service Organization	3
Church or Religious Group	2
College or University	2
State or Local Government	2

*All centers in the survey were sponsored by nonprofit organizations.
Source: New Chance Child Care Study surveys.

ally operating seven hours a day, five days per week. The centers' operating schedules conformed to the New Chance program schedule, with mothers and children generally arriving between 8:00 A.M. and 9:00 A.M. and leaving between 3:00 P.M. and 4:00 P.M. The overwhelming majority (98%) of caregivers at the New Chance centers were female, and 97% of the teachers worked full-time (35 to 40 hours per week). There was an average of eight caregivers (teachers in charge of a group or classroom) per center.

The New Chance centers closely resemble those in the comparison samples of child day care centers serving low-income populations in many, but not all, general characteristics. As seen in table 2, the New Chance child day care centers are comparable to the low-income PCS and NCCSS samples in size and in characteristics of the children they served. On average, New Chance centers enrolled 64 children; enrollment in each center ranged from 15 to 190 children. The average number of children enrolled in the low-income PCS sample (64) exactly matches that in the New Chance sample, while the average number of children in the low-income NCCSS sample is slightly higher (67).

The main characteristic differentiating the New Chance centers from the others was the substantially younger age group at New Chance. Over half (60%) of the children in New Chance

TABLE 2
General Characteristics of New Chance Child Care Centers, Low-Income PCS Sample, and Low-Income NCCSS Sample

Characteristic	New Chance	Low-Income PCS Sample	Low-Income NCCSS Sample
	(N=11)	(N=84)	(N=25)
Average Enrollment (# children)	64	64	67
Licensed Capacity (# of children)	78	64	n/a
Age of Children (%)			
Younger than one year old	22	3	—a
One year old	21	4	
Two years old	17	9	
Three years old	19	22	
Four years old, not in kindergarten	14	43	
Five years old, not in kindergarten	3	10	
Kindergarten/school age	4	9	
Ethnicity of Children (%)			
African American	50	60	55
Caucasian	31	26	21
Latino	15	11	14
Asian/Pacific Islander	1	3	5
Native American	2	<1	1
Other	2	<1	4
% of Children's Parents Who			
Receive Public Assistance	86	86	—b

aAvailable breakdown for low-income NCCSS sample: infants and toddlers, 26%; preschoolers, 50%; and kindergarten/school-age, 24%.
bSelected centers had 75% or more subsidized children.
Sources: Calculations from New Chance Child Care Study surveys; special computer run on data from Profile of Child Care Settings; special computer run on data from National Child Care Staffing Study.

centers were infants and toddlers, and almost one-quarter (22%) were less than one year old. In contrast, only 3% of the low-income PCS sample were this young. Forty percent of the children in New Chance centers were three years old or older, whereas 84% of the children in the low-income PCS sample and 74% in the low-income NCCSS sample were this age. The predominance of infants and toddlers in the New Chance sample is attributable to the relatively young age of the mothers in the New Chance program.

Quality of Care

Child-Staff Ratios and Group Size

Table 3 shows the child-staff ratios and group size in the New Chance centers, along with the NAEYC criteria for these two attributes for rooms for infants (0 to 11 months), young toddlers (12 to 23 months), older toddlers (24 to 35 months), and pre-schoolers (36 months and older). An examination of child-staff ratios reveals a positive picture of care in New Chance, with all ratios matching or exceeding the NAEYC standards.

In addition, the infant child-staff ratios based on enrollment in New Chance classrooms ranged from 1.6 to 8.3 children per staff member, the toddler rooms had from two to nine children per staff member, and the preschool rooms had from four to 13.5 children per staff member. A high percentage of New Chance classrooms met or exceeded the NAEYC standards for child-staff ratios: 72% of the infant rooms, 60% to 75% of the toddler rooms (using the NAEYC standard for younger and older toddlers, respectively), and 95% of the preschool rooms.

The quality of New Chance care does not appear to be as high when considering group size as when considering staff ratios, particularly among infant rooms. The average group size of 10 infants, based on enrollment, was larger than the NAEYC standard of eight infants. The average enrolled group size in New Chance toddler rooms met the NAEYC standard, however, and the average enrolled preschool group size was less than the NAEYC criteria.

The average figures conceal a considerable range in group size across the New Chance classrooms. Based on enrollment, group size in infant rooms ranged from six to 25 children; only 39% met or exceeded the NAEYC standard. Group size in toddler rooms ranged from six to 28 children, and 60% met or exceeded the NAEYC standard. Group size in preschool rooms ranged from four to 27 children; and 89% met or exceeded the NAEYC standard.

TABLE 3

Child-Staff Ratios and Group Size of New Chance Child Care Centers and NAEYC Accreditation Criteria

Characteristic	New Chance			NAEYC Criteria
	Enrolled	Attendance	Observed	
Child-Staff Ratios for Children Ages. . .				
0–11 months	4	3	2	4
12–23 months	5	4	4	5
24–35 months	—a	—a	—a	6
36–71 months	7	6	5	10
Average Group Size for. . .				
Infant (0–11 months)	10	7	7	8
Toddler (12–35 months)	12	9	7	12
Preschool (36 months and up)	14	11	10	20

aToddlers ages 12 to 35 months are included above.
Sources: Calculations from New Chance Child Care Study surveys; Accreditation criteria of the National Association for the Education of Young Children.

Observation showed that actual attendance was lower than the number of children enrolled, making enrollment-based measures conservative assessments. As table 3 reveals, average observed group sizes in New Chance rooms was well within NAEYC's maximum criteria for all age groups. In particular, the observed group size for toddlers and preschool children fell well under the relevant NAEYC limits. For example, NAEYC calls for no more than 20 preschool children per group; on average, observed group size across New Chance preschool rooms was half that number. Even for infants, the quality standards were met when attendance or observed figures were used.

The nationally representative, low-income sample from the PCS study of center-based care and the low-income NCCSS sample offer additional benchmarks for comparison. As seen in table 4, comparisons of child-staff ratios between the New Chance and PCS samples generally favor New Chance. For infants, the New Chance and low-income PCS centers each had child-staff ratios of about 4:1. For toddlers, the average child-staff ratio in New

Chance centers of 5:1 was less than the ratios in the low-income sample for the younger and older toddlers of 6:1 and 8:1, respectively. The New Chance ratio in preschool rooms of 7:1 was also lower than the ratios found across the low-income PCS centers of 9:1 and 10:1 for younger and older preschoolers, respectively.

The average enrolled group size in New Chance infant classrooms of ten children per group was larger than the average group size in the low-income PCS sample of eight children per group. On average, group size in New Chance toddler rooms fell between the average group size for younger and older toddlers in the low-income PCS sample. Group size in the New Chance preschool classrooms was, on average, smaller than the PCS groups.

New Chance centers had better child-staff ratios and group size than the low-income NCCSS sample. Ratios and group size from the NCCSS were comparable to the observed measures for New Chance classrooms. Ratios and group sizes of children of all ages in New Chance centers were favorable compared to the NCCSS for all age groups.

Education, Training, and Experience of Caregivers

Table 5 presents findings on the training and experience of caregivers. Those in New Chance child day care centers had lower levels of education than caregivers in the comparison child care studies. The highest level of education attained by 50% of New Chance teachers was a high school diploma or General Educational Development (GED) certificate; almost 20% had a B.A. or a B.S. degree or higher. In comparison, in the low-income PCS sample, only 11% had no education beyond a high school diploma or a GED, and 44% had completed college. Caregivers in the low-income NCCSS also had more formal education than the New Chance teachers.

Directors in New Chance centers also reported that 35% of the caregivers received formal education in the early childhood education field. Three percent received formal education in ele-

TABLE 4
Child-Staff Ratios and Group Size of New Chance Child Care Centers, Low-Income PCS Sample, and Low-Income NCCSS Sample

Characteristic	New Chance Enrolled	Low-Income PCS Sample	New Chance Observed	Low-Income NCCSS Sample
Child-Staff Ratio				
Infant	4	4	2	4
Toddler	5	6[a]	4	5
Toddler	—	8[b]	—	—
Preschool	7	9[c]	5	8
Preschool	—	10[d]	—	—
Group Size				
Infant	10	8	7	9
Toddler	12	11[a]	7	9
Toddler	—	15[b]	—	—
Preschool	14	18[c]	10	16
Preschool	—	17[d]	—	—

[a]In low-income PCS, refers to 12 to 23 months.
[b]In low-income PCS, refers to 24 to 35 months.
[c]In low-income PCS, refers to 36 to 47 months.
[d]In low-income PCS, refers to 48 to 59 months.
Note: Low-income PCS ratios and group size are comparable to New Chance enrollment measures. Low-income NCCSS ratios and group size are comparable to New Chance observational measures.
Sources: Calculations from New Chance Child Care Study surveys and observational data; special computer run on data from Profile of Child Care Settings; special computer run on data from National Child Care Staffing Study.

mentary education, 5% in another area of education or child care, and 4% in psychology or child care. A high percentage of caregivers (73%) received 15 hours or more of training during the past year, compared to only 44% of caregivers in the low-income NCCSS sample.

New Chance caregivers had considerable experience working in a child day care setting. Twenty percent had ten or more years of experience, and 44% had four to nine years of experience. New Chance caregivers' total experience in the child day care field roughly matched the experience of those from the low-income NCCSS centers. Thus, the New Chance caregivers

TABLE 5

Education, Training, and Experience of Caregivers in New Chance Child Care Centers, Low-Income PCS Sample, and Low-Income NCCSS Sample

Characteristic	New Chance	Low-Income PCS Sample	Low-Income NCCSS Sample
Educational Levels of Teaching Staff (%)			
Less than high school diploma	1	0	6
High school diploma or GED	49	11	17
Some college, no degree	22	12	53[a]
Associate of Arts (AA) degree	7	19	—
B.A./B.S. degree	13	31	25[b]
Some graduate work	4	—	—
Master's (graduate) degree	3	13	—
% of Teachers who Received 15 Hours or More of Training During Last 12 Months	73	—[c]	44
% of Teachers Experienced in Early Childhood Education			
Three years or less	36	—[c]	29
Four to nine years	44	—[c]	45
Ten or more years	20	—[c]	26

[a]Includes A.A. degree.
[b]Includes B.A./B.S. or more.
[c]Data not available.
Note: The New Chance percentages are based on a sample of 91 teachers. Samples for the other studies are not available.
Sources: Calculations from New Chance Child Care Study surveys; special computer run on data from Profile of Child Care Settings; special computer run on data from National Child Care Staffing Study.

had considerable experience and child day care training, but relatively little formal education in comparison with the staff in the PCS and NCCSS studies.

Staff Stability

The New Chance Child Care Study used annual rates of staff turnover to measure staff stability. Table 6 shows that the average turnover among staff members across the New Chance cen-

TABLE 6

**Staff Turnover and Compensation in New Chance Child Care Centers,
Low-Income PCS Sample, and Low-Income NCCSS Sample**

Characteristic	New Chance	Low-Income PCS Sample	Low-Income NCCSS Sample
Staff Turnover			
Staff turnover rate (% of staff)	13	29	26
Centers with no turnover (% of centers)	45	—[a]	56
Compensation[a]			
Average hourly wage	—[c]	$7.23	$8.15
Average hourly wage of:			
Lowest paid teachers	$5.59	—[c]	$ 8.09
Highest paid teachers	$8.69	—[c]	$10.22
% of Staff Receiving This Fringe Benefit			
Life insurance	73	57	59
Paid vacation	100	73	86
Education stipend	100	84	—[c]
Health insurance	100[b]	70	31
Paid sick time	100	78	89
Pension	73	51	44
Reduced fees	36	21	44
Paid parental leave	100	39	35
Yearly COLA	55	—[c]	67
Merit increases	45	—[c]	24
Paid preparation	91	—[c]	57
% of Centers' Budget Spent on Salaries and Benefits	75	64	76

[a]All wages in 1993 dollars.
[b]Health coverage fully paid at seven New Chance sites; partially paid at four sites.
[c]Data not available.
Note: The New Chance percentages are based on a sample of 91 teachers. Samples for the other studies are not available.
Sources: Calculations from New Chance Child Care Study surveys; special computer run on data from Profile of Child Care Settings; special computer run on data from National Child Care Staffing Study.

ters (13%) was less than half of that found in the low-income centers of the PCS (29%) or NCCSS samples (26%). Five of the 11 New Chance centers (45%) had no turnover at all in the preceding year, which is somewhat lower than the percentage of low-income NCCSS centers with no turnover (56%).

New Chance directors were also asked to report the lowest and highest hourly wages paid to caregivers at their centers (all wages have been converted to 1993 dollars). This range—$5.59 to $8.69—encompassed the average wage paid at low-income PCS centers ($7.23), but was somewhat lower than wages paid at the low-income NCCSS centers ($8.09 to $10.22, an average of $8.15). The average starting wage for New Chance teachers was roughly $6.00 per hour, which at maximum translates into $12,480 a year (assuming 40 hours per week for 52 weeks).

Though wages were relatively low, New Chance centers offered a more comprehensive package of fringe benefits than the other settings. Thus, the package of total compensation (wages plus benefits) may have in part accounted for the relatively low turnover rate. All New Chance centers gave teachers paid vacation, educational stipends, health insurance, paid sick time, and maternity leave. Centers in the PCS low-income sample most commonly provided educational stipends (84%) and paid sick time (78%). Centers in the low-income NCCSS sample provided roughly the same level of fringe benefits as the low-income PCS centers, except for health benefits. Health insurance (fully or partly paid) was provided to teachers at all New Chance centers, 70% of the low-income PCS centers, and only 31% of the low-income NCCSS centers.

Overall, New Chance center directors reported that they spent 75% of their budgets on salaries and benefits. This suggests that New Chance centers spent a larger percentage of their budgets on personnel than the low-income sample of centers in the PCS study, which spent an average of 64% of their budgets on personnel, but were roughly equal to the 76% spent by low-income NCCSS centers.

ECERS/ITERS Ratings

Tables 7 and 8 present the ECERS and ITERS quality ratings. On average, the overall quality rating for New Chance preschool classrooms using the ECERS was 4.87, just under a "good" rating (5) on the scale. These ratings, based on observations of six preschool classrooms, ranged from 4.28 to 5.64 (two sites scored above a 5). The ITERS ratings, based on observations of 11 New Chance infant and toddler classrooms, averaged 4.58. All of these centers scored better than a 3, which corresponds on the scale to "minimal" care; the ratings ranged from 3.91 to 4.97.

The ECERS subscale scores (the average score of all items in the subscale) were all close, suggesting that no element of these programs was particularly better or worse than others. The highest ECERS ratings were 5.67 for furnishings and display for children and 5.07 for personal care routines (i.e., meals/snacks, nap, toileting, and personal grooming). The lowest rating was for adult needs (4.51), a category that rates the separate areas for adults (e.g., restroom, lounge areas, meeting areas), opportunities for professional growth, and provisions for parents.

The ITERS subscale scores varied more widely than the ECERS scales. On the high end of the scale, the interaction category (i.e., peer interaction, caregiver-child interaction, and discipline) received a score of 5.76. On the low end, learning activities (i.e., materials and activities that enhance eye-hand coordination, active physical play, art, music, block play, pretend play, sand and water play, and cultural awareness) averaged 3.75.

The average New Chance ECERS rating (4.87) was better than the average ECERS score across the low-income NCCSS centers (4.48). The overall quality of the New Chance infant and toddler

TABLE 7
Quality Ratings of New Chance Child Care Centers—ECERS Ratings of Preschool Rooms (N = 6 classrooms)*

Average Rating Across All Centers	4.87
Lowest Score	4.28
Highest Score	5.64
Subscale Scores:	
Personal care routines	5.07
Furnishings and display for children	5.67
Language-reasoning experiences	4.63
Fine and gross motor activities	4.58
Creative activities	4.79
Social development	4.64
Adult Needs	4.51

*Scale:

  1 (inadequate)—care does not meet custodial care needs;

  3 (minimal)—care meets custodial and to some small degree basic developmental needs;

  5 (good)—basic dimensions of developmental care are met;

  7 (excellent)—high quality, personalized care.

Source: Calculations from New Chance Child Care Study ECERS ratings.

classrooms as determined by the ITERS (4.58) was also higher than the quality of the low-income NCCSS centers, which scored 3.94 and 4.1 across infant and toddler classrooms.

Correlational Analysis

Table 9 presents correlations of the observational ratings (ITERS and ECERS scores) of New Chance classrooms with survey-based characteristics of the caregivers and centers. This analysis determines whether the indicators of quality from the survey correspond to the quality ratings based on researchers' observations. It includes the following variables derived from the survey data:
- Percentage of teachers with a B.A. degree or higher;
- Percentage of teachers with more than three years of early childhood experience;

TABLE 8

Quality Ratings of New Chance Child Care Settings—ITERS Ratings of Infant & Toddler Rooms (N = 11 classrooms)*

Average Rating Across All Centers	4.58
Lowest Score	3.91
Highest Score	4.97
Subscale Scores:	
Furnishings and display for children	4.80
Personal care routines	4.62
Listening and talking	4.95
Learning activities	3.75
Interaction	5.76
Program structure	4.91
Adult needs	4.55

*Scale:

   1 (inadequate)—care does not meet custodial care needs;

   3 (minimal)—care meets custodial and to some small degree basic developmental needs;

   5 (good)—basic dimensions of developmental care are met;

   7 (excellent)—high quality, personalized care.

Source: Calculations from New Chance Child Care Study ECERS ratings.

- Lowest hourly wage of full-time teachers;
- Percentage of total budget spent on personnel;
- Annual turnover rate;
- Average enrolled group size (calculated for each age category, in a site); and
- Average enrolled child-staff ratio (calculated for each age category, in a site).

Although these results must be interpreted cautiously because of small sample sizes, this analysis reveals the importance of child-staff ratios and group size to the quality of child day care centers. As expected, the correlations show that, for all age groups, sites with larger group size, and to a lesser degree, larger child-staff ratios, had lower ITERS or ECERS ratings. This analysis did not, however, find strong associations between the other characteristics of the centers and the ITERS or ECERS ratings.

TABLE 9
Correlations Among Quality Variables

Survey-Based Variable	Correlation with ITERS		Correlation with ECERS
	(Infant Rooms) *(N = 8 centers)*	*(Toddler Rooms)* *(N = 5 centers)*	*(Preschool Rooms)* *(N = 5 centers)*
% of Teachers with B.A. Degree	−0.32	−0.44	0.10
% of Teachers with More than 3 Years Experience	−0.20	−0.14	0.66
Lowest Hourly Wage of Full-Time Teachers	−0.05	0.04	0.38
% of Total Budget Spent on Personnel	−0.34	−0.63	0.12
Annual Turnover Rate	0.00	−0.04	−0.23
Average Enrolled Group Size	−0.90***	−0.73*	−0.61
Average Enrolled Child-Staff Ratio	−0.76**	−0.42	−0.28

Notes: Correlations are Pearson correlation coefficients. The Pearson coefficient varies from −1, indicating a perfect negative association, to +1, indicating a perfect positive association. A zero indicates the variables have no linear relationship.

Statistical significance levels are indicated as: *** = 1%; ** = 5%; * = 10%.

Source: Calculations from New Chance Child Care Study ITERS ratings (for infant and toddler rooms) and ECERS ratings (for preschool rooms), and New Chance Child Care Study surveys.

Conclusion

The findings from the New Chance Child Care Study show that the children in the New Chance centers generally received good quality care, but not exceedingly high quality care. Child-staff ratios, observed group size, benefits provided to teachers, and turnover met the threshold level of quality based on the established NAEYC standards and were as good as or better than comparable centers serving low-income children.* When considering caregivers' educational levels and the enrollment-based group size of infant classrooms, however, New Chance centers fell below desired levels. The ITERS and ECERS ratings were slightly higher than those of comparable centers in the NCCSS sample, but still fell just below the "good" level of services, also indicating room for improvement.

The results of this study suggest that policies to enhance the quality of child day care should focus on improving structural characteristics such as group size, particularly in classrooms for infants. The correlational analysis, which showed the strong relationship that child-staff ratios and group size have with quality, reinforces the need to reduce the number of children per classroom.

Personnel considerations must also be taken into account, in particular the need to attract a highly educated and trained staff. Although the correlational analysis did not find the expected relationship between personnel attributes and quality, the relatively low level of the staff's formal education and the room for improvement on certain observed dimensions of quality (such as the relatively low ITERS rating for learning activities) are areas of concern. The study suggests the need for high quality in-service training and some wage progression so programs can keep caregivers as they gain new skills.

Although the New Chance child day care programs could be improved, this study shows that they are comparable to other programs for low-income families and that, in general, they meet accepted child day care standards. Integrating good quality child day care with programs for welfare recipients is feasible: the New Chance programs were selected for this study because of

---

*The findings from this study are consistent with the results of the cost analysis of New Chance, which found that a relatively high level of resources were spent on child day care provided as a part of New Chance. The cost per slot for the on-site child day care centers averaged $420 per month, or $5,040 per year.

the high quality of services they provide to teenage mothers—now it is known that these programs also provide decent quality child day care. Less obvious is whether the care is good enough to improve the development of children at high risk who may need the best quality programs. ♦

References

Berrueta-Clement, J. R., Schweinhart, L. J., Barnett, W. S., Epstein, A. S., & Weikart, D. P. (1984). *Changed lives: The effects of the Perry Preschool program on youths through age 19.* Ypsilanti, MI: High/Scope Press.

Bredekamp, S. (Ed.). (1984). *Accreditation criteria and procedures of the National Academy of Early Childhood Programs.* Washington, DC: National Association for the Education of Young Children.

Harms, T., & Clifford, R. M. (1980). *Early childhood environment rating scale.* New York: Teachers College Press.

Harms, T., Cryer, D., & Clifford, R. M. (1990). *Infant-toddler environment rating scale.* New York: Teachers College Press.

Hayes, C., Palmer, J., & Zaslow, M. (Eds.). (1990). *Who cares for America's children? Child care policy for the 1990s.* Report of the Panel on Child Care Policy, Committee on Child Development Research and Public Policy, National Research Council. Washington, DC: National Academy Press.

Hofferth, S. L. (1987). The children of teen childbearers. In S. L. Hofferth & C. D. Hayes (Eds.), *Risking the future: Adolescent sexuality, pregnancy, and childbearing* (vol. II) (pp. 174–206). Washington, DC: National Academy Press.

Kisker, E., Hofferth, S. L., Phillips, D., & Farquhar, E. (1991). *A profile of child care settings: Early education and care in 1990.* Washington, DC: U.S. Department of Education.

Pear, R. (1994, November 22). *G.O.P. proposal would overhall welfare system. The New York Times,* p. A1.

Ruopp, R., Travers, J., Glantz, F., & Coelen, C. (1979). Children at the center: Final report of the national day care study. Cambridge, MA: Abt Associates.

Smith, S., Blank, S., & Collins, R. (1992). *Pathways to self-sufficiency for two generations: Designing welfare-to-work programs that benefit children and strengthen families.* New York: Foundation for Child Development.

Whitebook, M., Howes, C., & Phillips, D. (1990). *Who cares? Child care teachers and the quality of care in America.* Final report of the National Child Care Staffing Study. Oakland, CA: Child Care Employee Project.

5

Predictors of Parent and Provider Satisfaction with Child Day Care Dimensions: A Comparison of Center-Based and Family Child Day Care

Preston A. Britner and Deborah A. Phillips

Predictors of satisfaction with specific aspects of child day care arrangements were evaluated for parents and care providers of children in full-time center-based child day care and family child care. Descriptive statistics for the predictors were compared by type of care. Hierarchical regression analyses revealed that perceived social support derived from the care arrangement was the best predictor of parental satisfaction in both types of care. For center-based providers, satisfaction was best predicted by parent-provider agreement about the importance of specific care characteristics. Parent-provider agreement about traditional child-rearing values was associated with satisfaction for family child care providers.

Preston A. Britner, M.A., is Ph.D. candidate, Department of Psychology, University of Virginia, Charlottesville, VA. Deborah A. Phillips, Ph.D., is Director, Board on Chil-

Almost universally, parents report that they are satisfied with their child day care arrangements [Bogat & Gensheimer 1986; Shinn et al. 1991]. Ninety-six percent of the parents in the 1990 National Child Care Survey (NCCS), for example, reported that they were satisfied with the arrangements they had made for their children [Hofferth et al. 1991]. This general finding applies across types of care, qualities of care, and regions of the United States [Mitchell et al. 1992]. At the same time, however, 26% of the parents in the NCCS said they wanted to change their child day care arrangements [Hofferth et al. 1991]. Single working parents living in poverty wanted to change their arrangements at even higher rates than did two-parent families [Brayfield et al. 1993]. This suggests that the literature on parental satisfaction with child day care is ambiguous at best. Little is known, for example, about what leads to parental satisfaction with care and whether these correlates of satisfaction vary by type of care arrangement.

What accounts for this apparent contradiction in the literature on parents' reactions to child day care? Is it primarily a methodological artifact? For example, do different questions elicit differing degrees of social desirability, and thus reluctance to acknowledge unhappiness with one's care arrangements? Or, does this contradiction reveal shortcomings in the frameworks that guide research on parental satisfaction with child day care?

The research reported here reflects the latter perspective. It departs from the majority of earlier research efforts in the following ways: (1) rather than focus on global assessments of satisfaction, we attempt to distinguish the specific dimensions of care

dren and Families, National Research Council, Washington, DC. Preparation of this article was supported in part by an individual grant to the first author by the University of Virginia's Developmental Training Grant, NIMH Grant MH18242. The authors gratefully acknowledge the assistance of the parents, child day care providers, and center directors who made this study possible.

that are associated with satisfaction from those that predict dis-satisfaction; (2) rather than focus exclusively on level of satisfaction, we examine several proposed aspects of care that can influence variation in satisfaction in center-based or family child day care settings; (3) rather than study parents in isolation from the providers on whom their own satisfaction with care is likely to be highly dependent, we include assessments of both the providers' satisfaction with the child day care settings in which they work, and the contribution to parents' satisfaction made by the degree of concordance between parent and provider child-rearing attitudes and views of the important dimensions of child day care; and (4) rather than limiting data collection to a single measurement period, we utilized a short-term longitudinal design in order to examine the role of dimensions viewed as important for the selection of the care arrangement (parents) and for good quality care (providers) at Time 1 in the prediction of satisfaction with the current care situation at Time 2.

Satisfaction with Dimensions of Care

Whereas previous research on parental satisfaction with care relied exclusively on assessments of overall satisfaction, recent studies have begun to use specific aspects of the care environment to assess satisfaction and to relate global and specific ratings [Mitchell et al. 1992]. In a study of 441 mothers using 46 child day care centers, for example, Shinn and her colleagues [1989] reported that mothers' overall satisfaction was associated with their child's experience (e.g., provider's warmth, daily activities, and opportunities for learning), the facility's attributes (e.g., amount of space, security, and safety), low teacher turnover, and the quality of their own interactions with the teachers. "Adult" concerns, such as cost, child day care location, flexibility of hours and rules, and opportunities for parents to influence program policies did not affect the mothers' overall satisfaction. Further, the mothers' perceptions of the quality of provider-child interactions were more strongly associated with their overall satisfaction than were structural dimensions of quality such as group size, staff-child ratio, and provider training [Shinn et al. 1991]. In a related study, Endsley and Bradbard [1987] identified a lack of educational and peer stimulation, provider undependability and neglect, and discrepant child-rearing values as the major sources of dissatisfaction among child day care center users who had changed their care arrangements.

Although only 30% of the children who are in nonrelative child day care in the U.S. are cared for in centers [Hayes et al. 1990], only in the last few years have researchers examined parent reports of satisfaction in noncenter settings. Bogat and Gensheimer [1986] found high levels of overall satisfaction among parents using both center-based and family child care arrangements, whereas in Fuqua and Labensohn's [1986] study, parents using family child care reported that they were more likely to choose another arrangement if it were available than were parents using centers. More recently, Hofferth and colleagues [1991] reported in the large-scale 1990 National Child Care Survey on the wide variability of care preferences and satisfaction for families using family child care or center-based care.

Results from a low-income subset of the NCCS [Brayfield et al. 1993], from a sample of teen mothers with children under two years of age [Kisker & Silverberg 1991], and from a three-site report on AFDC mothers of young children [Sonenstein & Wolf 1991] suggest that large percentages of mothers in poverty would change their child day care arrangements if they could. In low-income samples, choice of care may be a myth. Across these studies, center-based care was notably preferred over home-based nonrelative family child care arrangements. Such preferences for center-based child day care, even for young children, may stem from perceptions of centers as more safe and secure than homes in impoverished neighborhoods, or may reflect the effects of early intervention messages of the importance of school preparedness and screening. Parental satisfaction may also serve as a possible predictor of the effects of care. In Meyers' [1993] sample of 225 single mothers participating in a California employment and training program, for instance, one in three mothers indicated they would have preferred a different care arrangement: mothers who wished they could use a different child care provider were over twice as likely to drop out of the welfare-to-work transition program than were mothers who were satisfied with their provider.

Why do parents select a particular type of care arrangement? Research comparing parents' stated reasons for choosing care revealed that center users often cited the importance of intellectual stimulation and specific aspects of the program, whereas family child care users emphasized the child-rearing philosophy of the provider and the homelike nature of the setting [Pence & Goelman 1987]. In contrast to parents who used centers, users of family child care in a three-site study of care preferences reported more frequently that they chose their current arrangement because of its convenience than its perceived quality; parent preferences by type of care were also age dependent, with centers being preferred for older children [Kisker et al. 1991]. Bogat and Gensheimer [1986] found that parents cited health and safety and the provider's child-rearing philosophy as the most important dimensions in their care choice in both types of care. The researchers note that whereas parents choosing different types of care may value different aspects of care, parents were equally satisfied whether their children were in center-based or family child care settings and in preferred or nonpreferred arrangements.

These initial studies suggest that parental satisfaction is closely linked to comfort with the quality of care parents perceive their children to be receiving. Parents' own needs for convenient and flexible care, while undoubtedly important considerations when selecting an arrangement, appear to play a less salient role once the child is enrolled and the parents' concern turns to their child's well-being in child day care. Although interesting, this literature has remained highly descriptive, to the neglect of efforts to identify sources of variation in parental satisfaction. Absent attention to factors that account for differences in parental satisfaction with care, those who seek to improve satisfaction are left with minimal guidance about where to direct their efforts.

Another shortcoming of the literature on satisfaction is the absence of studies concerning care providers' satisfaction with care arrangements. Studies of center-based child day care workers have shown wages, provision for adult needs, education, and experience to be moderately associated with job satisfaction [Mullis et al. 1986; Phillips et al. 1991]. The quality of interactions with children also appears to be a source of job satisfaction among child day care workers [Kingsley & Cook-Hatala 1988; McClelland 1986]. It remains unclear, however, what leads to providers' satisfaction with the care they are giving, and whether parents' or providers' satisfaction is related to their agreement on child-rearing issues and views about what attributes of care are important. Use of parent and provider reports may yield a clearer picture of what leads to parents' selection of care and their satisfaction with the arrangement after the child has been in day care for some time.

Recent studies have given us some understanding of the levels and dimensions of parents' satisfaction with child day care. The work that has been done on satisfaction has had many limitations, however. To build upon the relatively less detailed, large-scale surveys of parental satisfaction with (and preferences for) types of child day care, it is necessary to study in added detail the various predictors of (or pathways to) satisfaction in both types of care and for both parents and providers, as the key players in children's interrelated environments of home and day care.

Predictors of Satisfaction: The Role of Home-Child Day Care Connections

Ecological theory affords a particularly promising direction for research on predictors of parent satisfaction with child day care.

In particular, Bronfenbrenner [1979] has called attention to the importance of studying the ecological mesosystem, or the interrelations between settings that the child is actively negotiating. Peters and Kontos [1987] have also written extensively about the role of continuity between the children's home and the child day care environments as an element of child day care.

Bronfenbrenner hypothesized that each environment's developmental potential for the child could be maximized when compatibility existed between the goals of the settings. On the assumption that family life provides an ideal developmental environment for children, as opposed to an intervention model stressing the need to remedy a "risk," continuity between home and caregiving environments has been touted as a goal for good child day care and viewed as a potentially important predictor of successful outcomes for children, parents, and care providers [McCartney & Phillips 1988; Powell 1989]. In the present study, the mesosystem is conceptualized as the intersection of the home and child day care environments and is believed to be a useful frame of reference for the study of satisfaction with the care environment for both parents and providers.

Past literature on continuity has been plagued with problems of operationalizing home-care continuity [Peters & Kontos 1987]. Continuity across child day care and home environments may reflect similarities or differences in the physical or social environment; behavior toward the child; beliefs about child development, rearing, or education; or perceptions of the child [Long et al. 1985]. The present study therefore focuses on four functional dimensions of continuity as possible predictors of satisfaction for parents and providers: (1) child day care as a social support to parents; (2) parent involvement in care; (3) parent-provider agreement on child-rearing beliefs; and (4) parent-provider agreement on the importance of dimensions of care that are important to parents in their choice of care and valued by providers as essential to good quality care.

Social Support

In response to Bronfenbrenner's ecological emphasis on the need
to strengthen bonds across environments, some recent work has
focused on family social support systems [Powell 1989]. Child
day care has been compared to an extended family because of its
potential to be a means of social support, especially when parent
involvement is common and communication is multidirectional
[Honig 1979]. By giving emotional support in addition to information and services, child day care providers can have a role in
the psychological well-being of employed parents [McCartney &
Phillips 1988; Schumacher & DeMeis 1992]. Howes and Stewart
[1987] found greater social support and maternal role satisfaction
to be associated with higher quality care. Parents' satisfaction
with care may be related to their perception of child day care as a
source of social support [Garbarino 1982].

Parent Involvement

Powell [1989] has supported the development of parent involvement programs aimed at improving levels of child competence,
parent satisfaction, and overall quality of child day care by increasing the amount of parent-provider interaction. Parent involvement has become a component in most provider training
programs [Honig 1979]. The National Association for the Education of Young Children (NAEYC) has stressed the importance of
parent involvement and parent-staff communication in its accreditation guidelines for centers [Hayes et al. 1990]. Despite the
relatively low levels of provider-parent interaction found in
studies of frequency of parent involvement [Deater-Deckard
1991; Endsley & Minish 1991], parent reports of the frequency of
communication and intensity of involvement have been linked to
their satisfaction with care [Kontos & Dunn 1989; Zigler & Turner
1982]. It is likely, however, that specific amounts and forms of
parent involvement that occur or are desired by parents and
providers may differ by type of care. For example, in Pence and

Goelman's [1987] sample, parents using family child care arrangements reported talking and feeling close to the provider more often than did parents using center-based arrangements. Parents using center-based care, however, were more likely to participate in informational exchanges with the providers than were family child care users.

Child-Rearing Attitudes

Child-rearing attitudes of parents and providers represent another area of potential continuity or discontinuity across environments that may influence satisfaction. Pence and Goelman [1987] suggested that differences in parents using family child care and center-based arrangements were defined more by caregiving philosophies and values than by socioeconomic factors. Schaefer and Edgerton [1985] reported that parents' attitudes about traditional versus progressive child-rearing styles were related to their children's motivation for learning, academic achievement, and instrumental independence. Kontos and Dunn [1989], in turn, found that mothers using center-based care who rated high on traditional values were less satisfied with the care their children were receiving than were those mothers who were less traditional. Whereas child-rearing beliefs in and of themselves may predict satisfaction with care, the agreement of parents and providers may be important to the satisfaction of both groups given the various role demands placed on children across environments [Powell 1989]. Because parents using family child care choose a particular provider, it may be the case that they select providers who have more similar child-rearing attitudes than do parents using center-based care [Kontos 1993].

Importance of Care Characteristics

Agreement between parents and providers on the importance of care characteristics that parents have cited as instrumental in their choice of care may also lead to satisfaction with specific aspects of care for parents and providers. To the extent that parents and providers value the same structural and functional care characteristics of the arrangement, the continuity of goals across the settings may translate into favorable child outcomes and satisfaction for parents and providers [Bronfenbrenner 1979; Endsley & Bradbard 1987].

Study Overview

The present short-term longitudinal study was designed to elucidate the pathways to satisfaction with child day care arrangements for parents and child day care providers in center-based and family child care settings. Ratings of satisfaction with specific aspects of the care environment were obtained from all four groups of respondents. Several aspects that were theorized to be predictors of satisfaction, including the reported frequency of parental involvement, the perceived social support derived from care, and the agreement between parents and providers regarding child-rearing values and important care characteristics, are described in detail, and their relative influence in accounting for the variance in satisfaction with care is quantified for each group of respondents.

Method

Participants

The participants were 27 center- and home-based child day care providers and 90 parents whose children were in the care of those providers. The 18 center-based providers were from six centers (three private, two church-affiliated, and one university-based); the nine home-based providers were from nine separate family child care homes (six regulated; three nonregulated), all located in two suburban areas in a mid-Atlantic state. All centers and family child care homes recruited for involvement in the study agreed to participate. Each of the participants provided full-time care for children under five years of age.

The parents of 225 children were asked to participate. Two hundred and five parents (140 mothers and 65 fathers) of 149 children returned the consent forms and questionnaires. Of these 149 children, 104 were in center-based care and 45 were in family child care homes. Child care providers completed questionnaires on the 149 children whose parents were participating. At a follow-up assessment approximately four months later, 111 of the 205 parents returned questionnaires, representing 90 children (60 in centers and 30 in family child care homes). All 27 care providers for these children completed the follow-up questionnaires, thus generating the final sample. In cases in which both parents completed the questionnaires, only the responses of the parent who was deemed the primary caregiver for the child were used in the analyses for this article. In the final sample, the responses of 85 mothers and five fathers were used.

The parents were predominantly Caucasian, college-educated (mean of 16.7 years of education), and middle- to upper-middle class (annual gross income of 67% of the families was in the $30,000 to $100,000 range). The care providers were predominantly Caucasian and had worked an average of six years in the field and two and a half years in their current position; approximately 40% belonged to a professional child day care or early childhood organization.

Measures

Care providers completed five measures and parents completed seven measures, as described below. The measures differed somewhat across the Time 1 and Time 2 assessments. Test-retest reliabilities for new measures were established with a pilot sample of 20 parents and 10 caregivers. Table 1 summarizes the Time 1 and Time 2 questionnaires for parents and care providers.

Demographics and experience. A number of demographic variables were obtained from background questionnaires completed by parents and providers. At Time 1, parents were asked about

TABLE 1
Measures Collected on Parents and Providers at Time 1 and Time 2

Measure	Parents		Providers	
	Time 1	Time 2	Time 1	Time 2
Demographics and Experience	X	X	X	X
Alternative Care Preferences	X			
Child-Rearing Attitudes	X		X	
Child Day Care as a Social Support		X		X
Importance of Care Characteristics	X		X	
Satisfaction with Care Characteristics		X		X
Frequency of Parent-Provider Involvement	X	X	X	X

their child's sex, age, initial age of entry into care, and amount of time in their current arrangement from first day of enrollment. Parents at Time 2 reported their own ethnicity, education, and family income level. At Time 1, care providers noted the age range and number of children in their direct care. Providers at Time 2 reported their own ethnicity, education, certification, training, involvement in professional organizations, and years of experience in child day care generally and in their current position. Family child care providers were also asked if they were licensed or registered and if they were sponsored by a family child care organization or met regularly with other family child care providers. The questionnaire was adapted from the caregiver interview of the National Child Care Staffing Study (NCCSS) [Whitebook et al. 1990].

Alternative care preferences. Three questions about initial types of care arrangements considered and preferred by parents at Time 1 were adapted from questions in Shinn and colleagues' [1989] study of parents, conducted in conjunction with the NCCSS, and from the National Child Care Consumer Survey (NCCCS) [Hofferth 1989]. Parents reported whether they had considered other similar programs or alternative types of care at the time they selected their current arrangement. Parents were also asked to note their preferred form of care at the time they made their selection, as well as their ideal arrangement if money were no object.

Child-rearing attitudes. Parents and caregivers at Time 1 completed Schaefer and Edgerton's [1985] 30-item Parental Modernity scale. Respondents rated their reactions from "strongly disagree" (1) to "strongly agree" (5) to a range of ideas about rearing and educating children. The modernity scale yields two scores on progressive and traditional child-rearing dimensions. The progressive dimension includes items that tap progressive democratic family and educational ideals, such as beliefs that children are basically good and learn actively and that the aim of education is learning how to learn. The traditional dimension includes items that tap traditional authoritarian family and educational ideology, such as an emphasis on obedience and respect for authority. Two summary scores, corresponding to the progressive and traditional dimensions, were created to describe the concordance between parent and provider ratings of modernity. The concordance scores were calculated by summing the absolute value of the differences between parent and provider ratings of the eight progressive items and the 22 traditional items.

Child day care as a social support. Belsky's [1991] 34-item revision of the Daycare as a Social Support Scale (DSSS) [Schumacher & DeMeis 1992] was completed by parents at the second assessment period as an outcome measure. The scale was designed to assess the emotional, instrumental, and informational support offered by child day care. Items are rated on a four-point scale from "never" (1) to "always" (4) based upon the frequency with which supportive actions take place. A composite was created to summarize the amount of support parents express. Items tap the parents' ratings of the care providers' supportiveness on issues such as willingness to set and work toward child care goals and respect for the parents' needs and opinions.

Importance of care characteristics. At the first assessment, providers rated a list of 32 characteristics of child day care for their importance as determinants of good quality care. The items were rated on a five-point scale from "very important" (1) to "very unimportant" (5). The same 32 items were rated at Time 1 by parents in terms of their importance when choosing their current care arrangement. Items were included to assess five hypothesized dimensions of importance: Structural Quality, Interactive Quality, Convenience, Communication, and Involvement. Some of the 32 items were derived from the caregiver interview used in the NCCSS [Whitebook et al. 1990], the Profile of Child Care Settings Study [Kisker et al. 1991], and the work of Deater-Deckard [1991]. The mean test-retest correlation for the 32 importance items in the pilot sample was .787 for parents and .781 for care providers.

To assess the internal consistency of the five hypothesized dimensions of importance with respect to parental choice, Cronbach's alpha coefficients were calculated separately for parents using center-based care and family child care. Four dimensions for parents using center-based care and three dimensions for parents using family child care demonstrated adequate internal consistency. Table 2 lists the items by dimension and the dimension coefficient alphas for center-based and family child care groups. Center-based and family child care providers' responses displayed patterns similar to parents' responses and are not reported in this article.

A summary importance score was calculated to describe the concordance between the importance ratings of parents and providers. The concordance composite score was created by summing the absolute value of the differences between parent and provider ratings on the importance items. This score captures the extent to which the dimensions of care considered by providers to be important to quality correspond to those that are considered by parents to be important when selecting care.

TABLE 2
Internal Consistency of Importance Dimensions by Type of Care

		Cronbach Alpha	
Dimension	*Item Description*	*Center-Based Care*	*Family Child Care*
Structural Quality	Physical Facility	.89	.87
	Health and Safety		
	Group Size		
	Security Precautions		
	Provider-Child Ratio		
	Space for Children		
	Compliance with State Standards (deleted for family child care)		
	Stability of Staff (deleted for all)		
Interactive Quality	Opportunity to Learn	.76	.87
	Parent Visiting Welcome		
	Warmth of the Provider		
	Day to Day Activities		
	Attention Child Receives		
	Discipline		
	Appropriate Toys and Equipment (deleted for family child care)		
Convenience	Cost	—	.76
	Hours Program Open		
	Flexibility to Come Late		
	Location Relative to Home or Work		
	Rules of the Setting		
Communication	Verbal Communication	.75	—
	Written Communication		
	Parent-Provider Conferences		
	Informal Conversation (deleted for all)		
Involvement	Volunteer (in Setting)	.84	—
	Fundraising		
	Attend Social Functions		
	Select Staff		
	Review Budget		
	Choose Activities		
	Volunteer (Outside Setting)		
	Attend Workshop		

Satisfaction. At the second assessment, the same 32-item list of child day care characteristics used to assess importance was rated by parents and providers to provide an assessment of the respondent's satisfaction with each characteristic of the caregiving arrangement. Parents rated items on a five-point scale from "very satisfied" (1) to "very dissatisfied" (5). Providers rated the quality of each item for their child day care setting on a five-point scale from "doing extremely well" (1) to "needs much improvement" (5). The 32 satisfaction items had a mean test-retest reliability correlation in the pilot sample of .934 for parents and .733 for care providers.

Satisfaction composite scores were created for parents and providers based upon the items that loaded on the "importance" dimensions. In center-based care, the parent and provider satisfaction score was created by summing the 25 items from the center-based care importance dimensions of Structural Quality, Interactive Quality, Communication, and Involvement, and then dividing by 25 (the total number of items used to compute the composites). The satisfaction scores for family child care parents and providers were created by summing the 17 items from the family child care importance dimensions of Structural Quality, Interactive Quality, and Convenience, and then dividing by 17 (the total number of items used to create the composites). All of the composite satisfaction scores ranged from "very satisfied" (1) to "very dissatisfied" (5).

Frequency of parent-provider involvement. The 13 items from the importance and satisfaction questionnaires that dealt with aspects of parent involvement and parent-provider communication were repeated at Time 1 and Time 2, on a questionnaire completed by both parents and providers, to assess the actual frequency with which these events took place. For example, parents and providers noted how frequently they conversed when the parent dropped off or picked up his or her child and how frequently an individual parent-provider conference was held.

The mean test-retest correlation in the pilot sample for the 13 frequency items was .714 for parents and .782 for providers. Composite scores for the frequency of parent involvement were created by summing the 13 frequency items, as reported by parents and by providers.

Procedure

Child day care providers were recruited from Office for Children and Youth lists of licensed centers and registered family child care homes and from a list of nonregistered family child care homes identified in previous research. For center-based child day care providers, center directors were initially contacted. All family child care providers were also the owners of the arrangements and so constituted the initial contact person. Initial visits were made to each center and home to obtain written consent and a listing of all children under the age of five years in the care of the provider for at least 20 hours per week. Children had to have been in the care of the provider for a minimum of two months to have their parents considered as eligible participants. A second visit was made to each participating arrangement to distribute the Time 1 questionnaires and to provide verbal instructions about their completion. Consent forms, questionnaires, and instructions were distributed by the child day care providers to a randomly-selected subset of parents from the lists they provided. Each parent packet was placed in a sealed envelope identified only by an ID number, which had been assigned by the first author. Parents returned completed consent forms and questionnaires to their providers, again in a sealed envelope identified only by an ID number. Parent and provider packets were collected on site.

Approximately four months after the initial questionnaire was completed, another visit was made to each participating arrangement for the purpose of distributing the Time 2 questionnaires to each provider and leaving the Time 2 parent questionnaires for providers to distribute to the participating parents. All

Time 2 questionnaires from parents and providers were mailed directly to the researchers in prestamped envelopes supplied by the researchers.

Results

Selection Effects

As a first step, it was important to assess whether there were significant differences between subjects in the original and follow-up samples on any of the Time 1 demographic variables and scale composites. Four separate one-way multivariate analyses of variance (MANOVAs) were conducted for parents using family child care, parents using center-based child day care, family child care providers, and center-based child day care providers. These MANOVAs had participation at Time 2 as the independent variable and the Time 1 composites (5 importance, 2 child-rearing, and frequency of involvement) and the demographic or structural markers (child age, child sex, group size, provider certification or training, and parents' initial preference for type of care) as the dependent variables. None of the MANOVAs approached significance, suggesting that there were no selection effects from Time 1 to Time 2 among any of the four groups of respondents.

Descriptive Statistics by Type of Care

Means and standard deviations are presented separately in table 3 for family child care and center-based child day care parents and providers on the predictor composites and the satisfaction composites.

Parent involvement. Parent involvement in the child day care setting was infrequent, according to both parents and providers in center-based and family child care arrangements, replicating the findings of previous studies [Deater-Deckard 1991; Endsley & Minish 1991; Zigler & Turner 1982]. Within type of care, the correlations of parent and provider composites of frequency of

TABLE 3
Descriptive Statistics for Composites by Type of Care

		Mean (Std. Dev.)	
Composite Score	*Range*	*FCDC*	*Center*
Frequency of Involvement	0 (infrequent) to 39 (frequent)		
(Parent)		8.2 (2.9)	11.8 (3.7)
(Provider)		9.9 (4.2)	13.8 (4.4)
Care as Social Support	34 (minimal) to 136 (extensive)		
(Parent)		126.0 (6.2)	122.7 (11.4)
Importance Ratings	1 (important) to 5 (unimportant)		
Structural Quality			
(Parent)		1.7 (.7)	1.5 (.4)
(Provider)		1.7 (.6)	1.5 (.9)
Interactive Quality			
(Parent)		1.5 (.7)	1.2 (.3)
(Provider)		1.6 (.7)	1.2 (.3)
Convenience			
(Parent)		2.0 (.7)	
(Provider)		1.7 (.5)	
Communication			
(Parent)			1.8 (.7)
(Provider)			1.6 (.9)
Involvement			
(Parent)			3.4 (.9)
(Provider)			2.7 (1.0)
Progressive Child-Rearing Concordance	0 (agreement) to 32 (disagreement)	2.8 (2.3)	4.4 (3.9)
Traditional Child-Rearing Concordance	0 (agreement) to 88 (disagreement)	17.7 (11.4)	12.2 (10.5)
Importance of Care Quality Concordance	0 (agreement) to 132 (disagreement)	37.8 (14.8)	29.0 (15.3)
Satisfaction with Care Quality	1 (satisfied) to 5 (dissatisfied)		
(Parent)		1.5 (3)	1.9 (.4)
(Provider)		1.6 (.5)	1.8 (.7)

parent involvement did not reach significance, suggesting that these ratings are tapping perceptions of involvement rather than accurate accounts of level of involvement. To examine differences in parents' reports of involvement by type of care at Time 2, a one-way MANOVA was conducted, with type of care as the independent variable and the 13 items about the frequency of parent-provider interaction as the dependent variables (F (13,76) = 8.79, $p < .001$), followed by univariate analyses of variance. Parents with children in center-based care reported that they received written communication, participated in formal parent-provider conferences, volunteered in the care setting, volunteered outside the care setting, helped raise funds, and chose activities for the setting more frequently than did parents of children in family child care. Family child care parents reported that they talked to their provider at drop-off or pick-up and received informal verbal feedback about their child more frequently than did parents using center-based care. All differences were significant at $p < .01$. There were no significant differences by type of care for the amount of time parents reported observing their children in care, participating in staff selection, reviewing the program budget, attending workshops, or attending social functions at the child day care setting. Similar patterns emerged for providers.

Social support. Parents in both types of care viewed their child day care arrangements as a form of social support. Parents using family child care and center-based care alike reported receiving high levels of instrumental, emotional, and informational support from the child day care providers. A comparison of the variances revealed that the responses of parents using center-based care to questions about support were more variable than were those of parents using family child care ($F(59, 29) = 3.41$, $p < .001$).

Importance. For family child care, parent and provider ratings of important quality dimensions yielded similar patterns. Interactive Quality, Structural Quality, and Convenience were rated by parents and providers as "important" to "somewhat important" dimensions, though Convenience was rated as slightly less important than the two Quality dimensions. For parents and providers in center-based care, Interactive Quality was rated as more important than both Structural Quality and Communication. For center-based care, involvement was seen as "neither important nor unimportant" for providers and parents, though providers rated it as somewhat more important than did parents.

Dimensions of care characteristics that were rated by parents as important to their choice of care varied by type of care. Convenience was not an internally consistent dimension of importance to parents who selected center-based care. Although Convenience was important to parents using family child care [Kisker et al. 1991], Interactive Quality and Structural Quality were more important than Convenience to all parents and providers in the present study. Quality—in terms of both the interactive provider-child relationship and characteristics of the provider and the structural characteristics of group size, provider-child ratio, and the like—was the most important consideration for both groups of parents in their choice of care and for both groups of providers in reporting what was necessary for good care.

Child-rearing attitudes. Contrary to the hypothesis that concordance of modernity ratings would be greater in family child care arrangements, center-based respondents agreed slightly more in their opinions about traditional child-rearing beliefs than did family child care respondents ($t(88) = 2.27$, $p < .05$). Family child care providers were more traditional in their child-rearing beliefs than were the other respondents, although all four groups were low on the composite of traditional values. Parents and providers in both types of care showed a high level of agreement about traditional child-rearing beliefs. With respect to progressive modernity, family child care respondents agreed slightly more in their opinions than did center-based respondents ($t(86) = 2.51$, $p < .05$). Overall, however, parents and providers displayed high levels of agreement about progressive child-rearing beliefs.

Parent-provider agreement on importance and associated satisfaction levels. Parent and provider ratings of the importance of care quality also showed high levels of concordance. In the context of good overall concordance, agreement between parents using center-based care on characteristics that were important to them in their selection of care and providers of center-based care on characteristics that were important to good care was somewhat higher than agreement between parents and providers of family child care ($t(88) = 2.57, p < .05$). Not surprisingly, parents and providers in both types of care arrangements expressed satisfaction with, respectively, the care being provided and the job they were doing in terms of the various dimensions of child day care quality.

Predictors of Satisfaction

What predicts satisfaction with aspects of child day care for parents and providers in center-based and family child care arrangements? As an initial step, the theorized predictors of satisfaction were intercorrelated. Sex of the child was uncorrelated with any other variable and was dropped from these analyses. Due to its high correlation with provider certification, the size of the care group (and thus the provider-child ratio) was dropped. The intercorrelations of the variables retained for the regression analyses are presented separately for family child care and center-based care groups in tables 4 and 5, respectively.

Each of the four satisfaction composites (center-based care parent, family child care parent, center-based care provider, and family child care provider) was regressed in a five-step hierarchical regression on the theorized predictors of satisfaction. Hierarchical regression was employed to see if the addition of markers of social support from the care provider, interactions between providers and parents, and, finally, parent-provider agreement about child-rearing attitudes would improve the prediction of satisfaction (for each of the four groups) over the traditionally employed markers of provider training, age of the child, and parental reports of initial preference for type of nonmaternal care arrangement if money were no object. In the first step, the child's

TABLE 4

Intercorrelations of Predictors of Satisfaction in Family Child Care

	Child Age	Certification	Ideal Care	Social Support	Frequency (Parent)	Frequency (Provider)	Traditional	Progressive	Importance
Child Age	1.00	-.683*	.180	.113	.165	.152	-.295	.138	-.255
Certification	-.683*	1.00	-.117	.016	-.233	.088	.584*	.052	.109
Ideal Care	.180	-.117	1.00	-.051	.331	.013	.138	.230	.320
Social Support	.113	.016	-.051	1.00	.312	-.089	.220	.118	.173
Frequency (Parent)	.165	-.233	.331	.312	1.00	.036	.292	.024	.064
Frequency (Provider)	.152	.088	.013	-.089	.036	1.00	-.020	-.109	-.394*
Traditional	-.295	.584*	.138	.220	.292	-.020	1.00	.314	.197
Progressive	.138	.052	.230	.118	.024	-.109	.314	1.00	.200
Importance	-.255	.109	.320	.173	.064	-.394*	.197	.200	1.00

*p < .05

TABLE 5
Intercorrelations of Predictors of Satisfaction in Center-Based Child Day Care

	Child Age	Certification	Ideal Care	Social Support	Frequency (Parent)	Frequency (Provider)	Traditional	Progressive	Importance
Child Age	1.00	−.303*	−.040	−.146	−.149	.063	−.205	.137	.188
Certification	−.303*	1.00	.081	.082	.310*	.300*	.190	−.320*	.192
Ideal Care	−.040	.081	1.00	−.157	.144	−.210	−.167	−.207	.161
Social Support	−.146	.082	−.157	1.00	−.134	.048	.043	.006	.057
Frequency (Parent)	−.148	.310*	.144	−.134	1.00	.097	.034	−.089	−.019
Frequency (Provider)	.063	.300*	−.210	.048	.097	1.00	.086	.007	.031
Traditional	−.205	.190	−.167	.043	.034	.086	1.00	−.030	.101
Progressive	.137	−.320*	−.207	.006	−.089	.007	−.030	1.00	−.339*
Importance	.188	.192	.161	.057	−.019	.031	.101	−.340	1.00

*$p < .05$

age and provider's certification in child day care/early education were entered as the independent variables. Parent reports of their preferred child day care arrangement type were entered second, and the extent to which parents viewed child day care as a source of social support was entered third. Parent and provider reports of the frequency of parent involvement were added in the fourth step. The variables of parent-provider concordance on traditional child-rearing beliefs, progressive child-rearing beliefs, and importance of quality care characteristics were entered in the last step. The results of the hierarchical regressions of satisfaction on the various theorized predictors are summarized in table 6.

For parents using centers, self-reports of social support and reported frequency of parent involvement were the only significant predictors of parents' satisfaction with the care arrangement. Parents were more satisfied with the center-based care arrangement if they viewed it as a source of social support and reported high frequencies of involvement in the center. Interestingly, parents' reports of the level of their involvement predicted their satisfaction with care, although parents had not rated involvement as an important dimension in their choice of care.

For parents using family child care arrangements, social support emerged as the only significant predictor of parents' satisfaction with care. Like parents using center-based care, parents using family child care who viewed their child day care as a source of social support reported greater satisfaction with aspects of the care arrangement.

Providers of center-based child day care were the only group for which satisfaction with care was significantly predicted by any of the demographic variables. The statistical interaction of the child's age and the provider's status as certified in child day care or early childhood education was significantly associated with the providers' reports of satisfaction with aspects of the child day care arrangement. Certification was more important to these providers' satisfaction with care characteristics for those in charge of older children than for those who cared for younger

TABLE 6

Hierarchical Regression of Satisfaction Composites on Predictors of Satisfaction by Type of Care and Respondent

Satisfaction Composite	Predictors	Beta	t	R^2	F (df)
Parent Using Center-Based Child Day Care	Social Support	-.018	-.4523***	.261	20.458*** (1,58)
	Social Support	-.017	-4.368***	.354	15.626*** (2,57)
	Frequency (Parent) of Involvement	.034	2.871**		
Parent Using Family Child Care	Social Support	-.032	-3.960***	.359	15.685*** (1,28)
Center-Based Child Day Care Provider	Training x Age	.369	3.519***	.187	12.381*** (1,54)
	Training x Age	.233	2.391*	.389	16.846*** (2,53)
	Concordance of Importance	.021	4.186***		
Family Child Care Provider	Concordance of Traditional Child-Rearing Beliefs	-.029	-5.266***	.498	27.736*** (1,28)

*p < .05
**p < .01
***p < .001

children. The explained variance in the providers' satisfaction increased significantly with the addition of parent-provider concordance on the importance of quality care characteristics. Greater concordance between the parents' important characteristics when selecting care and the providers' important characteristics when rating "good care" was related to relatively higher levels of satisfaction with care for providers of center-based care.

For family child care providers, the only significant predictor of satisfaction with care characteristics was parent-provider concordance on traditional child-rearing beliefs, which accounted for half of the variance in satisfaction. Relatively high levels of agreement between parents and providers about traditional child-rearing values were associated with satisfaction with characteristics of the child care arrangement for providers of family child care.

Discussion

The most important contribution of this study is the identification of different predictors of satisfaction with care characteristics for parents using center-based child day care, parents using family child care, center-based child day care providers, and family child care providers. Consistent with other research, overall satisfaction with care was high for all groups [Bogat & Gensheimer 1986; Shinn et al. 1991]. On the dimensions of the care setting's structural quality (e.g., health and safety, group size) and the quality of interactions between providers and children (e.g., provider's warmth, attention to children), parents using and providers of center-based child day care and parents using and providers of family child care were all equally satisfied. Contrary to the hypothesis that provider training and experience and child day care group size would predict satisfaction with care, these variables were significantly associated with satisfaction only for providers in centers. The importance of functional (e.g., parent-provider interaction) rather than structural (e.g., provider training) markers in predicting satisfaction with care in all groups in this study is in line with previous findings about what dimensions of care are important to parents' satisfaction [Shinn et al. 1991]. The traditional "quality" variables of academic research and licensing standards simply were not associated with parents' satisfaction with care. Whereas parents may view structural markers such as group size to be important in their selection of a care arrangement, their satisfaction with the arrangement is not associated with these same markers.

Although parents rated aspects of quality as more important than convenience in their selection of care arrangements, parents in this middle-class sample may have chosen their care arrangement on the basis of perceived quality of settings that were realistic options, given cost, hours, and location [Hofferth et al. 1991; Shinn et al. 1991], despite the fact that they may have had more options than low-income parents [Brayfield et al. 1993; Kisker & Silverberg 1991; Sonenstein & Wolf 1991]. Consistent with previous research [Hofferth et al. 1991], parents' reports of their preferred type of care arrangement were not related to their satisfaction with their current arrangement.

The finding that social support from the child care provider was the best predictor of satisfaction for parents using family child care *and* for those using center-based child day care is impressive and suggestive of a fruitful area for more extensive study. With respect to the role of support offered to parents, some investigators have suggested that the dynamic relations among children, parents, and care providers serve as a means of socializing children with a neighborhood exosystem, and function similarly to extended family networks in previous generations, especially when parent involvement is common and communication is multidirectional [Kontos & Dunn 1989; Peters & Kontos 1987]. Most parents using both types of care in the sample viewed their child day care arrangements as a source of extensive informational and emotional support. As a result of feeling supported, parents may experience less stress and be more satisfied with care than those who feel less supported [Schumacher & DeMeis 1992; McCartney & Phillips 1988]. As such, child day care may be more usefully viewed as a social support, rather than a replacement, for the family [Garbarino 1992].

The specific types of parent-provider interactions that were reported to occur differed across types of care. Informal conversations and feedback from providers were more often reported by parents using family child care, whereas written communication, conferences, and parent activities in the setting were more frequent for parents using center-based care. Overall levels of parent involvement in this sample, however, as in previous works [Deater-Deckard 1991; Endsley & Minish 1991; Zigler & Turner 1982], were low, suggesting the need for renewed and innovative efforts to get parents more involved in their children's care environments.

Child-rearing attitudes of parents and care providers represent another area of potential continuity or discontinuity across environments in the mesosystem. Cultural and subcultural values (such as the appropriateness of physical punishment) also represent patterns within the overarching macrosystem [Bronfenbrenner 1979]. In the present study, the compatibility of parents' and providers' child-rearing philosophies was high in each type of care, as was the agreement between parents' and providers' beliefs regarding what specific aspects of caregiving are important for good quality care. This suggests that parents seek out care providers and settings that espouse similar value systems, priorities, and expectations of what is important to their children [Kontos 1993; Powell 1989]. In the context of this high overall agreement, parent-provider concordance on what aspects of caregiving were most important for good care was predictive of satisfaction for providers of center-based care only, and agreement on child-rearing beliefs was related to satisfaction only for providers of family child care. In fact, agreement on child-rearing philosophies accounted for half of the explained variance in the satifaction of providers of family child care with the care they were providing. Concordance may lead to providers' satisfaction due to more favorable social outcomes for children as a result of the agreement on goals and role demands across the settings.

Several methodological problems in the present study should be noted. The small sample size, especially with respect to the number of registered and nonregistered providers of family child care, may limit the generalizability of findings of the study. Additionally, the centers and family child care homes selected for participation in the study may not be representative of arrangements in other geographic regions. Child day care arrangements from one state were studied for practical reasons and for the comparison of the importance of aspects of care to parents and providers under comparable standards of child care registration and licensing [Phillips & Howes 1987]. Additionally, family child care homes that are identifiable for research purposes may not be representative of all such homes. Replication of the study with larger samples in more diverse geographic areas is necessary to address these issues. Although no overall selection effects were identified for participants in the original and follow-up samples, participants in the original sample may have been reliably different from nonparticipants. This potential effect of nonrepresentative selection of participation is common in research using questionnaires [Berk 1983], but the implications for possible bias in the results should be noted. Future work in this area could also use observer ratings and survey methods to assess the role of various dimensions of quality of care in mediating the relationships between the predictors identified in the current study and parent and provider satisfaction in family child care and center-based child day care arrangements.

Despite its limitations, the present study describes some of the key variables, especially those on the nature of interactions and agreement between parents and providers, that are associated with their satisfaction with family child care and center-based child day care arrangements. One practical implication of this study is its demonstration of the importance of studying parents' and providers' satisfaction with specific aspects of the care arrangement to capture more fully their satisfaction with the setting. Another key finding is the identification of different predictors of satisfaction for parents and providers across type of care arrangement. Most importantly, the present study has emphasized the need to look at home and child care environments as interconnected settings. Child-rearing is, in fact, a collaborative effort between parents and child day care professionals. Rather than comparing "home" and "child day care" influences on child outcomes or ratings of satisfaction, it is important to look at the joint effects and interactions between these environments. Satisfaction with the child day care arrangement, if not the "quality" of the care, resides in the intersection of the two systems in which children are functioning, learning, and developing. ◆

References

Belsky, J. (1991). *Daycare as a social support scale*. Unpublished questionnaire.

Berk, R. A. (1983). An introduction to sample selection bias in sociological data. *American Sociological Review, 48*, 386–398.

Bogat, G. A. , & Gensheimer, L. K. (1986). Discrepancies between the attitudes and actions of parents choosing day care. *Child Care Quarterly, 15*, 159–169.

Brayfield, A. A. , Deich, S. G. , & Hofferth, S. L. (1993). *Caring for children in low-income families: A substudy of the National Child Care Survey, 1990*. Washington, DC: Urban Institute Press.

Bronfenbrenner, U. (1979). *The ecology of human development: Experiments by nature and design*. Cambridge, MA: Harvard University Press.

Deater-Deckard, K. (1991). *Mother-caregiver communication in center-based care* (unpublished master's thesis, University of Virginia, Charlottesville, VA).

Endsley, R. C., & Bradbard, M. R. (1987). Dissatisfaction with previous child care among current users of proprietary center care. *Child and Youth Care Quarterly, 16*, 249–262.

Endsley, R. C., & Minish, P. A. (1991). Parent-staff communication in day care centers during morning and afternoon transitions. *Early Childhood Research Quarterly, 6,* 119–135.

Fuqua, R. W., & Labensohn, D. (1986). Parents as consumers of child care. *Family Relations, 35,* 295–303.

Garbarino, J. (1992). *Children and families in the social environment.* New York: Aldine.

Hayes, C., Palmer, J. L., & Zaslow, M. (Eds.). (1990). *Who cares for America's children? Child care policy for the 1990s.* Washington, DC: National Academy Press.

Hofferth, S. L. (1989). *The national child care consumer survey* (unpublished questionnaire).

Hofferth, S. L., Brayfield, A. , Deich, S. , & Holcomb, P. (1991). *The national child care survey, 1990.* Washington, DC: Urban Institute Press.

Honig, A. S. (1979). *Parent involvement in early childhood education* (rev. ed.). Washington, DC: National Association for the Education of Young Children.

Howes, C., & Stewart, P. (1987). Child's play with adults, toys, and peers: An examination of family and child care influences. *Developmental Psychology, 23,* 423–430.

Kingsley, R. F., & Cook-Hatala, C. (1988). A survey of child care workers: Implications for administrators regarding job stress and satisfaction. *Child and Youth Care Quarterly, 17,* 281–287.

Kisker, E. E., Hofferth, S. L. , Phillips, D. A. , & Farquhar, E. (1991). *A profile of child care settings: Early education and care in 1990 (vol. 1).* Princeton, NJ: Mathematica Policy Research, Inc.

Kisker, E. E., & Silverberg, M. (1991). Child care utilization by disadvantaged teenage mothers. *Journal of Social Issues, 47,* 159–178.

Kontos, S. (1993, March). *The ecology of family day care.* Paper presented at the meeting of the Society for Research in Child Development, New Orleans, LA.

Kontos, S., & Dunn, L. (1989). Attitudes of caregivers, maternal experiences with daycare, and children's development. *Journal of Applied Developmental Psychology, 10,* 37–51.

Long, F., Peter, D. L., & Garduque, L. (1985). Continuity between home and day care: A model for defining relevant dimensions of child care. *Advances in Applied Developmental Psychology, 1,* 131–170.

McCartney, K., & Phillips, D. (1988). Motherhood and child care. In B. Birns & D. Hay (Eds.), *The different faces of motherhood* (pp. 157–179). New York: Plenum.

McClelland, J. (1986). Job satisfaction of child care workers: A review. *Child Care Quarterly, 15,* 82–89.

Meyers, M. K. (1993). Child care in JOBS employment and training program: What difference does quality make? *Journal of Marriage and the Family, 55,* 767–783.

Mitchell, A., Cooperstein, E., & Larner, M. (1992). *Child care choices, consumer education, and low-income families.* New York: National Center for Children in Poverty.

Mullis, A. K., Ellett, C. H., & Mullis, R. L. (1986). Job satisfaction among child care workers. *Journal of Child Care, 2,* 65–75.

Pence, A. R., & Goelman, H. (1987). Silent partners: Parents of children in three types of day care. *Early Childhood Research Quarterly, 2,* 103–118.

Peters, D. L., & Kontos, S. (1987). Continuity and discontinuity of experience: An intervention perspective. *Annual Advances in Applied Developmental Psychology, 2,* 1–16.

Phillips, D., & Howes, C. (1987). Indicators of quality child care: Review of research. In D. Phillips (Ed.), *Quality in child care: What does research tell us?* (pp. 1–20). Washington, DC: National Association for the Education of Young Children.

Phillips, D., Howes, C., & Whitebook, M. (1991). Child care as an adult work environment: Implications for job satisfaction, turnover, and quality of care. *Journal of Social Issues, 47,* 49–70.

Powell, D. R. (1989). *Families and early childhood programs.* Washington, DC: National Association for the Education of Young Children.

Schaefer, E. S., & Edgerton, M. (1985). Parent and child correlates of parental modernity. In I. E. Sigel (Ed.), *Parental belief systems: The psychological consequences for children* (pp. 287–318). Hillsdale, NJ: Lawrence Erlbaum.

Schumacher, J., & DeMeis, D. K. (1992). *Child care as a social support system for employed mothers* (unpublished manuscript).

Shinn, M., Galinsky, E., & Gulcur, L. (1989). *The role of child care centers in the lives of parents* (unpublished manuscript).

Shinn, M., Phillips, D., Howes, C., Galinsky, E., & Whitebook, M. (1991). *Correspondence between mothers' perceptions and observer ratings of quality in child care centers* (unpublished manuscript).

Sonenstein, F. L., & Wolf, D. A. (1991). Satisfaction with child care: Perspectives of welfare mothers. *Journal of Social Issues, 47*, 15–32.

Whitebook, M., Howes, C., & Phillips, D. (1990). *Who cares? Child care teachers and the quality of care in America*. Final report of the National Child Care Staffing Study. Oakland, CA: Child Care Employee Project.

Zigler, E. F., & Turner, P. (1982). Parents and day care workers: A failed partnership? In E. F. Zigler & E. W. Gordon (Eds.), *Day care: Scientific and social policy issues* (pp. 174–182). Boston: Auburn House.

6

The Importance of Curriculum in Achieving Quality Child Day Care Programs

Diane Trister Dodge

Quality child day care programs promote children's social competence, an important prerequisite of academic success. In high-quality programs, children develop a positive sense of identity, learn to trust others, and acquire the characteristics that enable them to succeed as learners. One effective strategy for achieving a quality program is the use of a developmentally appropriate curriculum. A well-defined curriculum framework, based on child development theory, provides early childhood educators with a structure for planning a program that encompasses all aspects of a child's development and meets professional standards.

Diane Trister Dodge, M.S., is President, Teaching Strategies, Inc., Washington, DC.

The components of a quality child day care program are no mystery. Quality programs are based on an understanding of child development, and on a recognition that each child is an individual with unique needs, interests, and learning styles. Children's safety and health are of paramount importance and never compromised. The physical environment of quality programs is well-organized and filled with a variety of age-appropriate and culturally relevant materials. In quality programs, relationships between staff members and families are positive and supportive, and the staff receives ongoing training and support.

These components of quality have been identified by numerous professional organizations including the National Association for the Education of Young Children [1991; Bredekamp 1987], Zero to Three/The National Center for Clinical Infant Programs [1992], the National Association for Family Child Care [Sibley & Shimm 1992], and the Child Welfare League of America [1992]. Although the field is in substantial agreement about the components of quality, a number of factors impede the achievement of quality: low wages and resulting high staff turnover; state regulations that require only the barest minimum conditions for safety and health, inadequate physical facilities, the cost of high staff-to-child ratios, and inappropriate curriculums.

Why Quality Is Important

According to the Bureau of Labor Statistics, 51% of mothers with infants under one year of age, and 63% of mothers with children of preschool age (three to four) currently work part- or full-time outside the home. Many of their children spend the majority of their waking hours in child day care programs and family child care homes, licensed and unlicensed.

The quality of the programs that serve children and families is important because it is during the early childhood years that children are forming a sense of identity, learning to trust others, and acquiring a sense of their own competence. If these early experiences are positive, children are more likely to succeed in school and in life.

Infants as young as a few months show the profound effects of early experiences on their sense of self and their interest in learning. Brazelton writes [Zero to Three 1992] that it is possible to determine, at age eight months, whether a baby expects to succeed or fail simply by observing how that child approaches a task.

> We offer two blocks to a seated eight-month-old, and then we demonstrate that we'd like her to place the two blocks together. A baby who expects to succeed, and who is used to the approval and encouragement of adults around her, will pick up one block, mouth it, rub it in her hair, drop it over the side of the table, watching to see whether you will retrieve it for her. When you do, she finally completes the requested task—place the two blocks together. Then she looks up at you with a bright-eyed look of expectancy that says: "Tell me how great I am!"
>
> But a baby who has an untreated learning disability, or who comes from an environment too chaotic or too hopeless to reinforce in him a feeling of success, will demonstrate an expectation to fail. The baby will accept the offered blocks, look dully at them, bring them close together dutifully as directed, but without excitement or enthusiasm. He has demonstrated his cognitive understanding of the task, then he pushes them past each other, apparently failing the task. Then comes the symptom: he looks at you with the hangdog look that says, "Hit me, I'm no good. See! I failed!" This child will expect to fail in school. He will expect no encouragement from teachers, and may shrink from encouragement if it is offered. He is likely to find school embarrassing and joyless and may eventually drop out.

If experiences within the first few months of life affect a child's future success, it is critical to ensure that these experiences are positive and nurturing.

Characteristics That Influence a Child's Future Success

The U.S. Department of Education has set forth a national educational goal that states, "By the year 2000, all children in America will start school ready to learn" [U.S. Department of Education 1991]. This goal challenges us to think about the characteristics that must be nurtured in children to ensure they are ready and able to learn in school.

The National Association of State Boards of Education interviewed more than 100 Head Start, child day care, and kindergarten teachers to discover what factors were key to early school success [1992]. Respondents identified such characteristics as self-confidence, ability to cooperate with peers and adults, strong self-esteem, curiosity, eagerness to ask and answer questions, and the ability to use materials in many different ways. It is significant that teachers did not talk about *what* children had learned (e.g., the alphabet, numbers, colors) but rather valued the competencies associated with being a good learner. These findings confirm why social competence is the underlying goal of early childhood education.

Head Start defines social competence as the child's everyday effectiveness in dealing with his or her environment and later responsibilities in school and in life. This includes the ability to initiate and maintain satisfying relationships with peers as well as with adults.

Research also confirms the importance of social competence. Children who fail to achieve social competence in relationships with their peers are at risk for a variety of social maladaptations later in life. The quality of a child's social competence in kindergarten is a good predictor of academic as well as social competence in later grades. Thus, programs that promote children's social and emotional development are in fact also advancing their cognitive development and future academic success [Pelligrini 1980; Pelligrini & Glickman 1991].

Teachers across the country find that many children today lack the characteristics associated with school success. "Children are different today than when I first started teaching," is a statement heard over and over again from teachers. When asked to describe what they see, teachers talk about children who are fearful and stressed, fall apart easily and need constant adult attention and direction, are angry or withdrawn and unable to say why they have these feelings, lack the social skills to work cooperatively with others, misuse materials or use them at a repetitive and elementary level, are aggressive in their relationships with others, or have few play skills.

Why do so many children today lack social competence? A number of possibilities can be identified:

- The increasing number of children living in poverty—now estimated to be 13 million or one in five—and the impact this has on children's health and emotional well-being.
- The increasing number of children with parents in the workforce and the resulting stress on families trying to sustain their children's basic needs.
- The loss of a sense of community in neighborhoods where people are strangers to one another and children are kept indoors for safety reasons.
- Unstable family situations where children are exposed to violence, abuse, and emotional stress at home.
- The impact of television, dominated by violent programming, which has replaced play in children's lives.
- Inappropriate school curriculums that focus on performance of cognitive tasks and fail to address other areas of development.

Children who have not developed social competence are in particular need of a high-quality child day care program. Social skills are developed in the context of caring relationships, where the content of the program is of interest to the children, children are encouraged to explore and exchange ideas, and adults model respect. Findings from the Perry Preschool Study [Schweinhart et al. 1993] and a study by Marcon in the District of Columbia public schools [1990] both demonstrate that when an early childhood education program emphasizes choice and active learning rather than direct teaching and drills, children's acquisition of basic skills and their social competence are enhanced. The Perry Preschool Study shows the long-term benefits of emphasizing social competence in early childhood. Graduates of the high-quality, active-learning preschool program, who are now in their late twenties, are significantly more likely to have completed a higher level of schooling, to be employed, to own their own home, and to be in stable relationships, and significantly less likely to have needed social services or to have been arrested, than their peers who attended academically and highly structured preschools.

Because quality child day care programs promote children's social as well as academic competence, they can make a critical difference for children who are at risk of academic failure. An effective strategy for achieving a quality program is the use of a developmentally appropriate curriculum.

The Role of Curriculum in Child Day Care

According to a survey of accredited centers by the National Association for the Education of Young Children, a major determinant of program quality is the use of a developmentally appropriate curriculum [Bredekamp 1993]. A clear curriculum framework, based on child development theory, is an invaluable guide for early childhood educators. Without an appropriate curriculum framework to guide staff members in their decision-making, programs might easily implement practices that are inappropriate and even harmful to children.

Curriculum guides for infant/toddler programs too often emphasize intellectual stimulation above other critical areas of development. Books promising to "build superior minds" are plentiful, as are toys designed to teach lessons. Yet experts in infant/toddler care recognize that *caregivers* are the most important element of any infant/toddler program. The relationships staff members develop with children and families and the countless program decisions they make every day color and shape the experience of the infants, toddlers, and families the program serves.

Similarly, traditional curriculum resources for preschool programs too often focus on "busy-work" activities, offer packaged lessons, a different theme each week, and ditto sheets. In addition to promoting inappropriate practices, these resources take the focus away from the child.

Given everything that we know about early childhood education today, it is important that we advocate for and use appropriate curriculum in all of our programs that care for young children.

Defining Appropriate Curriculum

The most appropriate curriculum for programs serving children under the age of five provides a framework for planning an age-appropriate program. Rather than simply defining what to teach (e.g., activities, games, songs), the focus is on creating an environment—both social and physical—that nurtures the growth and development of each child. Implementing curriculum is a dynamic process involving countless decisions on the part of early childhood educators. The adults who work with children daily ask themselves questions such as the following:

- What is this crying baby trying to tell me?
- Do I need to intervene, or should I step back and let the child try to resolve a problem?
- What questions can I ask to help the child think through the problem and come up with a solution?

- Is the child ready for these materials, or will they prove frustrating?
- Is the physical environment working, or should I modify it?

The answers to these questions are more likely to be appropriate if they are guided by a clear curriculum framework that takes into account the following elements [Dodge & Colker 1992]:

- **Philosophy:** A description of the educational theories and child development principles underlying the curriculum's approach to early childhood education that explains how young children learn and how they develop socially, emotionally, cognitively, and physically.
- **Goals and objectives:** Clearly defined and realistic goals and objectives that cover all areas of development and that outline what children can be expected to achieve as infants, toddlers, preschoolers, and school-age children.
- **Physical environment:** Practical guidance on arranging indoor and outdoor spaces, on selecting appropriate materials and equipment, and on grouping and displaying physical resources.
- **Educator's role:** Strategies and approaches to enhancing children's social competence and learning, including how educators can plan activities that respond to the abilities, interests, and needs of the children.
- **Partnerships with families:** Recognizing that parents are children's first and most important teachers, the curriculum should explain the instructional approach to parents and ensure a meaningful role for them in the daily program.

Philosophy

Quality programs are guided by a "developmentally appropriate" philosophy. As defined by the National Association for the

Education of Young Children, a *developmentally appropriate* program is both age-appropriate and individually appropriate [Bredekamp 1987; Bredekamp & Rosegrant 1992]. Planning a program that is *age-appropriate* means that all decisions are guided by an understanding of normal sequences of growth typical of children within a given age group. Programs serving infants and toddlers, for example, recognize that at their core are the relationships children develop with one or two primary caregivers who are warm and responsive to each child's needs. Adults who care for children under age three know that infants and toddlers learn about themselves and their world by experiencing the environment with all their senses—seeing, tasting, hearing, smelling, and feeling—and by moving around their environment as they develop the ability to crawl and walk. They understand that preschool children are active and social individuals who have lots of ideas they want to try out and share. Preschoolers benefit most when offered a variety of activity choices such as dramatic play, block building, art, table toys, sand and water, cooking, music and movement, and a rich selection of books.

The curriculum must also be *individually appropriate*, for each child is a unique person with his or her own temperament, interests, learning styles, and cultural background. Children have individual patterns of growth. Some may walk earlier but begin using words later than other children of the same age. Some can spend hours playing with blocks and wheel toys; others prefer quiet activities like puzzles and books. A developmentally appropriate curriculum allows for individual preferences and provides strategies for satisfying individual needs.

Growing out of a developmentally appropriate philosophy are five important principles that guide the decisions of early childhood educators as they plan and implement a program.

1. Children must feel safe and secure and have their physical needs met in order to learn.

Maslow's "hierarchy of needs" [1955] reminds us of the importance of addressing children's basic needs as a vital component of curriculum. The basic needs are: physical—the satisfaction of hunger and thirst, and a feeling of comfort; safety—feeling secure, safe, and out of danger; belongingness—feeling accepted and cared for; and self-esteem—a sense of one's own worth. These four basic needs must be met before a child can be receptive to, and interested in, learning and exploring.

2.   Children construct knowledge.

Piaget [1952] helps us understand that children actively work to make sense of their experiences and that their thinking changes over time. Learning is about making connections, applying what one has learned and experienced to a new situation, and constructing meanings that may or may not be "correct." For example, when a toddler calls every four-legged animal "doggie," she is applying what she has learned about a family pet to all animals that have a similar characteristic: four legs. When a preschooler tells his teacher to put more water in the fish tank because, "the fish are drinking the water," he is trying to explain why the water level has gone down. The fact that these responses are "wrong" is unimportant. They demonstrate that the child is applying knowledge and trying to make sense of experience. Such constructs also provide opportunities for further learning.

Understanding that children have different ways of viewing and making sense of the world and that their thinking changes over time reminds educators who are planning experiences to consider what stage a child is at. For example, to expect children to understand and use abstract symbols such as numbers and letters before they have had the experiences that enable them to make sense of these symbols and value their use is not only a waste of valuable learning time but also causes frustration and turns off children as learners.

3.   Children learn through social interactions.

For children, learning is a social event. Almost everything that happens in their lives involves and depends on relationships with others. In a developmentally appropriate program, chatter is constant. Infants and toddlers exchange smiles, sounds, gestures, and words with their caregivers. They observe adults and their peers and imitate what they see. Preschool children readily share information, ideas, and questions with each other and with adults. They talk about what they're learning, and they replay their experiences to gain a better understanding of them.

4.   Children learn through play.

Play isn't something that children get to do when they finish their "real learning"; play *is* learning. Play has different forms and each form contributes to a child's growing understanding of the world. Smilansky and Shefatya [1992] identify four different kinds of play and what children gain from each. In *functional play*, children learn what materials feel like, what they do, and what they taste like. During *constructive play*, children make something from materials. For example, they might use blocks to build an apartment house or sand to construct a castle. *Games with rules* teach children to remember rules and stick to them in playing a game. And in *pretend play*, children have to recall experiences they've had and reenact those experiences in such a way that they convince others that they really understand what they're talking about.

The ability to engage in pretend play has strong implications for children's academic success. Research findings indicate that a direct relationship exists between the ability to pretend and children's academic success [Johnson 1990]. To think abstractly means to create mental pictures or symbols that stand for real objects or events. Dramatic play teaches children to substitute symbols for real objects and events.

Goals and Objectives

The second component of a developmentally appropriate curriculum is a statement of goals and objectives that includes all areas of development: social, emotional, cognitive, and physical. Sample goals for a preschool program might comprise the following [Dodge & Phinney 1990: 5]:

- **Social:** To help children feel comfortable in the child day care environment, trust the new environment, make friends, and feel a part of the group.
- **Emotional:** To help children experience pride and self-confidence, develop independence and self-control, and gain a positive attitude toward life.
- **Cognitive:** To help children become confident learners by letting them try out their own ideas and experience success, and by helping them acquire learning skills such as the ability to solve problems, ask questions, and use words to describe their ideas, observations, and feelings.
- **Physical:** To help children increase their large and small muscle skills and feel confident about what their bodies can do.

Goals and objectives are used to plan experiences and activities that will further children's development. Goals and objectives are also used to guide appropriate assessment. For example, a checklist for documenting children's progress can be based on the curriculum's goals and objectives and can be completed two or three times a year. This form of assessment is invaluable in ensuring that a curriculum deals with all aspects of a child's development.

The Physical Environment

The third component of a developmentally appropriate curriculum is the physical environment. Because young children learn from their interactions with, and explorations of, their environment, the physical environment is like the "textbook" of an early childhood curriculum: the richer and the more interesting the environment, the more opportunities children have to learn.

An environment for infants and toddlers is homelike, soft, and comfortable. It offers interesting things to look at, a variety of levels and textures to explore, and spaces to creep on, crawl in and out of, and pull up on. Procedures for ensuring sanitary and safe conditions are established and followed by all staff members to protect children's health and safety.

The environment for preschool children is organized into well-defined interest areas that offer children clear choices and varied opportunities to explore and construct and to work individually or in small groups on projects and tasks that are of interest. Each area is stocked with age-appropriate toys and materials, including blocks, props for dramatic play, table toys, art, sand and water, books, and more. Labels for materials show that everything has a place and help children to choose activities and also share responsibility for the environment.

The Educator's Role in Promoting Learning

An appropriate physical environment structures the educator's role in promoting children's development and learning. In a program serving infants and toddlers, caregiving itself and unhurried time to explore and investigate the environment are central themes of curriculum. In a program serving preschool children, early childhood educators set the stage for children to initiate their own actions, and then talk with children about what they are doing and ask questions to extend their learning.

Because the building of relationships is the core of high-quality infant/toddler programs, the adults who provide care and education are of central importance. Who they are as individuals—their interests, their temperaments, their values, their style of caregiving—influences the relationships they build with infants and toddlers. These relationships develop in the context of daily routines—holding and talking to infants and toddlers, feeding and changing them, placing safe and interesting toys and objects within their sight and reach, encouraging their explorations, and responding with enthusiasm to their efforts and successes.

Infants and toddlers develop a sense of identity by imitating the important adults in their lives and by incorporating the traits of these individuals into their own sense of self.

Part of what infants and toddlers get from caregivers are perceptions of how people act at various times and in various situations (seen as how the infant should behave), how people act toward them and others (seen as how they and others should be treated), and how emotions are expressed (seen as how they should feel). These impressions are used by the infant, and often incorporated by the infant into the self they become. . . . More is happening than tender loving care and learning games. Values and beliefs are being witnessed and incorporated. [Lally 1994]

Given the central role early childhood educators play in promoting the growth and learning of infants and toddlers, it is evident why, in quality programs, children are assigned to one or two adults who provide consistent care. Continuity of care and small group size make it possible for responsive caregiving to be the focus of curriculum for infants and toddlers.

In preschool programs, early childhood educators are more likely to implement a developmentally appropriate program if they know how to use interest areas as the focus for curriculum planning [Dodge & Colker 1992]. Many inappropriate practices—relying on worksheets, practicing letters, drilling children on numbers and colors—are responses to pressures from parents and administrators to push academic learning at an early age so that children will be "ready for school." This type of program contradicts what we know from the research cited earlier. An environmental focus supports free choice and active learning. To plan for and ensure children's growth and learning, childhood educators must have a good understanding of what materials will interest and challenge children, and the skills to observe how each child uses the environment. Learning how to support children in making choices, what to say to help them clarify their understanding, and how to ask open-ended questions—"What do you think will happen if . . . ?" "How many different ways can you . . .?" "Why do you think that happened?"—are all essential aspects of the early childhood educator's role. When used effectively, the interest areas of the classroom become the laboratory for children to investigate, reconstruct, and share what they are learning. The educator's role is to help children develop socially (by building positive relationships and teaching social skills), emotionally (by nurturing pride, self-esteem, and self-control), cognitively (by allowing children to try out their own ideas, observe what happens, raise more questions, and express their feelings and understandings), and physically (by helping children develop muscle coordination and use all their senses in learning).

Building Partnerships with Parents

The most effective early childhood programs are those that involve children's families in meaningful ways. This is why the final component of curriculum concerns the role of parents. Although an educator works primarily with children, the needs of the child are always best met if parents feel that they are an important part of the program.

A partnership begins with mutual respect and trust. Staff members who convey the message that parents are welcome and who encourage them to visit the program set the tone for a positive relationship. Participating in the program enables parents to observe firsthand how their children are progressing so the parents can support and extend their children's learning at home.

Early childhood educators who take the time to explain developmentally appropriate practice to parents, to acknowledge their concerns about their children, and to build confidence and pride in what their children can accomplish, gain valuable allies in the effort to support quality child day care programs. It is an important step in getting the community at large to recognize, acknowledge, and demand access to quality services for children and families.

The Challenge Ahead

This article has presented the components of an early childhood curriculum and has identified such a curriculum's role in achieving high-quality child day care programs. The adoption of an appropriate curriculum, however, is only the first step. To successfully implement a curriculum, the following elements must be in place:

- Staff members receive ongoing training in child development and understand the curriculum.
- An experienced director or education coordinator sets standards and provides support and guidance to the staff in achieving these standards.
- Staff-to-child ratios meet the profession's standards— one adult for every three to four infants, one adult to every four or five toddlers, one adult to every eight or ten three- and four-year-olds [Child Welfare League of America 1992; NAEYC 1991].
- Facilities and materials are safe, sanitary, and developmentally appropriate.
- The workforce is stable because its members receive recognition for the importance of their work and are adequately compensated.

We are far from achieving the quality child day care we need in this country. According to the most recent study, the majority of the five million children in child day care centers are receiving care that is "poor to mediocre;" and infant care is rated the worst of all [Cost, Quality & Child Outcomes Study Team 1995]. These findings are consistent with a study that examined the quality of care in family child care homes [Families and Work Institute 1994]. Each of these studies confirms the necessity for states to put high standards for child day care into effect and to seek solutions to the inadequate wages and lack of staff training that stand as obstacles to quality. The long-term impact on children who do not receive high-quality care in their early years will be far more costly than making a commitment to invest in the best of care during the first five years of life. ◆

References

Bredekamp, S. (Ed.). (1987). *Developmentally appropriate practice in early childhood programs serving children from birth through age 8*. Washington, DC: National Association for the Education of Young Children.

Bredekamp, S. (1993, April 12). *Lessons on quality from national accreditation*. Paper presented at the annual meeting of the American Educational Research Association, Atlanta, GA.

Bredekamp, S., & Rosegrant, T. (Eds.). (1992). *Appropriate curriculum and assessment for young children* (vol. 1). Washington, DC: National Association for the Education of Young Children.

Child Welfare League of America, Inc. (1992). *Standards of excellence for child day care services (rev. ed.)*. Washington, DC: Author.

Cost, Quality & Child Outcomes Study Team. (1995, April). *Cost, quality, and child outcomes in child care centers, public report (2nd ed.)*. Denver, CO: Economics Department, University of Colorado at Denver.

Dodge, D. T., & Colker, L. J. (1992). *The creative curriculum for early childhood* (3rd ed.). Washington, DC: Teaching Strategies, Inc.

Dodge, D. T., & Phinney, J. (1990). *A parent's guide to early childhood education* (p. 5). Washington, DC: Teaching Strategies, Inc. (reprinted with permission).

Johnson, J. E. (1990). The role of play in cognitive development. In E. Klugman & S. Smilansky (Eds.), *Children's play and learning: Perspectives and policy implications*. New York: Teachers College Press.

Lally, R. J. (1994). *The impact of child day care polices and practices on infant/toddler identity formation*. Proceedings of the international symposium: Neue Entwicklungen in der Kleinkindpadogogik. Berlin, Germany: Freie Universitat Berlin.

Marcon, R. (1990). *Early learning and early identification: Final report of the three year longitudinal study*. Washington, DC: Office of Educational Accountability and Planning, District of Columbia Public Schools.

Maslow, A. H. (1955). Deficiency motivation and growth motivation. In M. R. Jones (Ed.), *Nebraska symposium on motivation.* Lincoln, NE: University of Nebraska Press.

National Association of State Boards of Education. (1988). *Right from the start* (report of the NASBE task force on early childhood education). Alexandria, VA: Author.

National Association of State Boards of Education. (1992). *Caring communities: Supporting young children and families* (report of the national task force on school readiness) (p. 10). Alexandria, VA: Author.

National Association for the Education of Young Children. (1991). *Accreditation criteria & procedures of the National Academy of Early Childhood Programs.* Washington, DC: Author.

Pelligrini, A. D., & Glickman, C. D. (1991). Measuring kindergartners' social competence. In *ERIC Digest.* Urbana, IL: ERIC Clearinghouse on Elementary and Early Childhood Education.

Pelligrini, A. (1980). The relationship between kindergartens' play and achievement in prereading, language, and writing. *Psychology in the Schools, 17,* 530–535.

Piaget, J. (1952). *The origins of intelligence.* New York: International Universities Press.

Schweinhart, L. J., Barnes, H. V., & Weikart, D. P. (1993). *Significant benefits: The High/Scope Perry Preschool study through age 27.* Ypsilanti, MI: High/Scope Press.

Sibley, A., & Shim, M. A. (1992). *Assessment profile for family day care study guide.* Atlanta, GA: Quality Assist, Inc.

Smilansky, S., & Shefatya, L. (1990). *Facilitating play: A medium for promoting cognitive, socioemotional, and academic development in young children.* Gaithersburg, MD: Psychosocial and Educational Publications.

U.S. Department of Education. (1991). *America 2000: An education strategy.* Washington, DC: Author.

Zero to Three/National Center for Clinical Infant Programs. (1992). *Heart Start: The emotional foundations of school readiness.* Arlington, VA: Author.

7

Utilizing a Statewide Training System to Improve Child Day Care Quality

Richard Fiene

This article describes Pennsylvania's comprehensive child day care and early childhood development training system, with particular attention to ECELS—the Early Childhood Education Linkage System of the Pennsylvania chapter of the American Academy of Pediatrics—and its immunization initiative. The innitiative was established with the state Bureau of Child Day Care Services to improve the overall immunization status of all children in child day care in Pennsylvania. An early childhood education/ child day care quality improvement model is briefly discussed to demonstrate how licensing/monitoring data can be tied to a training and technical assistance program.

Richard Fiene, Ph.D., is Research Psychologist, Bureau of Child Day Care, and Adjunct Professor of Psychology and Education, Penn State, Harrisburg, P.A.

With the advent of the federal Child Care and Development Block Grant (CCDBG) in 1991, states have implemented initiatives to promote program quality that range from loans to child day care programs to large-scale training systems.* Allowable projects are in five major areas: resource and referral activities, training, licensing improvement, staff salaries, and child day care loans. Many states have used this funding to establish and implement training systems [Morgan et al. 1993].

This article describes Pennsylvania's development of a comprehensive child care and early childhood development training system and the system's initial results, followed by a discussion of the Early Childhood Education Linkage System (ECELS) of the Pennsylvania chapter of the American Academy of Pediatrics. The Pennsylvania chapter has established an innovative system for monitoring and improving childhood immunization status that can serve as a model of how states can link licensing/monitoring data to technical assistance/training system interventions [Fiene 1992].

In 1992, the Pennsylvania Department of Public Welfare (DPW) instituted several collaborative projects to increase training opportunities for child care providers in the Commonwealth. These initiatives were begun for several reasons: (1) DPW wanted to assure that high-quality training would continue to be offered; (2) periodic, ongoing training (six hours per calendar year) was mandated by DPW for all child care workers; and (3) DPW was able to subsidize the training to make it affordable for more child care providers. Pennsylvania used federal and state funds[1] during state fiscal year 1991–1992 to support the statewide training system. Only Texas spent more CCDBG funds on training [Morgan et al. 1993] than Pennsylvania.

---

*In 1991, CCDBG set aside 6.25% of $731,915,000 of federal funds for program quality initiatives.

During 1992–1993, Pennsylvania's training system was expanded and renamed the Child Care and Early Childhood Development (CCECD) training system. Approximately 50,000 training encounters were provided during that period, garnering immediate national attention for Pennsylvania for its training initiatives. ECELS, the Keystone University Research Corporation Home-Based Project, and the Southeast Regional School-Age Training Project were all recognized nationally for their innovation and leadership in the early childhood development and child day care training field [Morgan et al. 1993]. It is these initiatives that are described in this article.

During 1993–1994, the major training initiatives continued, with much fine tuning and expansion in areas such as mentoring projects with local programs, additional articulation agreements with local colleges and universities, experimentation with video training, increased input from the Child Care and Early Childhood Development Training Advisory Committee, shared resources and information with the Alliance of Early Childhood Professional Preparation (the state higher education advisory committee) and the Family-Focused Early Intervention System, and expansion of technical assistance opportunities. In all, approximately 40,000 training encounters were provided by eight training contractors during 1993–1994.

Some training programs were arranged or delivered by Marywood College, Keystone Junior College, and Pennsylvania State University. A school-based program was housed within the Central Intermediate Unit in the state college area. Other training programs were housed with nonprofit or corporate entities, such as Community Services for Children, Keystone University Research Corporation, Pittsburgh YMCA, Montgomery Child Care Association, and the Pennsylvania chapter of the American Academy of Pediatrics. Funding and contracts were awarded on a competitive basis.

Other major initiatives were developed as a result of the Pennsylvania Child Care and Early Childhood Development

(CCECD) training system. An early childhood development curriculum continues to be refined and expanded as courses are offered to graduate level teachers and directors. The Child Development Associate (CDA) scholarship program continues to grow. A new early childhood education loan forgiveness program has been instituted and should attract additional highly qualified staff members to teach in child care programs.

At present, training contractors offer classes and courses to child day care staff members across Pennsylvania in the following seven categories: developmentally appropriate practices; emergent literacy; child development; discipline, growth-producing relationships, and interpersonal skill development; health and safety; program administration; and collaboration with community resources and parents.

A description of each of the initiatives and projects follows, with types of services, targeted populations, and service areas noted. The Early Childhood Education Linkage System (ECELS) is highlighted because its major immunization initiative is of special interest to state agencies.

The CCECD Training System

Child Day Care Centers

Licensed child day care centers employ the greatest number of child day care staff. Two providers of training are responsible for assuring that high-quality training sessions on child development and child care operations are available and accessible to child care center staff members (teachers, aides, directors, etc.). Louise Child Care (the Training Connection) serves the western and central regions of Pennsylvania (47 of its 67 counties); Marywood College serves eastern Pennsylvania (the remaining 20 counties).

From July 1993 to June 1994, these two training contracts served over 25,000 child day care employees. Trainees could choose from several options: general workshops, agency-specific workshops, subsidized early childhood college courses, on-site mentoring sessions, and subsidized conference attendance.

To provide the many training programs needed for licensed child care teaching staff members and to maintain cost-effectiveness, Marywood College and the Training Connection forged partnerships with other organizations and subcontractors. Using regionalized subcontractors enabled them to hold training sessions simultaneously at several sites. Both Marywood College and the Training Connection provided training outlines to subcontractors and reviewed course materials to ensure the quality and consistency of training. All curriculum content was approved by the State Training Director. As of January 1995, over 400 trainers were in the CCECD training system.

Additionally, the two training providers developed articulation agreements (contractual arrangements with local colleges and universities) with several colleges to offer child day care staff members college credits for attending a specified series of training workshops. Thus, child care staff members could advance on the career ladder while implementing quality programs and practices. Helping staff members obtain training necessary for promotion within the child day care and early childhood education field may reduce staff turnover.

School-Age Child Day Care

School-age child care (SACC) programs were developed to provide children from five to 15 years of age with a safe and developmentally appropriate alternative to nonsupervised care. Child day care for school-age children is provided through a diverse network of organizations that includes churches, synagogues, Boys and Girls Clubs, YM/YWCAs, traditional child day care centers, family child care homes, municipal recreation departments, schools, community organizations, and neighborhood centers.

The Pennsylvania Department of Public Welfare funds four organizations to implement, administer, and assure the quality of services for latchkey children: Community Services for Children (Northeast Region Training Contractor), Day Care Association of Montgomery County (Southeast Region Training Contractor), YMCA of Pittsburgh (Western Region Training Contractor), and Central Intermediate Unit (Central Region Training Contractor). All offer training and technical assistance for quality improvement of existing SACC programs. The four organizations have conducted 300 training programs, educating 4,466 staff members.

Family Child Care Homes

A significant number of children in Pennsylvania receive child day care services in the homes of family child care providers rather than in child day care centers and nursery schools. These providers run small programs that serve from four to as many as 12 children. Home-based providers may receive training through workshops, a training refund program, or a Child Development Associate (CDA) scholarship assistance program [Fiene 1993].

Keystone University Research Corporation (KURC) has served family child care providers with refund/voucher and CDA scholarship programs for over seven years. The refund/ voucher program allows providers to attend preapproved training programs of their choice and submit bills for reasonable costs to KURC for reimbursement. Acceptable training options include conferences, seminars, college courses (reimbursed at $250 per course), workshops, and on-site training. To receive reimbursement, providers must submit evidence of their family child care home registration (family child care homes) or license (group child day care homes), the training must be "appropriate," and the training must last at least six hours. Appropriate training topics include health matters such as first aid and CPR, child development, business management, working with parents, and developmentally appropriate practices and curriculum. A total of 896 reimbursements were approved in 1993–1994.

For child care providers and staff members with low incomes, KURC offers scholarships and scholarship assistance to help them obtain a CDA credential. The CDA credential indicates that the provider has completed a prescribed course or series of training sessions related to child day care and early childhood education. During 1993–1994, 176 child care staff members and providers received scholarships or financial assistance.

In addition to these ongoing services, KURC offered 300 direct training workshops. With the addition of more direct trainers, the program was able to serve a total of 4,865 child care employees in 1993–1994. KURC also distributes a newsletter and operates a toll-free telephone hotline to make information accessible to child day care providers. The use of both services continued to increase during 1993–1994.

Many families purchase child day care services from unregulated and/or minimally certified providers. It is difficult to assess, improve, or maintain quality at these sites because they rarely come to the attention of officials. In fact, it is virtually impossible to determine the number of providers who operate this way. During the 1992–1993 fiscal year, the Pennsylvania Department of Public Welfare became partners with the Penn State Cooperative Extension to implement the Better Kid Care program in response to the needs of these parents and providers.

The Better Kid Care program offers educational materials—a kit with information on health and safety, child development, and age-appropriate activities for children, along with six learn-at-home programs called "Caring for Kids." Child care workers or parents can obtain the materials by writing or calling, via toll-free hotline, the Penn State Extension offices, which are located in all 67 counties in Pennsylvania. Parents are encouraged to share information with child care providers who might be reluctant to draw attention to themselves by requesting information. More then 5,000 people were enrolled in the project during 1993–1994.

In addition, the 67 Penn State Cooperative Extension county offices conducted workshops for child care providers. Training in various topics in early childhood development and education was provided to more than 2,400 people.

Third-Party Evaluation

A third-party evaluation [Johnson 1994] is being completed at this writing on the overall CCECD system. It has been apparent that the six hours of inservice training per year are not adequate to produce significant program improvements in the classroom by teachers. Regulatory recommendations from the evaluation call for an increase in the six hours of inservice training to the 24 hours per year recommended by the National Association for the Education of Young Children or—preferably—to the 40 hours per year recommended by the Child Welfare League of America.

The evaluation does indicate improvement in classroom implementation of developmentally appropriate practices on the part of staff members who had 20 or more hours of classes and/or workshops on these subjects. Staff members who had fewer than 20 hours of this kind of training did not demonstrate the same level of change in their classroom implementation skills—a key finding.

The evaluation has also uncovered a need to tie training to ongoing monitoring and licensing. This interface of data and technical assistance, which few states use, can serve as a critical link in improving the quality of all child care programs. ECELS— the Early Childhood Education Linkage System—a national demonstration project, has been successful in providing many of these linkages.

The Early Childhood Education Linkage System

The Early Childhood Education Linkage System (ECELS), funded in part by the Pennsylvania Department of Public Welfare and the Pennsylvania Department of Health, collaborates with public and private agencies to improve the well-being of children in the state's early childhood programs. ECELS services include a registry of professional health consultants for technical assistance and local linkage with child care providers; a toll-free information hotline; a free lending library; a quarterly newsletter;

and an arrangement of linkages among community-based trainers and child day care providers.

The early childhood program quality improvement model (PQIM) drawn from ECELS is a conceptual model for interfacing the child care licensing system with the training and technical assistance system [Fiene 1992]. The licensing system literally drives the training and technical assistance system by the use of information derived from licensing data. Appropriate technical assistance and training modalities can be targeted to major areas of noncompliance with regulations. Interventions can be determined by type of provider (center-based or home-based), by geographic area (urban or rural), by size of program, and so on.

Training opportunities include information on evaluating data from immunization and preventive health service records, preventing traffic injuries, and promoting general health and safety. The American Red Cross Child Care Course and self-learning modules on health and safety for family child care providers are also offered. Child day care providers participated in 7,772 units of ECELS training during 1993–1994.

Other noteworthy accomplishments of ECELS in 1993–94 included responding to over 4,000 requests for health information; conference presentations on infection control, health policies, and illness prevention; publication of the quarterly HEALTH LINK newsletter (circulation 15,000+); and recruitment of health professionals consultants to assist child day care programs with specific health-related issues and problems.

The Immunization Initiative

The immunization initiative is the product of a unique relationship between ECELS and Pennsylvania. The Bureau of Child Day Care Services licensing staff regularly collects licensing information from providers of child day care services, including sampling records to check the immunization status of children. Over the past several years, the state licensing office determined, both from a sample of programs studied by ECELS and from the ongoing efforts of the licensing staff, that children in child day care settings lacked up-to-date immunizations, contrary to the state's child day care regulations. Regulatory compliance was only 80% to 85% statewide, in contrast to a national goal of 95% for group child day care settings. Based upon these results, a partnership was forged between the Pennsylvania Bureau of Child Day Care Services and ECELS to increase compliance regarding immunizations in child day care programs.

On a quarterly basis, data gathered by the licensing staff are aggregated by the research division of the bureau and shared with ECELS for follow-up. ECELS follows up with those programs that have the greatest noncompliance with immunization regulations and provides technical assistance and linkage to pediatric services in the community. The director of ECELS is a past president of the Pennsylvania chapter of the American Academy of Pediatrics. Her success in following up with her peers is much greater than what licensing staff members might achieve with the same pediatricians.

This monitoring system has great potential, especially when the federal government's CCDBG efforts to increase the monitoring of the immunization status of children in federally supported child day care are considered. It is an example of how licensing data can be used to drive the focus of a state's training and technical assistance efforts, a subject that has been reviewed extensively [Fiene & Nixon 1985; Fiene 1988, 1992; Aronson 1994] in the early childhood program quality research literature.

The early childhood program quality improvement model has other components that can be used to improve programs that are not a formal part of the training and technical assistance system. Self-assessment as used in accreditation of early childhood programs provides one example of such an approach; site inspection findings from licensing observations or through Head Start performance reviews is another. This program quality improvement model offers a multidimensional approach to the quality enhancement of early childhood programs. A critical component of the model is the linking of data from monitoring systems to training and technical assistance systems so that interventions can be customized to the needs of individual programs.

Conclusion

The Pennsylvania Child Care and Early Childhood Development training system has offered all early childhood personnel numerous training opportunities to achieve quality practice. Focus groups have been established to obtain feedback from trainees, providers, agencies, and trainers on improving the existing system. Moving toward a seamless early child care and education professional development system is the goal. Expansion of articulation agreements with local colleges and universities is occurring throughout the state. Additional linkages between the licensing and technical assistance/training systems will be explored.

As is true with any statewide training system, constant improvements are always being considered. The Pennsylvania CCECD training system is no exception. For fiscal year 1995–1996, the training system has been locally based by using the Penn State University Cooperative Extension offices as resource training centers in each county. This administrative change moves Pennsylvania's CCECD training system one step closer to a seamless early child care and education professional development system by establishing one statewide training contractor where previously there were eight .

Finally, ECELS's successful tying of licensing/monitoring data to a technical assistance/training system demonstrates that this approach is both cost efficient and effective for program quality improvement in child day care and early childhood programs. The new National Health and Safety Performance Standards for Out-of-Home Child Care Programs [American Public Health Association/American Academy of Pediatrics 1992] are being given priority by the National Center for the Education in

Maternal and Child Health. With selected high-priority standards, it will be possible to target technical assistance and training to key risk areas. ♦

Note

1. Child Care and Development Block Grant (CCDBG) funds ($2,105,178) as well as state funds ($617,607) and other federal funding (Child Development Associate (CDA) Scholarship funds = $100,000 and federal Dependent Care Block Grant funds = $366,000) were used to fund the Pennsylvania Child Care/Early Childhood Development (CCECD) training system. The CCDBG block grant is a major child care and early childhood development federal funding stream that provides direct child day care service funds and program quality funds to states. The CDA program offers scholarships to low-income and needy students who are pursuing their CDA credential. The Dependent Care Block Grant is a federal funding stream earmarked for programs for school-age children.

References

American Public Health Association/American Academy of Pediatrics. (1992). *National health and safety performance standards*. Arlington, VA: National Center for Education in Maternal and Child Health.

Aronson, S. (1994). The science behind the American Public Health Association/American Academy of Pediatrics national health & safety guidelines for child-care programs. *Pediatrics, 84*, 1101–1104.

Fiene, R., & Nixon, M. (1985). Instrument-based program monitoring and the indicator checklist for child care. *Child Care Quarterly, 14*, 198–214.

Fiene, R. (1988). Human services instrument-based program monitoring and indicator systems. In B. Glastonburg, W. LaMendola, & S. Toole (Eds.), *Information Technology and the Human Services* (pp. 185–190). Chichester, England: John Wiley and Sons.

Fiene, R. (1992, June). *Measuring child care quality*. Paper presented at the International Conference on Child Day Care Health: Science, Prevention, and Practice, Atlanta, GA.

Fiene, R. (1993). *Child care and early childhood development annual report*. Harrisburg, PA: Office of Children, Youth and Families.

Johnson, J. (1994). *Child care training and developmentally appropriate beliefs and practices of child care employees in Pennsylvania*. Harrisburg, PA: Center for Schools and Communities.

Morgan, G., Costley, J. B., Genser, A., Goodman, I. F., Lombardi, J., & McGimsey, B. (1993). *Making a career of it*. Boston: The Center for Career Development in Early Care and Education, Wheelock College.

8

Factors Related to the Recruitment, Training, and Retention of Family Child Care Providers

Charles W. Mueller and Lisa Orimoto

Using a multifaceted program evaluation strategy, this paper identifies factors related to recruitment, training, and retention of family child care providers in two rural communities. Findings point to the relative success of efforts to recruit and train high quality family child care providers and the relative difficulty of retaining these providers over time.

Charles W. Mueller, Ph.D., is Associate Professor, School of Social Work, University of Hawaii at Manoa, Honolulu, HI. Lisa Orimoto, M.A., is Research Associate, Social Welfare Evaluation and Research Unit, School of Social Work, University of Hawaii at Manoa, Honolulu, HI. The authors thank the staff members at the state of Hawaii's Office of Children and Youth and at the two program sites for their support and cooperation throughout this study.

Family child care is generally the first choice for alternative care arrangements for infants and young children whose parents are not available during working hours [Galinsky et al. 1994b]. Child advocates and child development specialists have worked to establish standards for quality family child care (FCC) and a supply of family child care providers. The success of these efforts, however, has been hampered by difficulties in attracting providers to come into and remain in licensed FCC. Although most states regulate family child care, a significant underground of unregulated and unlicensed providers exists [Kontos 1992]. Many children no doubt receive quality care from unlicensed providers, but at least one report suggests that licensed providers deliver superior child care [Galinsky et al. 1994b]. Developing ways to recruit, train, and retain qualified FCC providers is a continuing concern.

Regulation and/or licensing alone do not guarantee quality child care, and stringent requirements may actually serve as a disincentive for becoming licensed. Many states therefore provide some form of training and assistance, which can also help individuals meet accreditation standards established by national organizations (e.g., the National Association for Family Day Care). Although there are a great many FCC training programs throughout the United States, not much has been published about their efficacy. Kontos [1992] identified 22 monographs, journals, or accessible databases that describe FCC training programs. Of these, 15 include an evaluation component. Training needs have been identified [Aguirre 1987] and include a variety of topics—health and safety, food and nutrition, child development, discipline, educational methods, techniques and games, first aid, activity planning, and various business aspects (e.g., record-keeping, taxes, insurance, business contracts). Such investments in training are believed to lead to a higher quality of child day care on average and better quality assurances overall, and to increase the likelihood that high quality providers will remain in the field. Although the existing research has technical weaknesses, FCC training programs have generally been found to be highly rated by participants, to have produced moderate increases in pertinent knowledge, to have had little effect on provider attitudes, and to have improved the quality of FCC [cf. Kontos 1992]. A recent three-state study found that FCC training improved overall quality of care and enhanced provider's commitment [Galinsky et al. 1994a].

The retention of FCC providers has proven to be a great challenge. The annual turnover rate is estimated to be between 40% and 60% [Kontos 1992]. As pointed out by Bollin [1993], high turnover of FCC providers may have a variety of negative effects, including adjustment reactions in children, decreased confidence and increased stress in parents, and difficulties in establishing FCC as a viable vocation. Providers who see FCC as their chosen work report the greatest job satisfaction [Kontos 1988], but job satisfaction is only marginally related to retention of FCC providers [Bollin 1993]. Perceived social support may relate to retention, especially support from the provider's parent clientele [Bollin 1993]. FCC providers who also are caring for their own children are less likely to stay in the work than are those who do not have their own young children [Bollin 1993]. Although this finding has been interpreted as evidence of stress related to boundaries between FCC providers' own families and the children they care for, it might also indicate a difference in the reason that certain women enter FCC initially. They may see FCC as a short-term opportunity to earn income while also providing care and companionship for their own children. When their children enter center-based care or school, these women may tend to move on to other careers (including careers interrupted by their FCC experience).

To date, only one study has examined the impact of an FCC development program on the retention of FCC providers. Lawrence et al. [1989] attempted to contact program participants 12 to 18 months after initial recruitment into the program. Of those reached for a telephone interview, 69% reported still being in FCC. Nearly one-quarter of the participants were not reached, however. If these latter participants are considered non-providers, then this study found about a 50% retention rate for program participants, which is comparable to the typical rates cited earlier. This study also found that participants with large household incomes from a spouse or partner were more likely to have continued as FCC providers than those with less financial support from partners.

The present study describes a mixed-method evaluation of two rural programs designed to recruit, train, and retain FCC providers. Using both qualitative and quantitative techniques, the study examined a wide range of factors. This article deals with the following questions: What impact did the programs have on the recruitment, training, and retention of participants? What individual and societal factors influenced recruitment, training, and retention success?

Method

Participants

Over the two-year course of the two demonstration projects, 356 individuals inquired about the two FCC programs and 140 entered training. The first 125 who entered the training program serve as the primary participants in this study.[1] Across the two sites, 16 training groups were conducted, with an average of sightly less than nine participants in each group. While a given group was participating in the training sequence, participants for the next training sequence were being recruited.

Nearly all the participants (96%) were female, 64% were married (or remarried), 16% were single, 13% were divorced or separated and not remarried, and 7% were together but unmarried. Participants' ages ranged between 19 and 65 years ($\overline{X}$ = 32.28, SD = 9.04). Participants' average educational achievement was about one year post-high school ($\overline{X}$ = 13.09 years, range = 9–20, SD = 1.99). On average, participants had about two children of their own ($\overline{X}$ = 2.18, range = 0–7, SD = 1.55) and had about three to four siblings ($\overline{X}$ = 3.61, range = 0–10, SD = 2.12). About 47% of the participants were Caucasian, with the vast majority of the remainder of Asian and/or Pacific Islander ancestry.

Programs

Both programs were funded by the state's legislature as demonstration projects to train FCC providers to become economically self-sufficient small-business operators. These programs were set in a state that regulates FCC through licensing of FCC providers who care for between two to six children unrelated to themselves. Caregivers for six to 13 children come under the purview of a different (group home) set of licensing guidelines. Other requirements for licensure include an FBI background check of all adults living in the FCC home, a safety inspection of the FCC facility, first aid and CPR certification of the FCC licensee, and health clearance of individuals living in the FCC home. Child care training is recommended but not mandated for licensure.

Each program developed ongoing recruitment strategies, including formal and informal notifications about the program and interorganizational relationships for referrals. Once a sufficient number of participants were enrolled in a program, they were organized into a small group and provided with classroom didactic training based on the Dodge and Colker [1991] curriculum, modified to accord with the cultural diversity of the participants. Arrangements for child care while in the training program were provided, as were one or more home visits from an experienced FCC provider, opportunities to observe and interact with a mentor delivering FCC, peer support activities (e.g., support groups), small grants to help defray business start-up costs (e.g., licensing fees, provision of safety devices, yard fencing), help in coordinating with appropriate state and community agencies (e.g., zoning offices, insurance companies), and ongoing consultations. The programs were multifaceted and emphasized informal training (e.g., small-group didactics, in-home observation, discussion and support groups). Participants were required to attend all didactic sessions (or make up missed sessions), observe a mentor, and be visited one or more times in the potential FCC home to graduate from the program.

Data Collection

A variety of data collection measures were used throughout the study.[2] A strategic data collection design was used, where different measures were collected at different times throughout the course of the study (see table 1). The effects of recruitment activities were measured by recording every inquiry received by the programs on an initial contact form that included the inquirer's name, address, telephone number, interest in the program, and source of referral. The impact of the training program was assessed by pretraining and posttraining measures of seven categories of knowledge; by posttraining self-reports about changes in attitudes and beliefs about one's own child-care skills, interests, and intentions, and about perceived usefulness of various components of the program; by in-person or telephone interviews of randomly selected participants within two months of completion of the training; and by face-to-face interviews with a smaller stratified sample of participants between 12 and 18 months after completion of the program. Initial entry of providers into the work was assessed by identifying the status of each program participant approximately two months after completion of the program. Retention was assessed by identifying the status of first-year program completers approximately 15 to 18 months after program completion. A stratified random sample of program completers who were and were not providing FCC at follow-up were identified and interviewed using an open-ended semistructured interview schedule.

TABLE 1
Data Collection Schedule

Data Collection Period	N	Comment
I. Before Training		
Initial inquiry form	356	Annotated telephone log
Preassessment	125	Demographics, motivation for FCC, belief about FCC
Pretest knowledge	88*	Seven knowledge categories, 44 total items
II. At Completion of Training		
Posttest knowledge	88*	Repeat of pretests
III. Two-Month Follow-Up		
Status check	125	Provider status
Provider interview	41	Program feedback, utilization of resources, self-efficacy as FCC provider
Dropout assessment	36	Structured telephone interview
IV. Fifteen-Month Follow-Up		
Status check	61	Provider status
Provider/nonprovider interviews	22	Semistructured interview

*Represents total number of trainees with complete pretests and posttests.

Results

Recruitment

Both programs were able to successfully recruit the targeted number of participants. Interorganizational referrals, primarily from existing FCC referral agencies, produced nearly one-half (44.1%) of all referrals. Flyers, local media announcements, and news articles produced another 20.1% of referrals. Graduates from earlier training groups served as the primary referral source for 4.0% of initial inquiries; the remaining inquiries were from other referral bases or were unknown. Inquiry patterns were seasonal, with peaks in the fall and spring and lulls in the summer months. Participants who were referred by the established FCC referral organizations or by earlier program participants were more likely to begin and to complete the training than were participants who heard about the programs from other sources (programs A and B, $\chi^2 = 4.07$ and 3.88, respectively, both $p < .05$).

Program Impact

Knowledge gain. Knowledge about FCC was assessed before and at the completion of the program. Slightly different questionnaires and assessment procedures were developed for each program to accommodate differences in curriculum content across sites.[3] Participants at both sites demonstrated significant gains in knowledge related to schedules and routines, group guidance and child management, bookkeeping and taxes, and child development (see table 2). No significant gains were observed in the other three knowledge categories.

Perceived child care skills. This dimension was assessed indirectly via Likert-style self-reports of changes in attitudes and beliefs about one's own FCC provision, using open-ended questions at two-month follow-up, and using open-ended questions and direct but unstructured observations at 18-month follow-up.

Table 3 summarizes the responses to closed-ended questions scored on a six-point disagree-agree scale. Overall, participants reported strong agreement with statements indicating gains in confidence, commitment, interest, and skills. Participants' answers to open-ended questions supported these findings. Participants spontaneously indicated greater confidence in their child-caring skills and in their patience with children (related to a better understanding of child development), and a better awareness of children's abilities and needs. It was noteworthy that while many providers felt the curriculum on business aspects of FCC was very important, no participants spontaneously reported confidence in this area. During the 15-month follow-up, this component was investigated further. Even the most competent providers (as judged by our interviewers) voiced little confidence in their ability to manage the business side of FCC.

TABLE 2
Mean Percent of Correct Answers on Knowledge Tests Across Programs

Content Area		Posttest			Pretest	
	Pretest	Program A	Change		Program B	Posttest	Change
Schedules and Routines	54.73	64.74	10.01*		55.79	60.53	4.74*
Health and Safety	83.89	87.78	3.89		87.18	90.77	3.59
Room Arrangement	82.10	86.84	4.74		86.50	87.00	.50
Group Guidance and Child Management	71.79	77.24	5.45*		65.13	72.04	6.91*
Building a Partnership with Parents	87.84	85.13	−2.71		86.91	86.31	−.60
Bookkeeping and Taxes	61.26	72.97	11.71*		56.01	73.26	17.25*
Child Development	63.63	72.63	9.00*		45.00	72.00	27.00*
Total Score	70.73	76.98	6.25*		60.86	66.84	5.98*

*Indicates significant differences between pretest and posttest scores ($p < .05$).

TABLE 3
Mean Level of Agreement with Self-Judgments after Training*

Statement	Mean	Standard Deviation
I feel more confident in my ability to take care of children.	5.71	.56
I feel very committed to the child care profession.	5.47	.90
I feel good about the things which I have learned and the skills which I've received.	5.90	.37
I feel confident that I will make a good child care provider.	5.78	.53
I feel more interested in joining child care professional organizations.	5.29	1.19
I feel challenged to take more child care training courses if offered.	5.67	.57
I want to read more about child care and child development.	5.66	.69

*Responses to a 1–6 (disagree-agree) Likert scale.

Furthermore, many of these providers expressed a desire for ongoing support and advanced training on business topics.

Job satisfaction. During the 15-month follow-up interviews, providers were asked to describe the three most and the three least satisfying aspects of FCC. All responses were transcribed, coded, and subjected to a content analysis. Table 4 presents the results of this analysis. Participating in the healthy development of the FCC children was a unanimously cited satisfaction. Typical responses included, "to know that I'm doing a good job mothering the kids" and "watching the children grow and learn." Two-thirds of the providers described the opportunity to be with their own children (e.g., "getting to stay home with my own children") or to provide companionship to these children as a major satisfaction (e.g., "having another playmate for my child"). Indeed, all but one of the providers with children of their own at home (and under the age of five) cited this as a major satisfaction. The remaining responses fell into one of three other categories: FCC provider's own growth and development (e.g., "getting love in return"), the convenience or independence of the job (e.g., "I'm

TABLE 4
Percent of Providers Identifying Most and Least Satisfying Aspect of FCC at
15-month Follow-up

Content Area	Percent of Providers
Most Satisfying	
FCC children's development	100.0
Benefit own children	66.7
Own growth and development	41.7
Convenience/independence	33.3
Service to others	25.0
Least Satisfying	
FCC child difficulties	50.0
FCC parent difficulties	50.0
Low pay/difficult work	50.0
Restrictions on freedom	25.0
Lack of adult contact	16.7
Paper work/licensing requirements	16.7

my own boss," "getting to do what I like . . . cooking"), or service to other families (e.g., "I like providing a service to the community," "providing peace of mind for parents").

There was less consensus about the least satisfying aspect of FCC. Fifty percent of the providers reported difficulty with the FCC children's behavior or with periods when children are sick (e.g., "having a bad day when the kids are in a bad mood," "when kids get sick"). Similarly, one-half of the providers described problems with parents (e.g., "parents may not respect me," "telling parents when they have a problem"), and 50% described difficulties about the day-to-day job of FCC (e.g., "too much repetition of menial tasks," "having things broken [by the children]," "diapers"). The remaining responses fall into three content areas, as shown in table 4.

Placement and retention. Ninety-two of the initial 125 program participants completed the training program by the end of this study. Of these 92, 48 graduates were providing FCC two months after matriculation (initial placement rate = 52.17%). Although not statistically significant, the second-year placement rate was higher than the first year of the program (59.46 vs. 42.62%, $\chi^2(1) = 1.98, p > .05$).

Long-term retention rates were available for first-year graduates only. The short- and long-term placement rates for these graduates are shown in table 5. About 30% of those who completed the first-year program were providing FCC at both two and 15 months. An additional 26% were providing FCC either at two or 15 months, but not both. Overall then, 55.74% of the first-year graduates provided FCC at one of these two points, while 44.26% were not providing FCC at either time.

Potential Influences on Program Success

Participant characteristics. The impact of a wide variety of demographic, attitudinal, and motivational variables on program completion, entry into FCC (within two months after graduation), and retention in the field (at 18 months) was studied. Ethnicity, marital status, age, years of education, number of children, and number of siblings had no reliable impact on program completion, field entry, or field retention (all but one $p > .05$).[4]

Previous research suggested that having one's own children at home would lead to higher turnover in FCC. No such effect, however, was discovered in this study. Presence of the FCC provider's own children in the home did not predict retention at 15 months. Nevertheless, open-ended interview responses at 15 months strongly suggested that many providers intended to change careers once their own children entered school. These providers indicated that this was why they were in the work, and that their reasons for entering and exiting the field were closely related. Consistent with the previous literature, many of these women report high job satisfaction working with children, but a number of the best providers spontaneously spoke about an unfulfilled need for more stimulating adult contact and thought

TABLE 5
Number and Percent of First-year Graduates Providing FCC Two and 15 Months
after Program Completion

Providing FCC	Number	Percent
At two and 15 months	18	29.51
At two but not 15 months	8	13.11
At 15 but not two months	8	13.11
Neither at two or 15 months	27	44.26

about moving into other child-care careers, such as center-based or school-based care.

Ecological factors. Throughout the research and evaluation of this project, a strong sense emerged that ecological factors influenced program results. Telephone interviews at two months and face-to-face interviews at 18 months failed to identify any uniformity of factors influencing the initiation and maintenance of a FCC business. Instead, many respondents described a variety of macrosystem factors affecting their decisions about pursuing or remaining in FCC. These factors include landlord disapproval, zoning regulation prohibitions, liability and lack of affordable liability insurance, unavailability of fringe benefits, instability of FCC income, and inability to compete with underground (or nonlicensed) provider fees.

Discussion

This study describes findings generated from an evaluation of two rural family child care demonstration projects. Results indicate that these projects were successful in recruiting potential providers into the program and training the participants. Graduates demonstrated reliable knowledge gains, reported increased confidence in their skills, and were judged to provide high quality family child care by informal direct observations. Nevertheless, the programs were less successful in getting graduates started in the business and retaining providers over the first 18 months. Individual provider factors did not reliably relate to program success. Environmental factors seemed most influential, yet these factors affected individuals differently. As such, we interpreted these findings as evidence of a dynamic ecology, where certain macrosystem factors are present for many or all trainees but have individualized impacts.

Although lacking a control group comparison, the positive changes in FCC knowledge over the course of training confirm and extend previous findings [Kontos 1992]. Using a well-known published curriculum, participants at both sites demonstrated statistically significant gains in knowledge in four content areas. Furthermore, high pretraining scores in the other three knowledge categories likely precluded measuring improvement in those areas.

Participants reported increased self-confidence and commitment about providing FCC and generally reported a high level of job satisfaction [see also Galinsky et al. 1994a]. As reported in the earlier literature, these FCC providers were most likely to point to the development of the children in their care and of their own children as major sources of job satisfaction [Atkinson 1988]. In addition, the provider's own growth and development, job convenience, and service to others were cited as sources of satisfaction. Interestingly, these reported benefits have been found to be predictors of quality child care in another study [Galinsky et al. 1994b].

Contrary to the previous literature, none of these FCC providers reported conflict between their own and their FCC children as a problem [Bollin 1993; Pence & Goelman 1987]. This may have to do with local cultural norms, which emphasize extended families and caring for children other than one's own, or may relate to program selection or training. In accord with other studies, low pay, problems with parent clients and child discipline, and caring for sick children were common sources of job dissatisfaction [Kontos 1992].

The initial data on placement and retention provide an interesting picture. It is noteworthy that the two- and 15-month provider rates for first-year graduates were exactly the same. About 70% of those who were providing care at two-month follow-up were still doing so at 15 months. In addition, the 30% who dropped out after initially providing care were fully replaced by providers who did not start until after the first assessment.

These data suggest two points. First, there is a substantial amount of fluidity into and out of FCC, even for many trained providers. Second, trained graduates may delay entry into the FCC workforce. Programs are therefore well advised to maintain supportive contact with these nonproviders for at least one year after graduation.

The present results support the finding in the literature that indicates it is difficult to predict a priori who will and will not become stable FCC providers. Although subject to the flaws of null hypothesis reasoning, these findings may have implications for the future development of similar programs. First, programs and policies supporting a variety of different levels of training and support may hold the most promise. The flexibility offered by such programs allows potential FCC providers to choose from an array of training opportunities and support services that best fit their individual needs. Such programs have been successfully developed and implemented elsewhere [Lawrence 1987].

Second, measures selected to evaluate program success have to be flexible and multifaceted. For example, this study found substantial movement of FCC providers into and out of the field. Programs incorporating this information into their own program and evaluation design may choose to target individuals with both short- and long-term FCC career potentials for program inclusion. In these programs, long-term retention of FCC providers would not be an appropriate sole measure of success. Instead, programs that adopt a flexible model might be better considered by a cost-benefit analysis. Components of the program that have more limited benefits should consume fewer resources per participant than program elements with larger and more lasting benefits. This analysis would help program planners and developers focus on specific targets. It has the additional benefit of allowing prospective participants temporary or gradual entry into the field. This gradual entry might help participants themselves determine their long-term suitability for FCC.

Finally, the negative impact of FCC attrition may be reduced by supporting providers in their bid to move into other positions within the child care field. Incentives offered in the form of job or educational training that are directly tied to the number of years of provider service may increase provider service longevity. Such incentives may also provide career-advancing opportunities that have been so sorely lacking in the field. ♦

Notes

1.   Due to the planned termination of the evaluation contract, the remaining 15 trainees were not included in the study.

2.   All measurement instruments are available upon request.

3.   One of five items from the child development subscales and four of eight items from the guidance/group management subscales differed across programs. Also, Program A staggered the administration of the pretests so that each subtest immediately preceded classroom didactics on that topic. The comparability of findings across the two programs, however, suggest that these differences did not affect the results.

4.   Participants who completed the training program reported greater perceived family support than did those who did not finish; no such effect was found, however, for entry or retention in FCC. This may therefore represent a chance finding.

References

Aguirre, B. E. (1987). Educational activities and needs of family child care providers in Texas. *Child Welfare, 66*, 459–465.

Atkinson, A. M. (1988). Providers' evaluations of the effect of family day care on family relationships. *Family Relations, 37*, 399–404.

Bollin, G. G. (1993). An investigation of job stability and job satisfaction among family child care providers. *Early Childhood Research Quarterly, 8*, 207–220.

Dodge, D. T., & Colker, L. J. (1991). *The creative curriculum for family child care.* Washington, DC: Teaching Strategies, Inc.

Galinsky, E., Howes, C., & Kontos, S. (1994a). *The family child care training study.* New York: Families and Work Institute.

Galinsky, E., Howes, C., Kontos, S., & Shinn, M. (1994b). *The study of children in family child care and relative care.* New York: Families and Work Institute.

Kontos, S. (1992). *Family child care: Out of the shadows and into the limelight* (research monograph vol. 5). Washington, DC: National Association for the Education of Young Children.

Lawrence, M. (1987). *California child care initiative: Year-end report (October 1, 1985—September 30, 1986).* San Francisco: California Child Care Resource and Referral Network.

Lawrence, M., Brown, J., & Bellm, D. (1989). *Helping family child care providers stay in the business: Retention strategies from the California child care initiative.* San Francisco: California Child Care Resource and Referral Network.

Pence, A. R., & Goelman, H. (1987). Who cares for the child in day care? An examination of caregivers from three types of care. *Early Childhood Research Quarterly, 2*, 315–334.

9

Children in Court: A Troubling Presence

Lucy Hudson and Patricia Hrusa Williams

The rise in domestic and community violence and criminal activity has brought with it a noticeable increase in the number of children who are present in the nation's courthouses. This article details the reasons children come to court and the effect the experience has on their well-being. Drop-in child day care is discussed as a possible program model to support families and counteract the risks to children.

Lucy Hudson, M.S., is Senior Associate, Center for the Study of Social Policy, Washington, D.C. Patricia Hrusa Williams is Ph.D. candidate, Eliot Pearson Department of Child Study, Tufts University, Medford, MA.

179

For almost all children, going to court is a frightening experience which occurs at a time of family crisis already fraught with anxiety. Courthouse corridors and even courtrooms are full of children: they accompany adults who need to be there and have no other place to leave their children, or they are there because they themselves need to appear in court.

Courts should provide friendly environments, including trained staff, for children who are waiting to testify in court cases, child victims who are attending hearings and other court proceedings, and children who have merely accompanied their parents to court because there was no one to look after them. Friendly environments and trained staff can provide a safe, nurturing alternative to the tension, conflict, and verbal violence that often characterize courtrooms. [Higginbotham et al. 1992]

Drop-in child day care can offer a safe haven to children who increasingly find themselves in courthouses around the country, where the potential is great for exposure to disturbing and possibly dangerous situations. Judges, attorneys, and other court employees in several states have recognized the harm that children may suffer by virtue of their presence in court, and have organized efforts to provide court-based child day care settings for the children of litigants and for children who are themselves court-involved. This article documents the reasons children are appearing in court and why child welfare and related professions should take steps to limit children's exposure to this intimidating adult environment.

The presence of children in courthouses is escalating due to several factors. An increasing number of parents and other adult guardians are getting divorced and thus arguing about custody and child support. Parents are seeking restraining orders to protect themselves from abusive spouses. Substance abuse is wracking the integrity of the family, resulting in criminal charges and abusive or neglectful parenting. The court is deciding the fate of children in the custody of the state's child welfare system. Parents and children are victims of, or witnesses to, violent crime.

Many court-involved families lack the personal and financial resources to arrange for alternative care for their children while they are in court, leaving them with no choice but to bring their children with them to court. The presence of children in courts is cause for serious concern for two major reasons. First, children can disrupt the timely administration of justice by behaving as one might expect them to behave in such stressful circumstances: they cry, shout, run, taunt, laugh, argue, complain, and fidget, and they throw things. Second, the presence of children in courts may subject them to testimony and/or situations potentially disturbing or even damaging to them. They may hear their parents and other adult guardians accused of vicious crimes; they may hear a parent describe the torture inflicted by a vindictive spouse; they may hear sobs from victims of rape still distraught from their traumatizing experience. Adults find such situations anxiety-provoking at best; children can easily be traumatized.

While common sense firmly supports the notion that children are easily harmed by the adult events that unfold in courthouses, a review of the literature showed that this particular aspect of harm to children has received little attention. (The bulk of the research on children's presence in court focuses on the children as witnesses.) Most of the research illustrates the damage children experience when exposed to violence in their homes or communities; because there are parallels, this literature is briefly reviewed.

Children who witness violence and trauma are likely to exhibit aggressive behavior themselves. Theoretical work suggests that exposure to environments that (1) provide aggressive models, (2) reinforce aggression, and (3) frustrate and victimize the child, contribute to the development of aggressive tendencies [Perry et al. 1990]. Applied research supports this view and expands our understanding of the variety of negative consequences experienced by children exposed to violence. School-age children exposed to violence in both their home and community are more likely than those not so exposed to engage in aggressive acts themselves. Teens have an increased likelihood of perpetrating a violent act if they have been a victim of or a witness to violence [Bell & Jenkins 1993; Jenkins & Thompson 1986; Jenkins et al. undated; Shakoor & Chalmers 1991; Uehara et al. 1990]. Thus, early exposure to adult aggression may perpetuate the cycle of criminal behavior, making a court-based child day care center an especially valuable resource inasmuch as it reduces children's exposure to adult aggression.

Court Activity and Usage

> It's very distracting. Children cry. They run around. Parents concentrate on the children instead of the case and everything takes longer. They go back and forth between Mommy and Daddy like it's a tug-of-war. Not to mention the mess they make. I've seen children bite court officers. I've seen children watch as parents hyperventilate or go into cardiac arrest. [West 1995]

Each year, a growing number of children are brought into court as increases in criminal activity require more adults to appear in court. In 1991, 14,475,613 criminal offenses were committed—a 10% increase since 1987 [Federal Bureau of Investigation (FBI) 1992]. This translates into a crime every two seconds. On average, someone is robbed every two seconds, raped every five minutes, and murdered every 21 minutes [FBI 1992]. In 1991, over one million people were arrested in the U.S. for drug abuse violations, a 56% increase in such arrests since 1982.

The rising crime rate has resulted in the presence of millions of persons brought into court as victims, witnesses, defendants, and jurors. Many of these adults bring their children with them.

In addition, the number of cases specifically involving families and children have increased. Civil matters such as divorce, child custody, and support cases involve some ten million children [Hewlett 1991]. The legal establishment of paternity is estimated to affect another five million children born to single mothers [Hewlett 1991].

Criminal cases also involve children and families. Violence in the home increasingly claims the attention of courts as they adjudicate restraining orders and determine parental suitability to care for neglected and abused children. The incidence of domestic violence is substantial: 20% of American families can expect to experience some kind of spouse-on-spouse abuse [Coalition Against Rape & Abuse 1992].

In many instances, children do not need to be present in the courtroom, but simply accompany their parents and other adult guardians because of a lack of child day care. In the courtroom, they become spectators while the trauma they have privately suffered at home becomes a topic for public consumption.

Children Who Appear in Court: A Profile

The children who come to court constitute a particularly vulnerable segment of America's children. They are likely to come from impoverished families. Living in poor communities, they have probably been exposed to criminal activity and/or violence in their homes or neighborhoods [Garbarino et al. 1992]. Their parents' involvement with the courts suggests troubled home environments—stressful places where financial stability is uncertain, where marriages or other adult relationships are dissolving, and where the future custody of children is an open question.

For example, at the Roxbury District Court Child Care Center in Boston, 60% of the children served in 1992 came from low-income families and 40% lived in publicly subsidized housing [Associated Day Care Services of Metropolitan Boston 1992]. A group of studies examining the backgrounds of abused and neglected children whose cases were being adjudicated in Boston Juvenile Court found that the families of these children were impoverished, mostly headed by single mothers. More than half of the parents had a serious psychiatric disorder, and 81% had an average of four reports of abuse and neglect over a three-year period [Jellineck et al. 1990; Murphy et al. 1991; Taylor et al. 1991]. A child day care needs-assessment conducted by the New York Permanent Judicial Commission on Justice for Children confirmed the daily presence of hundreds of children in the courts, the majority of whom were from New York's lowest income and most vulnerable families [Heidt 1992].

The threat to healthy growth and development is exacerbated for these children because of their socioeconomic status. Exploration of the relationship between child development and poverty [Kaplan-Sanoff et al. 1991; Tarnowski & Rohrbeck 1993] finds that impoverished children are more likely than their more affluent counterparts to experience health problems such as low birth weight, intrauterine growth retardation, failure to thrive, infant mortality, chronic ear infections, pediatric AIDS, lead exposure, accidental injury, learning disabilities, adolescent pregnancy, asthma, and problems secondary to vaccination; stress in the form of disruptions, moves, and losses; parenting risks including drug use; and behavioral disturbances including high rates of child and maternal pathology. Not only do children living in poverty encounter more risks to their healthy development than their middle- and upper-class counterparts, but they experience more serious consequences from their exposure to those risks than do middle- and upper-class children [Kaplan-Sanoff et al. 1991].

Children's Exposure to Traumatic Events in Courthouses

Courthouses and court rooms can be incredibly intimidating places for children, especially when their future is at issue. Children, even very young ones, understand that serious subjects are discussed in court. Parents, if present, are often tense and preoccupied. As a result, children in court are often frightened, and in many cases have little to take their minds off the grave proceedings at hand. Observers who have taken the time to really notice how children spend their time in court have seen them playing on dirty floors and in trash cans for lack of anything else to do. They have also observed children creating disturbances after long hours of waiting for their cases to come up, and in some cases, have seen exasperated parents discipline harshly, which only worsens matters. [Burke 1995]

Courthouses are intimidating places, especially for children. Experimental work suggests that simply being questioned in a courtroom about something as familiar as a school lesson is stress inducing for children [Saywitz & Nathanson 1993]. Institutional surroundings coupled with events that frighten children can do significant damage. Even very young children are harmed by exposure to violence and other traumatic events. In courthouses, children are often witnesses to disturbing events. Altercations between court officers and prisoners, angry voices, and wild gesticulation are adult behaviors that young children are not able to put into a context that would defuse their anxiety.

When the children are themselves parties to the events transpiring in the courthouse, the court's need to go over the incident in detail can cause a secondary victimization. The fear and confusion the child felt when the incident took place are repeatedly called to mind. Child victims of sexual assault and their families often experience continued stress and trauma as cases make their way through the legal system. Children may experience recurrent trauma as they are repeatedly required to recount events to authorities. As stories are questioned in court, the child's emotional well-being may further be jeopardized, because the courtroom cross-examination seems to be a betrayal by the adults who said they believed the child's story [Higgins 1988].

Inappropriate and frightening adult behavior is not limited to family court. Williams [1993] found that there were nearly as many children under the age of 12 present per hour of court time in an inner-city municipal court (seven children) as during a family court session (nine children). During two hours of observation at the municipal court, an average of 3.4 children under the age of 12 were exposed to six cases involving neighborhood violence (assault, breaking and entering, etc.), five cases involving substance abuse (driving while intoxicated, drug possession and sale), and two domestic violence cases (assault on a family member and violation of a restraining order) [Williams 1993].

Courtroom proceedings are not the only cause for concern. Courthouses pose a distinct threat to children's physical safety. The nation has seen an epidemic of violence in courthouses in recent years. Newspaper articles around the country detail the myriad security issues facing the courts. In Massachusetts, for example, data reported by the district courts over a three-year period indicated the occurence of 35 escapes, 29 attempted escapes, 10 attempted suicides, 69 violent struggles or assaults on court officers, and 42 incidents where court officers were injured [Wong 1992]. Gang presence has heightened the threat of violence. The District of Columbia's Superior Court has been plagued by the presence of teenage gangs who wait in corridors next to women with young children, disrupting proceedings and heightening the potential for violence and intimidation of witnesses [Lewis 1994]. No one incident better illustrates the potentially devastating events children may experience than a case in California: in court, a mother took the law into her own hands and shot to death a man accused of molesting her son, fearful that the man would receive a light sentence and return to hurt her family again [Adams 1993].

Some courts have devised means to shield child witnesses from courtrooms [Higgins 1988; Lloyd-Bostock 1988]. Research has revealed, however, that technological advances such as closed circuit television and videotaped testimony are not often used, and, even if used, do not deal with the problem that court involvement is an ongoing process that continues to challenge the coping resources of children and families long after the testifying is over [Whitcomb 1986]. These issues are even more pressing for children and families in inner-city areas who are coming to court in increasing numbers due to escalating domestic and community violence.

Children who are forced to witness violence and traumatic events in their homes and communities are at tremendous risk for a host of problems, including depression, behavior problems, and decreased developmental opportunities [Martinez & Richters 1993; Osofsky et al. 1993; Pagelow 1990; Jaffe et al. 1986; Caesar 1988; Adalist-Estrin 1994; Widom 1992; Emde 1993]. Garbarino and his colleagues described the effects of violence in the following way:

> In the developmental process, the child forms a picture or draws a map of the world and his or her place in it. As children draw these maps, they move forward on the paths they believe exist. If a child's map of the world depicts people and places as hostile, and the child as an insignificant speck relegated to one small corner, we must expect troubled development of one sort or another: a life of suspicion, low self-esteem, self-denigration, and perhaps violence and rage. We can also expect a diminution of cognitive development and impediments to academic achievement and in-school behavior. [Garbarino et al. 1992]

Counteracting the Risks to Children

There is little disagreement that court is not a good place for young children, under almost any circumstances, and that steps should be taken to minimize the trauma of the experience when it cannot be avoided. Children are dramatically affected by family crises, even when the crisis doesn't directly involve them, and in times of turmoil, parents and other family members are the persons least available to comfort and support their children. Offering care and support to these children and their families at a critical time may have long-term preventive benefits for the children. [Carter 1993]

The harmful effects of courthouse events can be mitigated by an innovative form of child day care currently practiced in 23 courthouses in six states around the country. Court-based, drop-in day care originated in the Municipal Court of Philadelphia in 1915 with the establishment of a nursery where children could wait while their parents and other adult guardians transacted their court business. Not until 1973 was the idea translated to new settings when courts in Chicago (1973), Washington, D.C. (1974), and New York City (1975) initiated similar programs. Since then, additional programs have opened in California, Illinois, Massachusetts,* and New York State. Though each program implements the concept in unique ways, they all share certain characteristics—at least one staff person whose sole function is the management of the court-based child care program, and a self-enclosed site designed as a child care center. The U.S. Department of Justice, under the leadership of Attorney General Janet Reno, grew interested in this development and subsequently funded the National CourtCare Demonstration Project to examine it and to provide technical assistance to court jurisdictions interested in establishing such programs.

The Center for the Study of Social Policy (CSSP) in Washington, D.C., launched the National CourtCare Demonstration Proj-

---

*The two Massachusetts programs are operated by agency members of the Child Welfare League of America: at Roxbury District Court by Associated Day Care Services of Metropolitan Boston, and at the Hampden County Courts by Springfield Day Nursery.

ect as a way of demonstrating the utility of court-based, drop-in child day care and family support centers in the courts. The project seeks to provide pertinent information to judges and court administrators so that they can evaluate the efficacy of court-based child day care programs and, if needed, establish their own programs. The center became interested in the National CourtCare Demonstration Project* because it provided a potentially important forum to contribute to three related efforts: improving the administration of justice, shielding children from traumatizing experiences, and linking needy families with other support services.

What makes this project unique is that court-based child care brings together two very disparate professional systems—the judiciary and the social services system for children and families. Jointly, they offer the promise of integrated services that can simultaneously benefit both the courts and the families. ♦

References

Adalist-Estrin, A. (1994). Family support and criminal justice. In S. L. Kagan & B. Weissbourd (Eds.), *Putting families first* (p. 161). San Francisco: Jossey-Bass Publishers.

Adams, J. M. (1993, April 18). Killing of accused child molester stirs justice debate. *Boston Globe*, pp. 1, 24.

Associated Day Care Services of Metropolitan Boston. (1992). *1992 annual report to the United Way of Massachusetts Bay; Roxbury District Court Child Care Center*. Boston, MA: Author.

Bell, C. C., & Jenkins, E. J. (1993). Community violence and children on Chicago's south-side. *Psychiatry, 56*, 46–54.

*For more information about the National CourtCare Demonstration Project or a copy of the annotated bibliography that further details our review of the literature, contact: Lucy Hudson, Project Director, National CourtCare Demonstration Project, Center for the Study of Social Policy, 1250 Eye Street, NW, Washington, DC 20005, (202/371–1565).

Burke, A. (1995, January 31). *A small step* (pp. 14 and 16). Speech to the Illinois Joint Task Force on Gender Equality. Chicago: Office of the Special Counsel to the Governor for Child Welfare Services.

Caesar, P. L. (1988). Exposure to violence in the families-of-origin among wife-abusers and maritally nonviolent men. *Violence and Victims, 3* (1), 49–63.

Carter, J. L. (1993, December 1). Personal correspondence. Family Resource Coalition, Chicago, IL.

Coalition Against Rape & Abuse Inc. (1992). *Always on call* [flier]. Cape May, NJ: Author.

Emde, R. N. (1993). The horror! The horror! Reflections on our culture of violence and its implications for early development and morality. *Psychiatry, 56,* 119–123.

Federal Bureau of Investigation. (1992). *Crime in the United States 1991; Uniform crime reports* (pp. 4–5). Washington, DC: U.S. Government Printing Office.

Garbarino, J., Dubrow, N., Kostelny, K., & Pardo, C. (1992). *Children in Danger: Coping with the consequences of community violence* (p. 10). San Francisco: Jossey-Bass Publishers.

Heidt, J. (1992). *Report of a survey of families that bring children to court* (p. 1). New York: Permanent Judicial Commission on Justice for Children.

Hewlett, S. A. (1991). *When the bough breaks: The cost of neglecting our children* (p. 88). New York: Basic Books.

Higginbotham, A. Jr., Ross, C. J., Abromowitz, D. M., Asher, J. D., Barber, M. E., Barkett, R., Clanton, D. M., Day, K. A., Determan, S. A., Dohrn, B., Donald, B. B., Duffly, F. R. V., Foscarinis, M., Franklin-Suber, S., Godfrey, L. A., Goldstein, L. N., Green, I. M., Hartog-Rapp, F., Hornak, K., Hostetler, Z. F., Mallory, B. T., Morales, J., Neuhard, J. R., Popilek, J. L., Ramsey, B., Roberts, P. J., Schenk, D. H., Schmidt, L. W. Jr., Schwartz, R. G., Segal, D., Shor, N. G., Skinner, T. E., Skoler, D. L., Stillwaggon, J. M., Toal, J. M., Turnbull, H. R. III, Wilson, M. B., Wolf, M. J., & Yu, D. C. (1992). *America's children at risk; A national agenda for legal action.* (p. 57). Chicago: American Bar Association, Presidential Working Group on the Unmet Legal Needs of Children and Their Families.

Higgins, R. B. (1988). Child victims as witnesses. *Law and Psychology Review, 12,* 159–166.

Jaffe, P., Wolfe, D., Wilson, S., & Zak, L. (1986). Similarities in behavioral and social maladjustment among child victims and witnesses to family violence. *American Journal of Orthopsychiatry, 56,* 142–146.

Jellinek, M. S., Murphy, J. M., Bishop, S., Poitrast, F., & Quinn, D. (1990). Protecting severely abused and neglected children: An unkept promise. *New England Journal of Medicine, 323,* 1628–1630.

Jenkins, E. J., & Thompson, B. (1986). *Children talk about violence: Preliminary findings from a survey of black elementary school children.* Paper presented at the Nineteenth Annual Convention of the Association of Black Psychologists, Oakland, CA.

Jenkins, E. J., Thompson, B., & Mokros, H. (no date). *Correlates of self-perceived aggression for black children* (unpublished manuscript).

Kaplan-Sanoff, R. J., Parker, S., & Zuckerman, B. (1991). Poverty and early childhood development: What do we know and what should we do? *Infants and Young Children, 4* (1), 68–76.

Lewis, N. (1994, May 2). D.C.'s clogged corridor of justice: In hallway-turned-waiting room, cases are imperiled. *Washington Post,* p. A1.

Lloyd-Bostock, S. (1988). The benefits of legal psychology: Possibilities, practice, and dilemmas. *British Journal of Psychology, 79,* 417–440.

Martinez, P., & Richters, J. E. (1993). The NIMH community violence project: II. Children's distress symptoms associated with violence exposure. *Psychiatry, 56,* 22–35.

Murphy, J. M., Jellinek, M. S., Quinn, D., Smith, G., Poitrast, F. G., & Goshko, M. (1991). Substance abuse and serious child maltreatment: Prevalence, risk, and outcome in a court sample. *Child Abuse and Neglect, 15,* 197–211.

Osofsky, J. D., Wewers, S., Hann, D. H., & Fick, A. C. (1993). Chronic community violence: What is happening to our children? *Psychiatry, 56,* 36–45.

Pagelow, M. D. (1990). Effects of domestic violence on children and their consequences for custody and visitation agreements. *Mediation Quarterly, 7,* 347–363.

Perry, D. G., Perry, L. C., & Boldizar, J. P. (1990). Learning of aggression. In M. Lewis & S. M. Miller (Eds.), *Handbook of developmental psychopathology* (pp. 135–146). New York: Plenum.

Saywitz, K. J., & Nathanson, R. (1993). Children's testimony and their perceptions of stress in and out of the courtroom. *Child Abuse and Neglect, 17,* 613–622.

Shakoor, B. H., & Chalmers, D. (1991). Co-victimization of African-American children who witness violence and the theoretical implications of its effects on their cognitive, emotional, and behavioral development. *Journal of the National Medical Association, 83,* 233–238.

Tarnowski, K. J., & Rohrbeck, C. A. (1993). Disadvantaged children and families. In T. H. Ollendick & R. J. Prinz (Eds.), *Advances in clinical child psychology* (vol. 15) (pp. 41–79). New York: Plenum.

Taylor, C. G., Norman, D. K., Murphy, J. M., Jellinek, M., Quinn, D., & Poitrast, F. G. (1991). Diagnosed intellectual and emotional impairment among parents who seriously mistreat their children: Prevalence, type, and outcome in a court sample. *Child Abuse and Neglect, 15,* 389–401.

Uehara, E., Chalmers, D., Jenkins, E. J., & Shakoor, B. (1990). Youth encounters with violence: Results from the Chicago Community Mental Health Council Violence Screening Project (unpublished manuscript).

West, D. (1995, January 29). In family court, caring for children. *The New York Times,* p. 39.

Whitcomb, D. (1986). Assisting child victims in the courts: The practical side of legislative reform. *Response to the Victimization of Women and Children: Journal of the Center for Women Policy Studies, 9*(1) 9–12.

Widom, C. S. (1992, October). The cycle of violence. *National Institute of Justice Research in Brief, 1.*

Williams, P. H. (1993, Summer/Fall). Child care improves the administration of justice. *State Court Journal,* 35–37.

Wong, D. S. (1992, September 10). SJC to secure courts: Laws suspended to allow deployment of officers. *Boston Globe,* pp. 31, 39.

10
Family Child Care and New Immigrants: Cultural Bridge and Support

Elizabeth Schnur, Rebecca Koffler, Nicola Wimpenny, Helayne Giller, and Eileen Nagel Rafield

Immigrants usually face an array of problems and stressors in the United States. After the Immigration and Naturalization Service and the local department of social services, family child care providers may be the primary external influence that new immigrants experience. This article describes a program for new immigrants from the former Soviet Union designed to buffer some of the stressors confronting the new immigrant, to act as a bridge between cultures, and to facilitate employment or vocational training of immigrant parents. Client descriptors from the past three years of the program are presented, and the experiences of four randomly selected clients are profiled. General implications for family child care for immigrant families are discussed.

Elizabeth Schnur, Ph.D., is Director, Research and New Program Development; Rebecca Koffler, ACSW, is Program Director, Family Day Care Services; Nicola Wimpenny, M.A., is Research Associate; Helayne Giller, M.S., is Director, Early Childhood Programs; and Eileen Nagel Rafield, M.S.W., is Associate Executive Director, Jewish Child Care Association, New York, NY.

The effects of child day care on young children's social and cognitive development have been hotly debated in both the academic and political arenas, and have been the focus of the bulk of child day care research. Studies variously indicate that child day care may have negative, disruptive effects on aspects of young children's development [Belsky 1988], or positive, protective effects [Caughy et al. 1994]. A striking feature of much of this debate is that it contrasts child day care with maternal home care, with the implicit assumption that the use of the former is a choice. In light of the growing number of women in the labor force, however—more than half of all women with children under the age of six work outside the home [Chilman 1993]—child day care is a necessity and not an option for the majority of parents of the six million children currently using such services [Adams 1990]. Studies that focus on how various factors in child day care differentially affect outcomes [e.g., Phillips 1994] are likely to prove the most useful in designing effective policy.

Mirroring much of the field of child welfare, studies of child day care have tended to deal almost exclusively with outcomes for individual children, and generally have not closely examined the impact of child day care on the family system. In regard to new immigrant families, for example, child day care can play a major role in facilitating their adjustment to a new country. The impact of child day care services on new immigrants seems particularly worth scrutiny since the majority of new immigrants to the United States are in their child-bearing years and are members of the working poor [Bouvier & Gardner 1986]. For many of these new immigrants, child day care serves as the primary point of extrafamilial contact. This article discusses how family child care can help immigrant families, and describes a family child care program designed to serve a particular group of immigrants—families from the former Soviet Union.

Even under the best of circumstances, recent immigrants may face such stresses as culture shock, communication difficulties, status and social-role upheaval, and isolation [Lequerica 1993]. With the added stress of pervasive economic struggles, new immigrant families often are at risk for interpersonal and mental health problems [Kelley 1994]. Child day care in general, and family child care in particular, may serve as a buffer for these young families and ease their introduction to the new culture.

Family child care, in which a provider cares for a small group of children in her or his own home, is particularly well suited for serving the needs of immigrant families. When matched to the cultural and linguistic background of the immigrant family, providers are intrinsically culturally sensitive. This matching creates a familiar, accessible point of entry for both the immigrant parents and their young children, reducing stress and strangeness. A culturally supportive environment fosters a child's sense of security and self-concept [Washington 1985]. In addition, according to Lequerica [1993], contact with people of similar ethnic/cultural background minimizes some of the stress and strangeness for the new immigrants. Perhaps most importantly, as Isralowitz and Saad [1994: 880] note, family child care offers the immigrant "an opportunity to make social contacts, whereas [for the immigrant] full-time parenting leads to social isolation."

In addition to serving an important buffer function, family child care can serve an important bridging function, connecting immigrants to the new culture. In family child care, relationships typically develop between providers and parents that go beyond the focus on the children. Providers who are able to manage effectively in both cultures may be models and mentors to immigrant parents, helping them to navigate and cope. In addition, children frequently learn to speak English in the providers' homes, which eases the children's subsequent move into school and often supports the parents' efforts to learn English as well.

A family child care program that draws on the immigrant community for providers may also be an instrument of change both for the providers and for the larger immigrant community. In becoming a family child care provider, an immigrant takes on the new role of entrepreneur, acquiring prestige, a measure of independence, and business skills (records must be kept, clients billed, etc.). The community benefits because jobs are created and maintained. In some instances, immigrants who have been consumers of family child care services become providers. As discussed below, however, training and supervision are essential for new providers.

Within the past three decades nearly half a million people have immigrated to the United States from the former Soviet Union; the majority are young families with children. According to the U.S. Department of Health and Human Resources [Chiswick 1993], roughly one-third of these refugees are children and another third are between the ages of 25 and 44. The largest proportion of these immigrants (36%) have settled in New York City. In what follows, we consider a family child care program designed to meet some of the needs of this immigrant population, and describe the characteristics of the program and its participants at one site (located in the borough of Queens in New York City), based on the past three years of client intake and recertification records, and provider information files. In addition, several Queens program participants were interviewed to provide a personalized perspective, and parents of children who aged out of the program were queried about their children's adjustment to school.

Program Description

The family child care program of the Jewish Child Care Association of New York (JCCA) was designed to serve low-income immigrant families from the former Soviet Union. The program is publicly funded, and provides child day care at no charge, or on a sliding scale, to parents of young children who are on public assistance or who have very low incomes. Subsidized parents are required either to be employed, in training programs (the most common training program is English as a Second Language), or looking for employment; however, a small number of subsidized parents who don't fall into the employment/training categories also receive assistance due to their mental or physical incapacitation.

JCCA administers a network of providers who are trained, supported, and monitored by the agency; both the training and monitoring are necessary to the success of the program. Providers receive an orientation from the New York City Department of Health before submitting a final application to practice as providers. Once the city has approved them, providers must have 15 hours of training during their first year, and 15 hours of training every two years thereafter. Material is presented in the native language of the providers, and concentrates on mandatory requirements and the basics of caring for children in the United States.

Providers also attend lectures and workshops at JCCA to increase their knowledge of Jewish culture, heritage, and traditions (all of the former Soviet Union clients at Jewish Child Care Association are Jewish, and many are refugees from religious persecution). The inclusion of programming concerning the children's cultural heritage is in response to a point frequently articulated with respect to preschool programs such as Head Start, that is, that valuing a young child's cultural heritage and traditions may prove critical to developing and enhancing a child's self-concept [Washington 1985]. The cultural training of providers helps them develop age-appropriate games, learn about arts and crafts projects, and gain exposure to a range of print materials. Providers also are visited in their homes to help them carry out activities related to holidays or other cultural traditions.

Providers are monitored in their homes at least eight times per year by JCCA's staff members, many of whom are bilingual. During visits, staff members observe both the children and the provider, review health and safety equipment, and monitor meals. Staff members also function as mediators if conflicts arise between providers and parents, and as consultants for both parents and providers when developmental questions or problems arise.

The program currently offers family child care to 330 children (280 families) in the New York City boroughs of Brooklyn and Queens. Each provider has two to five children in her home, ranging in age from six months to six years. All of the providers to families from the former Soviet Union are originally from the Soviet Union and were recruited in Brooklyn and Queens neighborhoods with large concentrations of immigrants from the former Soviet Union.

The Queens program currently has 62 providers (all of whom are women) serving 170 families. All providers are fluent in Russian and many are fluent in English as well; a large proportion of providers also speak Hebrew (28%) and Bukharian (31%); a few speak Farsi, Persian, Hindi, Spanish, or Bengali. Providers range in age from 26 to 66 years (mean = 44). The providers' education varies greatly, with 40% having finished high school and 26% having some college. Most of the providers are married (88%) and have school-age children of their own.

The Queens Program Clients

An examination of reasons at intake for seeking family child care services showed that families had a high degree of stress and disruption. Most striking in the intake data is the pervasive sense of depression in nearly every record. Stressors named include difficulty adjusting to American life, financial struggles, marital conflicts, generalized depression and anxiety, "culture shock," linguistic/cultural communication problems, and inability to manage parenting and household responsibilities.

The depressed affect of parents is often mirrored in the young children entering family child care, who may show dysphoric or withdrawn affect. Although the parental affect may be seen as a direct reaction to the experience of being in a new and alien culture, it is difficult to isolate a major cause for the children's affect. They may be reflecting their own sense of displacement in a new culture, their parents' affect, their first out-of-home separation, other family problems, endogenous sources, or a combination of these factors. When a child's depressed behavior lasts beyond an initial adjustment period, the family child care worker is able to use her supervisor as a professional resource. The supervisor will work with both the parents and the provider to deal with the problem. This will often result in a supervisor's visit to a provider home and more intensive supervision of the worker in the home. A small number of children who do not appear to respond to the additional supports are referred for counseling.

The majority of the Soviet immigrants in the family child care program came from the south Asian regions, including Tashkent and Samarkand; a few came from the region of Kharkov, and several families came to the United States via Israel. A little over half (57%) of the immigrant families have two parents in the home, with the remaining families headed by separated or never-married mothers. Since no information was available on fathers who did not live with their children, all data reported for fathers is based on the 57% in the home. The average age of the mothers, at the time of this writing, was 28 years (ranging from 19 to 46), and the average age for fathers was 32 years (ranging from 24 to 50). Family size ranged from one to four children, with an average of two children per family. The majority of families (66%) had one child in family child care; one-third had two children in family child care (one family had three children in family child care). More than half (57%) of the families had no school-age children, and the remaining 43% had between one and three children in public school.

Both mothers and fathers had relatively high levels of educational attainment, with mothers having a mean of 12.5 years in school (ranging from eight to 18), and fathers a mean of 12 years (ranging from eight to 19). It should be noted that the Soviet educational system is quite different from the United States system, and a direct comparison of educational attainment may not be valid. Nearly two-thirds (62%) of the mothers were employed, with the majority of working mothers (74%) working part-time; 60% of the fathers were working, with the majority (63%) working full-time. Seventy-four percent of all the families received some form of public assistance and/or Medicaid.

The formal immigrant status of the parents varied across families. Mothers were more likely than fathers to be classified as legal immigrants. The largest proportion of mothers were classified as legal immigrants (39%), with the next largest number being refugees (34%). The largest proportion of fathers (45%) were classified as refugees and the next largest proportion (32%) were legal immigrants. A roughly equal proportion of mothers (26%) and fathers (22%) were resident aliens; 1% of mothers and fathers were parolees (not eligible for citizenship benefits), and 1% of the mothers were U.S. citizens.

It is of interest that the families in the program do not fit the typical profile of immigrants from the former Soviet Union [Chiswick 1993]. Although the parents in this sample have relatively high education levels, on average they have more than two years less education than the average Soviet immigrant. Likewise, the occupational attainment of this group falls well below the norm for Soviet immigrants, who tend to reach occupational parity with other European immigrants after a few years [Chiswick 1993]. The likely explanation for these differences is that, unlike the majority of Soviet immigrants, the families in the family child care program came chiefly from the non-European parts of the former Soviet Union—areas that are economically depressed. These immigrants have fewer resources and contacts in the United States than do their European counterparts.

Parent Interviews

Four parents (mothers) were randomly selected from the Queens program participants who were coming to the JCCA family child care office to recertify their children in the family child care program, and were asked about their impressions of the program. Half of those interviewed were fluent in English, and half were interviewed with the assistance of an interpreter. Informed consent (in either Russian or English) was obtained from all participants, and interviews were audiotaped. In addition, parents of children currently in the program, who also had another child who had graduated from the program, responded to brief phone interviews about their older children's adjustment to school. This sample is far too small to be representative, but offers an illustration of the parents' experience.

The one theme that runs through every interview is the pressure that the mothers all seem to be under, whether from illness or economics, and how the program has helped them to cope with the stress. Mothers seem to have developed close relationships with the family child care providers. In some cases, respondents were explicit about how the program provided support and countered isolation. For example, one parent spoke of how alone she felt when her own mother died, and said that other than her husband, she "has no one in the U.S." but "because of the program [I] survived—otherwise I wouldn't know what to do."

The mothers also seemed to value the relationships of their children with the providers, without any apparent ambivalence. Said one mother, "My child is in love with her . . . on Saturday and Sunday when he's playing he wants to go to her house." Mothers also frequently mentioned the value they saw in the opportunity for children to play together in a group—"I want [my child] to be in groups . . . they do everything together . . . it's good." They were often specific about what their child had learned (e.g., counting). The mothers were uniformly enthusiastic about the religious/cultural features of the program, and had attended holiday celebrations in the family child care homes, but two of the mothers wanted even more content. Finally, one of the Russian-speaking mothers emphasized that she appreciated how her child had learned to speak English, "so well that when I talk he wants to correct me!"

A brief telephone interview with 12 current client families about their older children who had previously been in the program revealed several ways in which parents felt that their children had benefited from the experience. Interestingly, parents' comments did not reflect anything unique to the immigrant experience, but rather described benefits of child day care and preschool experiences that commonly are cited for all children (e.g., facilitating peer interaction). Given the commonly noted problems that immigrant children have in adjusting to school, however, the lack of any such problems in the parents' reports can be viewed as evidence of the benefit of the program for immigrant families. It is important to note, however, that this group of parents was most likely to consider family child care to be beneficial since they had decided to enroll a second child in the program.

An advantage frequently cited by the parents of "graduates" was that the children had learned to adjust to a routine and structured setting in family child care, and that this had eased their adjustment to public school. Parents also felt that the experience helped their children relate to peers and to follow directions on both group and individual levels. Many of the parents felt that the children's exposure to the alphabet and to numbers gave them an advantage when they entered public school, that their children were better able to separate from them when they began school, and that they themselves were helped by the program to feel more comfortable about leaving their children to pursue their careers.

Conclusion

Bouvier and Gardener [1986] suggest that immigration has become the primary population growth factor in the United States, and is likely to continue to be so in the coming decades. Child day care is a critical need for new immigrants, as it enables parents to pursue the development of linguistic and occupational skills and to become independent, productive members of the new country. When programs are designed in a culturally sensitive way, they can meet the basic child day care needs of immigrant families, and perhaps as importantly, serve as a bridge for the immigrant to the new culture.

The first priority for evaluating the relative benefits of chid day care always will be ensuring that programs foster children's social, emotional, and cognitive growth. It also is important, however, to understand the role that child day care plays in the lives of families and the ways in which it inhibits or facilitates the family's functioning. This descriptive study of one family child care program represents a small step in identifying factors that might optimize a family's experience. It is hoped that future child care research will further explore factors in child day care settings that affect family functioning. ◆

References

Adams, G. C. (1990). *Who knows how safe? The status of state efforts to ensure quality child care*. Washington, DC: Children's Defense Fund.

Belsky, J. (1988). The effects of infant day care reconsidered. *Early Childhood Research Quarterly, 3*, 237–272.

Bouvier, L., & Gardner, R. (1986). Immigration to the U.S.: The unfinished story. *Population Bulletin, 41*(4), 3–50.

Caughy M., DiPietro, J. A., & Strobino, D. M. (1994). Day-care participation as a protective factor in the cognitive development of low-income children. *Child Development, 65*, 457–471.

Chilman, C. S. (1993). Parental employment and child care trends: Some critical issues and suggested policies. *Social Work, 38*, 452–460.

Chiswick, B. (1993). Soviet Jews in the United States: An analysis of their linguistic and economic adjustment. *International Migration Review, 27*, 260–285.

Isralowitz, E., & Saad, I. (1994). Attitudes of Russian immigrant and Israeli-born women toward child-care services. *Psychological Reports, 74*, 880–882.

Kelley, P.(1994). Integrating systemic and postsystemic approaches to social work practice with refugee families. *The Journal of Contemporary Human Services, 75*, 541–549.

Lequerica, M. (1993). Stress in immigrant families with handicapped children: A child advocacy approach. *American Journal of Orthopsychiatry, 63*, 545–552.

Phillips, D. (1994). Child care for children in poverty: Opportunity or inequity? *Child Development, 65*, 472–492.

Washington, V. (1985). Head Start: How appropriate for minority families in the 1980s? *American Journal of Orthopsychiatry, 55(4)*, 577–590.

11

Out-of-School Time: A Study of Children in Three Low-Income Neighborhoods

Beth M. Miller, Susan O'Connor, and
Sylvia Wolfson Sirignano

This article reviews the research on the effects of out-of-school time on children's development and school achievement, and describes the results of one study that examined the out-of-school time of children between the ages of four and seven who were enrolled in two federally funded programs. The research team investigated the activities of the children and the resources available in the community from a variety of perspectives, including those of parents, Head Start and Transition Program staff members, and key community informants. Findings are discussed in light of the employment of low-income parents.

Beth M. Miller, Ph.D., is Project Director and Co-Principal Investigator; Susan O'Connor, M.S.W., is Project Co-Director; and Sylvia Wolfson Sirignano, Ph.D., is Co-Principal Investigator, School-Age Child Care Project, Center for Research on Women, Wellesley College, Wellesley, MA. This research was supported by a grant from the Ford Foundation and another national foundation that prefers to remain anonymous. The authors thank Pamela Joshi, graduate student, and Alexandra Bermudez and Molly Kaplowitz, undergraduate students, for their help with the study. We are also immensely grateful to the many families and service providers in the three study communities for sharing their thoughts, lives, and dreams with the researchers.

Out-of-school time is critically important to children's development. It encompasses over 90% of a child's time in a given year, and gives children the opportunity to learn social skills, develop new interests and competencies, and form meaningful relationships with caring adults. For many children, it is also a time fraught with risks to healthy development. What children are doing, where they are, and the quality of adult supervision they receive during their out-of-school time affect children's school achievement and their success as adults.

As an increasing number of mothers join the labor force, concern for the presence and quality of supervision for their school-age children grows. Studies of labor market decision-making find that lack of child day care is a major impediment to employment, especially among low-income women [Bane & Ellwood 1994; Blank 1994; Hargreaves et al. 1994]. Studies of care for preschool children find that many children, especially those from low-income families, receive care that is barely adequate or completely inadequate to meet their developmental needs [Whitebook et al. 1989; Galinsky et al. 1994]. In addition, research on parent satisfaction with child care generally finds higher levels of dissatisfaction among low-income mothers, who rarely feel that they have a choice of child care arrangements [Sonenstein & Wolf 1991; Meyers & van Leuwen 1992; Brayfield et al. 1993].

This article reviews the major research related to the effects of out-of-school time on children's development and describes findings from a recent study, "Children in Head Start and Transition Programs: Experiences During Out-of-School Time," which examined the out-of-school time of children between the ages of four and seven who were enrolled in two federally funded programs. The research team investigated the activities of the children and the resources available in three communities from a variety of perspectives, including those of parents, Head

Start and Transition Demonstration Programs, and key community informants.*

What Children Do During Out-of-School Time

The most common activities of children not in school are watching television, playing with friends, and doing homework, with children spending the most time watching television. Recent estimates suggest that children spend an average of about three hours per day watching television or playing video games [Peterson & Zill 1980; Medrich et al. 1982; Timmer et al. 1985]. Liebert and Sprafkin [1988] found that some children spend a great deal more time: one study found that 25% of sixth-graders watched television for at least 8.5 hours daily on weekends and 5.5 hours on school days. In addition, children from low-income families spend more time, on average, watching television than children from middle- or high-income families.

The effect of television viewing on children has been the subject of a large body of research that began with the advent of the technology itself. Dozens of studies of the effects of television on children cover almost every topic imaginable, including the impact of program content (ranging from snack foods to violence), and children's behavioral outcomes (aggressiveness, sex role attitudes, understanding of fantasy versus reality) [for example, see Palmer & Dorr 1980; Singer & Singer 1981; Bryant & Anderson 1983; Manley-Casimir & Luke 1987; Liebert & Sprafkin

*With funding from the Administration for Children and Families, Transition Demonstration Programs in 32 sites across the country provide children with the comprehensive services and developmentally appropriate education through the early elementary school years that they received from Head Start. The Transition Demonstration Program began in September 1991, and now supports children in kindergarten through third grade. The Programs are being evaluated to test the hypothesis that the provision of continuous, comprehensive, Head Start-like services in education, health, parent involvement, and social services, delivered over an extended period of time, will help maintain the benefits of Head Start.

1988; Palmer 1988]. Two major elements of television viewing may affect children's development: the time children spend watching television and the content of the programs they watch. Despite continuing debate as to the strength, causes, and consistency of television's effects, most studies find that either watching a great deal of television or watching television shows with violent content has negative consequences for the educational achievement of large numbers of children [Lefkowitz et al. 1977; Gerbner & Gross 1980; Singer & Singer 1980; Milavsky et al. 1982; Williams et al. 1982; Fetler 1984; Turner et al. 1986; Beentjes & Van der Voort 1988; Liebert & Sprafkin 1988; Wiegman et al. 1992].

Some evidence suggests that children who are heavy television viewers (those who watch more than three hours per day) have lower reading achievement and more behavior problems than their peers [Chall et al. 1982; Dorr 1986; Beentjes & Van der Voort 1988]. Imaginative play and language skills may also be negatively affected [Peterson & Zill 1980; Singer & Singer 1981].

What children watch is as important as *how* much television they watch. Research indicates that children who watch violent programs (both cartoons and reality-based shows) are more likely to engage in aggressive behavior [Lefkowitz et al. 1977; Comstock 1980; Gerbner & Gross 1980; Singer & Singer 1981; Condry 1993]. This is especially true of children who watch many hours of such programs. Boys are more likely to be affected than girls, and highly aggressive children are especially vulnerable to such negative effects. Some research also suggests that children who watch many hours of violent programs may become desensitized to real-life violence [Cline et al. 1973; Drabman & Thomas 1974; Thomas et al. 1977].

Children who spend a relatively small number of hours per day watching televised educational programs may experience some positive effects. Several important studies have examined the potentially positive effects of educational television [Coates et al. 1976; Liebert & Sprafkin 1988; Palmer 1988; Marazon 1994]. These studies have found increases in prosocial behavior linked to viewing of programs such as "Sesame Street" and "Mr. Roger's Neighborhood." Studies examining the long-term effects of such viewing, however, have generally found that positive results are maintained over time only when television content is reinforced through other means, such as classroom teaching.

Playing with friends is the second most common activity for children during out-of-school time. Studies completed in 1976 and 1981 concluded that school-age children spend between 60 and 90 minutes playing with friends on a typical weekday [Peterson & Zill 1980; Timmer et al. 1985]. Children who do not spend time playing with friends during out-of-school time lose important opportunities to develop social skills, which are strongly associated with adult success and school achievement [Berndt & Ladd 1989; Hartup & Moore 1990]. Patterson and her colleagues examined the relationship between peer companionship outside of school and family income level, ethnicity, household composition, and gender. They found "that children from low-income homes experienced less peer companionship overall, and were isolated from peers in more out-of-school activities than were children from middle-income homes" [Patterson et al. 1991: 447].

Homework takes an estimated 30 to 45 minutes of children's time each day, making it the third most common out-of-school activity [Peterson & Zill 1980; Timmer et al. 1985]. Other common activities in a child's typical day include playing by oneself, doing chores, reading, and playing sports. Children who spend much time reading during their out-of-school time tend to have higher achievement in reading and writing skills, a larger vocabulary, and better overall school performance than those who do not [Peterson & Zill 1980; Chall et al. 1982; Dickinson & Tabors 1991; Snow et al. 1991; Nimon 1992].

The importance of out-of-school time is built on not only what children are doing but also on the interactions in which they are engaged. For example, conversations with parents and other adults have been strongly associated with literacy achievement [Anderson & Stokes 1984; Snow 1993]. Studies of children who are high achievers find that they often come from families in which there is a warm, supportive home environment and regular routines and expectations [Clark 1983, 1987, 1990; Dornbusch et al. 1987]. Benson and his colleagues [1980] found that among children with low socioeconomic status, parent participation in organized activities, having dinner together, and doing things on weekends all contributed to children's school achievement.

Where Children Are During Out-of-School Time

For children of dual-earner or employed single-parent families, child day care is a critical issue. The National Child Care Survey 1990 (NCCS) [Hofferth et al. 1991] documented the school-age child care arrangements of working families. Figure 1 illustrates the *primary* child day care arrangements for children ages five to 12 with employed mothers. The NCCS found that the most common arrangements were informal, with over half of the children cared for by either a parent or relative.

Most children spend their out-of-school time in a variety of settings, however. The National Child Care Survey 1990 found that 76% of school-age children with employed mothers spent time in two or more different child care arrangements each week. They may go to different places on different days, or go from one setting to another in a single afternoon. For example, although self-care is not common as a primary arrangement, the NCCS found that 14.6% of children ages five to 12 with employed mothers spend some time each week in self-care.

A tabulation by the U.S. Bureau of the Census [1994] of the results of nationally representative surveys dating back to 1958 found that the percentage of children reported to be in self-care ranged from 4% to 22%. Estimates based on smaller, more intensive research projects than the Census project generally estimate the percentage of latchkey children at 22% to 67% [Medrich et al. 1982; Vandell & Corasaniti 1985; Messer et al. 1988; Dwyer et al. 1990].

FIGURE 1

Primary Care for Youngest School-Age Child of Employed Mothers*

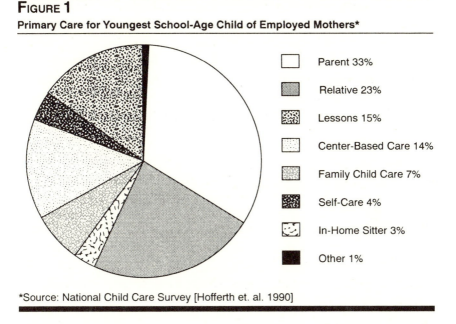

☐ Parent 33%

▨ Relative 23%

▨ Lessons 15%

☐ Center-Based Care 14%

▨ Family Child Care 7%

▨ Self-Care 4%

☺ In-Home Sitter 3%

■ Other 1%

*Source: National Child Care Survey [Hofferth et. al. 1990]

These results indicate that the number of latchkey children in the U.S. may range from less than one million to over 14 million.

Obviously, such wide variations in estimates are problematic not only for researchers but also for policymakers and the public at large. Two related considerations make it difficult to reach a sound estimate of the number of children in self-care [Hofferth 1994; Miller 1994]. First, parents are often extremely reluctant to report that their children are regularly left alone or in the care of school-age siblings. Second, in some states, such arrangements may even be statutorily defined as criminal neglect [Murphy 1995]. Therefore, unless researchers use very careful and thorough methods when questioning parents about such arrangements, they are likely to significantly underestimate the number of children spending time alone.

For low-income children in urban neighborhoods, self-care is associated with a number of negative outcomes, including fear and social isolation [Zill et al. 1977; Long & Long 1983; Belle et al.

1990], risk of diminished academic achievement [Woods 1972; Entwisle 1975], and increased risk of truancy, substance abuse, stress, and risk-taking [Dwyer et al. 1990].

Increasing evidence indicates that afterschool programs may play an important role in developing children's social and academic skills. Posner and Vandell [1994] compared children who were cared for after school by their mothers to children in four afterschool programs, children in self-care, and children cared for at home by a babysitter. They found that children attending the after-school programs had better work habits and peer relationships, were less antisocial, and were rated as having better emotional adjustment than the other groups of children.

The findings related to peer relations are supported by a study of a high-quality extended day program for kindergartners. It found that children who were enrolled in the program received more positive peer nominations than their nonprogram peers [Howes et al. 1987]. Three studies have examined the effects of academically oriented after-school programs on reading and math achievement; each found that enrollment was associated with increased test scores [Entwisle 1975; Mayesky 1980; Sheley 1984].

Very little is known about where school-age children spend their summer and vacation time. The NCCS [Hofferth et al. 1991] asked parents to indicate up to four arrangements used during the summer for their youngest children who were of school age. Nearly a third of respondents indicated that they had no arrangement, 25% stated that their child attended summer camp, 23% used a community recreation program, and 17% had some care provided by relatives. Smaller percentages of children (10% or less) spent time being cared for by a sibling, child care center, school program, family child care provider, or neighbor, or were in self-care or some other arrangement. Many children were in a number of different arrangements over the course of the summer.

What Determines Where Children Spend Their Time?

Where children spend their out-of-school time depends on a number of factors, including characteristics of the child and family, as well as the community context. For example, parental decisions about care arrangements are constrained by the availability of providers, the costs of care, and the availability of transportation to various care arrangements.

Social class influences the choice of child care arrangements. According to the NCCS [Hofferth et al. 1991], low-income families (incomes under $15,000 per year) are more likely to use relatives or family child care arrangements, and less likely to enroll their children in center-based care than families with higher incomes. The NCCS found that families in which the mother has less than a high school education are less likely to enroll their children in formal programs than are families in which mothers have relatively higher educational attainment. One reason for the differences in enrollment in formal programs may be the lack of subsidies available to low-income families seeking school-age child care. The National Study of Before and After School Programs [Seppanen et al. 1993] found that school-age child care programs derive an average of 83% of their income from parent fees; 86% of parents pay the full tuition fee.

The greatest difference between families of different income levels is seen in enrollment in lessons (i.e., music, organized clubs, sports). While 20% of children in families with incomes of over $50,000 per year take lessons, only 6% of children in families earning between $15,000 and $25,000 and 8% of children in the lowest-income families do so [Hofferth et al. 1991]. In addition, families with college-educated mothers are much more likely to enroll their children in lessons.

Studies of preschool children have found wide variation in use of child care arrangements by different racial and ethnic groups [West et al. 1993]. Care of school-age children also differs [Hofferth et al. 1991], with African American families more likely to rely on relative care than Caucasian and Latino families (42% versus 19% and 31%, respectively). Latino children are about half as likely as both Caucasian and African American children to attend formal child care programs in centers or schools.

Parents' work schedules may also affect the type of care used. Mothers who work only when school is in session are available to supervise their children during out-of-school time. Rodman and Pratto [1987] found that mothers who worked full-time were more likely to have their children in self-care than part-time workers. In addition, a large and growing number of young families work jobs that require evening, night, or irregular hours. Analysis of data from the 1980 Current Population Survey indicates that one-third of dual-earner couples with children under age five had one spouse working a regular day shift and the other working an evening, night, or rotating shift [Presser 1988]. Although working evening, night, or irregular shifts may be a good child care strategy for some parents, the proliferation of such jobs in the growing low-wage service sector means that an increasing number of young families may not have access to the formal child care system.

The care arrangements of younger school-age (under age eight) and older school-age children (age eight and older) differ widely. Younger children are much more likely to be enrolled in a center-based before- and/or after-school program and less likely to be taking lessons than older children [Hofferth et al. 1991]. As figure 2 illustrates, the proportion of children in self-care rises sharply as the children's age increases.

Parental preferences, values, and access to information may also have an impact on where children spend their time. A number of studies of parental choice and satisfaction focus on parents of preschool-age children [Lein 1979; Pence & Goelman 1987; Sonenstein & Wolf 1991; Meyers & van Leuwen 1992; Mitchell et al. 1992]. These studies have found that parents look for situations that they feel are of high quality and consonant with their own values regarding child-rearing. In addition, cost and conve-

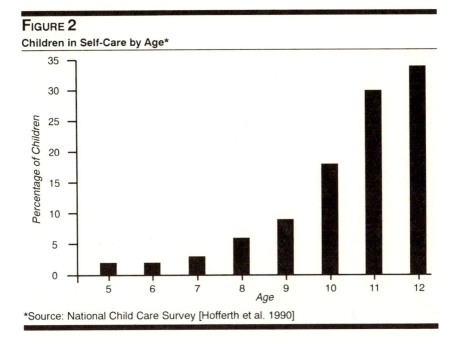

FIGURE 2

Children in Self-Care by Age*

*Source: National Child Care Survey [Hofferth et al. 1990]

nience are important considerations. In one of the few studies of child day care decision-making of parents of school-age children, Gravett and colleagues [1987] found that many of the single mothers' decisions regarding care arrangements were severely constrained due to job inflexibility, affordability problems, transportation problems, limited access to information, and lack of community networks.

Use of after-school arrangements is also affected by aspects of the community in which families live. Little is known about the community context for school-age child day care, but there is evidence that the supply of preschool-age child day care varies dramatically among communities, depending on region of the country, state, population density (urban versus rural or suburban), and per capita income of the local community [Fuller & Liang 1993]. In addition, transportation can be a major obstacle to access for school-age children, since parents are not available to transport their children from school to another location in the midafternoon.

Purpose of the Study

The present study, "Children in Head Start and Transition Programs: Experiences During Out-of-School Time," sought to examine the out-of-school (or out-of-program, in the case of Head Start) experiences of children from low-income communities. We were interested in what children were doing, how their activities varied with their mothers' employment status, and what impediments families faced in making the most of their children's out-of-school time. Our main research questions were:

- What do children do during their out-of-school time? What do they do in the summer?
- Where are children during their out-of-school time? What kinds of child care arrangements do they participate in?
- How do parents and program staff members feel about children's supervision and activities during out-of-school time? Are they able to provide the experiences they feel are important? If not, what obstacles stand in their way?
- What factors are linked to maternal employment? How does mothers' employment status affect children's out-of-school time?

Methods

The research team chose three sites from among the 32 Transition Demonstration Program sites funded by the Administration for Children and Families.* The sites were chosen to represent mid-

*A national evaluation of the outcomes of the Transition Demonstration Program is currently being conducted by the Civitan International Research Center at the University of Alabama at Birmingham.

sized cities with geographic diversity (one each from the north-east, the midwest, and the west). At each site, researchers worked with Transition Demonstration Program families whose children were in kindergarten or first grade, as well as families with children attending the local Head Start programs.

Personal interviews were conducted at each site by inter-viewers who shared the families' linguistic and cultural back-grounds. Interviews were conducted with the target child's mother or other primary caregiver at a meeting at either the family's home or the child's school, as parents preferred. One hundred and eighty randomly selected families (60 per site), with sampling stratified by child's age, racial/ethnic background, and gender, participated in interviews lasting between 60 and 90 min-utes. In addition, the senior research team observed 17 children during the afternoon hours. Six focus groups with parents were held to enrich the interview data. Social service staff members of all participating Transition and Head Start sites completed ques-tionnaires and participated in group discussions. Key informants were also interviewed in each community, including city plan-ners; school principals; personnel from after-school child care, recreational, and tutorial services; child care resource and referral agency staff members; and social service organization directors.

Measures

The Family Interview was developed by the senior research team, with some sections based on revisions of existing instru-ments, including the interview schedule developed by Marshall and colleagues for the Boston After School Experiences Study [1994], the Parent's Perception of Safety of Neighborhood [Medrich et al. 1982], and a subset of measures from Block's Child-Rearing Practices Report [Block n.d.].

Characteristics of the Study Sample

The study sample represented an ethnically diverse population (see table 1). Nearly half of the 180 respondents were not born in

TABLE 1
Characteristics of Study Sample

Characteristic	Percent* (N = %)
Ethnic Background	
Caucasian	28
Asian	19
African American	16
Latino	34
Native American	2
Mixed	2
Income	
Under $10,000	36
$10,000–$15,999	33
$16,000–$29,999	20
Over $30,000	11
Education	
Less than 8th grade	25
Less than high school diploma	28
High school diploma	25
Some college/degree	22
Marital Status	
Married, partner	59
Not married (divorced, separated, or widowed)	41

*May not total 100% due to rounding

the United States. Within the Latino group, the most common countries of origin were Mexico (on the west coast) and Puerto Rico. Three Asian groups had substantial representation in the study: immigrants from Vietnam and Cambodia, and the Hmong ethnic group from Laos. Most of the families had low incomes, with 57% of the respondents reporting that their families received income from Aid to Families with Dependent Children (AFDC). The education levels of respondents were generally low, reflecting in part the immigrant condition of the respondents. As is discussed in greater detail below, one-third of the mothers were employed.

Findings

What Children Are Doing

Parents were asked in an open-ended question to list all the activities in which their children participated during after-school time, and then to name the three activities on which their children spent the most time. Television was by far the most frequently cited activity of the three, mentioned by 59% of respondents. Other frequent activities were fantasy play, including playing with toys, dolls, and guns (listed by 40% of respondents); playing with friends or siblings (39%); academic skill learning, including homework, practice reading, educational toys, and lessons (34%); and language arts, including drawing, music, and recreational reading (34%). Typical responses included, "He plays with Nintendo, does homework, plays with his cousins and sister." "Coloring, watches cartoons, plays video games." "Watches TV a lot, plays with brother, plays with cars and trucks."

During the summer, children participated in an increased number of outdoor activities, such as biking, swimming, and going to the park, and decreased their school-related learning, with less than 10% of parents mentioning skill-related learning either inside or outside the home as one of the three most common activities.

Without the benefit of objective measures of how children spend their time, it is not possible to ascertain how accurately parents report their child's activities. The research team, however, was able to collect data from other sources that generally supported the information obtained from parents. One source was the focus groups conducted with social service staff members from Head Start and Transition Programs in the three sites, as well as questionnaires completed by the same staff members. Although these individuals do not have firsthand knowledge of how children spend their time when they are not in the program, their jobs requires extensive contact with families. In many cases, they are the persons helping parents manage issues related to their children's out-of-school time. In addition, the senior research team conducted two-hour child observations of a subsample of 17 children during the afternoon hours, observing how a number of children in each site spent their after-school time on a typical afternoon.

Program staff members listed watching television and playing with friends or siblings as the two most frequent activities of children during their out-of-school time. Asked to choose which activities children spent the least time on, the staff responded that hobbies, reading, and community activities were engaged in relatively infrequently. In our observations of the children, a majority of them spent most or all of the two-hour observation period in front of the television screen. Programming watched varied, and included violent video games, adult programming (usually soap operas), and, in one case, a videotape of the child's recent Head Start graduation ceremony. Little viewing of educational television was observed. In a number of cases, the television was turned on for the entire observation period, but the target child watched intermittently, going back and forth to a range of other activities and/or engaging in other activities, such as coloring, simultaneously with television viewing.

Where Children Are

The majority of study children (64%) spend all of their out-of-school time at home with their mothers. Of children who spend time in another arrangement, the most common primary care arrangement during the after-school hours is care by an older sibling or by the child's father, followed by other care situations. *Primary care arrangement* is defined as the nonmaternal care arrangement in which children spend the most time (see figure 3).

Of those who are in some type of nonmaternal care as their primary care arrangement, nearly half (48.9%) are cared for by relatives. The likelihood of being cared for by relatives varies

FIGURE 3

Primary Care Arrangement During Out-of-School Hours*

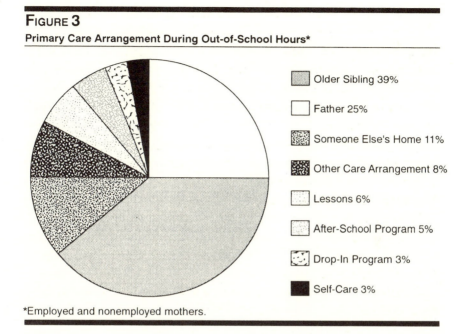

Older Sibling 39%

Father 25%

Someone Else's Home 11%

Other Care Arrangement 8%

Lessons 6%

After-School Program 5%

Drop-In Program 3%

Self-Care 3%

*Employed and nonemployed mothers.

depending on a number of child characteristics. Latino and Asian children are more likely to be cared for by relatives than either Caucasian or African American children; children whose mothers do not speak English are significantly more likely to be cared for by relatives than children with English-speaking mothers; children whose mothers were not born in the U.S. are more likely to be in relative care than children whose mothers were born in the U.S.; and children whose mothers have less than a high school education are more likely to be cared for by relatives than children whose mothers have a high school diploma or post-high school education.

Although it is not the primary care arrangement for most children, a relatively high percentage of the children between four and seven years of age spent at least some of their out-of-school time without adult supervision. Of the 180 children in the survey, 15.6% are reported by their parents to regularly spend time alone or in the care of a sibling under the age of 12. In the course of the researchers' child observations, we arrived several times at homes where the mother was out running an errand or retrieving a sibling from school. Given the lack of access to transportation in many neighborhoods, some mothers apparently feel that they have little choice but to leave their child alone or with other children for at least limited periods of time.

Summer care consisted primarily of the same care arrangements that children experienced during the school year. Families took special trips to nearby parks or swimming areas, but less than 10% of the children spent time during the summer in any formal program, such as a recreation program or summer camp.

Parent Satisfaction

Most parents said that they are satisfied with how their children are spending their out-of-school time. While less than one-quarter say they are "extremely satisfied" (23%), many parents are "very satisfied" (44%) or "somewhat satisfied" (29%). Only 3% of parents report being "not too satisfied," and only 1% say they are actually dissatisfied. Past studies, however, have shown that parents are generally uncomfortable suggesting that their children are spending time in inappropriate activities or environments. When we asked parents whether they would change the situation if they could, 54% said that they would like to make changes. The most common desire was for their child to be involved in community activities or lessons during out-of-school time. Typical parents' comments were, "I would like my child to be in some type of activity after school,"; "I would have liked her to go to the Girl's Club, but I can't afford it"; "He could be doing something else, but I can't get myself to trust people, to take him out to someone else." Among employed mothers, a common desire was for more time with their children.

We also asked parents on what activities they would like their child to spend additional time. The majority of parents want their child to be spending less time watching television and more time reading books than they actually were (see figure 4). Parents

FIGURE 4

Selected Activities: What Parents Want Their Children to Do More or Less of Than They Currently Do

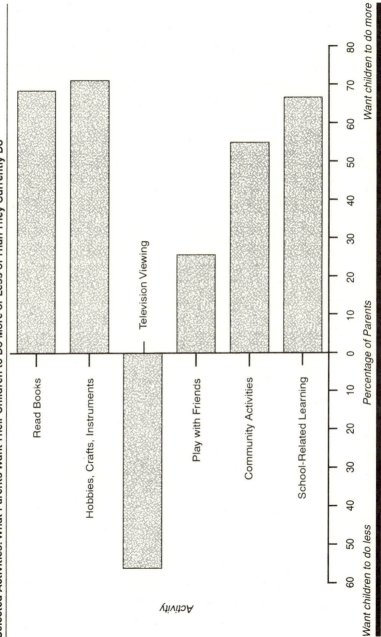

Want children to do less

Activity

Percentage of Parents

Want children to do more

Read Books

Hobbies, Crafts, Instruments

Television Viewing

Play with Friends

Community Activities

School-Related Learning

want their children to have additional access to community activities, and to spend additional time in skill-building activities such as learning musical instruments and school-related learning.

What obstacles prevent parents from providing children with the experiences and opportunities they wanted them to have? In response to open-ended questions, the most frequent obstacles mentioned by parents are affordability and transportation problems. Program staff members were asked to rate the extent to which a list of potential obstacles limited families' access to experiences. The most important obstacle, according to the staff, is cost, which 80% of respondents said limited families' access a lot, followed by neighborhood safety (72%), transportation (68%), lack of knowledge of existing resources (51%), and lack of quality of existing resources (40%).

Employment

As mentioned above, 31% of the mothers in the sample are employed. Of these women, 61% work full-time and 15% work on more than one job. The availability of accessible child care that mothers feel they can trust is strongly associated with the mother's work status, as shown in table 2. Mothers who are employed are significantly more likely than nonemployed mothers to have access to a car, have fewer children, have children who are older, live in safer neighborhoods, have more adults living in the household, and be married or living with a partner. In addition, those mothers with greater employment potential— who are more highly educated and speak English as their primary language—are more likely to be in the labor force. Mothers work in a wide variety of jobs, including curtain seamstress, teacher's aide, mail clerk, cannery laborer, and police officer. Many mothers work irregular hours, with 45% working on weekends, 34% working evening hours, and 13% working nights (after midnight).

Child care arrangements for children of employed mothers are similar to those for the entire group of children, although, of

TABLE 2
Characteristics of Employed and Nonemployed Mothers*

Characteristic	All Mothers (N = 180)	Employed Mothers (N = 56)	Nonemployed Mothers (N = 124)
Perception of Neighborhood Safety			
Very safe	18%	25%	15%
Fairly safe	47%	55%	44%
Fairly unsafe	22%	16%	25%
Very unsafe	12%	4%	16%
Access to a Car			
Yes	63%	73%	58%
No	37%	27%	42%
Average Number of Children in Home	3.5	2.9	3.7
Average Age of Youngest Child	3.5	4.3	3.1
Average Number of Adults in Home	1.9	2.2	1.9
Marital Status			
Married, partner	59%	70%	54%
Not married, divorced, separated, widowed	41%	30%	46%
Trust Considerations			
Parent Tries to Keep Child Away from Families with Different Values			
Strongly agree	34%	27%	37%
Somewhat agree	29%	20%	33%
Not sure	5%	5%	5%
Somewhat disagree	15%	25%	11%
Strongly disagree	17%	23%	15%
Employment Opportunities			
Education			
Less than 8th grade	25%	9%	33%
Less than high school	28%	14%	34%
High school diploma	25%	34%	21%
Some college/degree	22%	43%	12%
English Is Primary Language			
Yes	58%	78%	50%
No	42%	22%	50%

*May not total 100% due to rounding.

course, few children of employed mothers are exclusively in maternal care arrangements. As can be seen from figure 5, children of employed mothers are somewhat more likely to spend time in formal care arrangements than children whose mothers are not employed, and less likely to spend time at a drop-in recreation center. Concentrating solely on primary care arrangements, however, presents an inaccurate picture of children's out-of-school lives, since most children spend time in a variety of arrangements each week. Considering *all* the arrangements during the after-school hours, we find that, among children of working mothers, 79% of children are cared for at least part of the time by their fathers, 71% by older siblings, 29% by other adult relatives, 29% participate in some lessons or remedial programming, 11% care for themselves or are with younger siblings, 8% are taken care of by a babysitter, and 4% attend an after-school or recreational program.*

Three-quarters of the nonemployed mothers said that they expect to join the labor force within the next two years. By far the most important reasons for not working are that they do not want to work when their children are young (69% of nonemployed) and they don't want to leave their child with someone they don't know (65%). Though many nonemployed mothers had never looked for child day care, a number responded that they had problems finding child day care (see table 3).

Discussion

This study has a number of limitations that should be noted. First, it considered the experiences of children in three communities that may or may not be similar to other communities in the United States. Second, all the study sites were midsized cities, limiting the generalizability of the findings to other localities, especially those that are in rural, suburban, or large urban envi-

*Totals exceed 100% due to multiple arrangements.

FIGURE 5
Primary After-School Arrangement by Mother's Employment Status

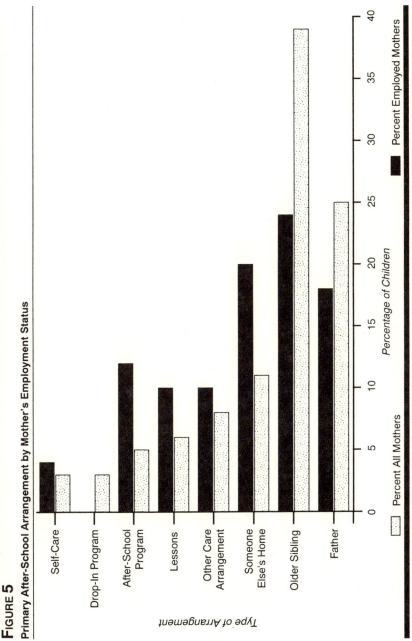

TABLE 3
Child Care Obstacles for Nonemployed Mothers

Obstacle	All Nonemployed Mothers (N = 124)
Children Are Too Young	
Don't want to work when children are young (Average age of youngest child = 3.1)	69%
Trust Considerations	
Don't want to leave child with someone they don't know	65%
Tries to keep child away from families with different values	70%
Access Considerations	
Problems finding satisfactory child day care	36%
Don't know person or program that provides child day care	40%
Can't get to available child day care easily	27%
Child day care is too expensive	37%

ronments. Finally, only children who attended Head Start or Transition Demonstration Programs were included in the study. The lack of a comparison group limits our ability to detect whether the findings apply only to children in these programs or to other children in the community.

Overall, the results of this study support earlier research suggesting that watching television, playing, and spending time with friends are children's major activities during their out-of-school time. Though time diaries were not collected in this study, due to resource limitations, both the family interviews and child observations bore out expectations regarding activities. The study does not examine directly the effects of the children's use of time on their development, but parent's desires for change reflect the findings of previous research. Parents want children to watch less television and spend more time in enrichment activities, both at home and in the community, than the children currently do. In addition, parents want their children to spend additional time reading.

What prevents parents from making such changes? A study of two Chicago neighborhoods suggests that organized activities are much less commonly available in urban low-income communities than in the middle-class suburbs [Chapin Hall Center for Children 1992]. Not only are relatively fewer enrichment opportunities available, but paying for them can be a major obstacles to utilization. In addition, transportation problems impede parental efforts to make the most of children's out-of-school time. For example, one study mother with a child in Head Start and two other preschool-age children was encouraged by the child's teacher to provide reading opportunities during the winter break. To get to the closest public library—the local branch had been closed several years previously due to budget cuts—required taking two buses each way. The mother had to prepare the three children for the winter weather, navigate to and from their third floor walk-up, and wait for the infrequent buses to arrive. The mother reported that the trip took the entire morning. Even when resources are in the community, obstacles such as cost, safety, transportation, trust, language and cultural difficulty, and scheduling often prove insurmountable.

Employed parents face an additional set of challenges. The two most striking findings of the present study are the lack of utilization of formal resources and the large percentage of children spending time without adult (or even teenage) supervision. The quality of these care arrangements was not measured as part of the study, but observations and interviews with both parents and community representatives suggest that in some cases supervision is inadequate to provide for even basic developmental needs. For example, one of the child observations took place in a setting where a five-year-old boy is under the supervision of his grandfather. The boy spends nearly all day alone in an apartment while his grandfather works in the adjacent garage. The child can and does get himself breakfast and dress himself, and he entertains himself for entire days with minimal contact with his grandfather. What these findings point to is the lack of options available to families in the study communities. Parents who had access to relative care, especially fathers and older siblings, were much more likely to be in the labor force.

Another employment-related finding was the strong emphasis many mothers placed on being home with their children during their early years. Mothers felt that they were their children's best provider, and while they often desired additional enrichment and learning-oriented activities, they did not want their child to spend many hours away from their supervision.

These findings suggest that, when they feel care is available, low-income mothers want to join the labor force to enhance the standard of living of their families. When such care is not available, however, mothers are extremely reluctant to leave their children with those they cannot depend upon to provide good supervision. Given the lack of accessible formal child care options in the communities involved in this research, such findings should be seriously considered by those who are concerned with both the labor force participation of low-income mothers and the well-being of children and families. ◆

References

Anderson, A. B., & Stokes, S. J. (1984). Social and institutional influences on the development and practices of literacy. In H. Goelman, A. A. Oberg, & F. Smith (Eds.), *Awakening to literacy* (pp. 24–37). London, England: Heinemann Educational Books.

Bane, M. J., & Ellwood, D. T. (1994). *Welfare realities.* Cambridge, MA: Harvard University Press.

Beentjes, J. W. J., & Van der Voort, T. H. A. (1988, Fall). Television's impact on children's reading skills: A review of research. *Reading Research Quarterly,* 389–413.

Belle, D., Burr, R., & Ozer, D. (1990). *Mothers' and children's views of children's after-school arrangements.* Paper submitted to the Department of Psychology at Boston University.

Benson, C. S., Medrich, E. A., & Buckley, S. (1980). A new view of school efficiency: Household time contributions to school achievement. In J. W. Guthrie (Ed.), *School finance policies and practices. The 1980s: A decade of conflict* (pp. 169–204). Cambridge, MA: Ballinger Publishing Company.

Berndt, T., & Ladd, G. (Eds.). (1989). *Peer relationships in child development.* New York: Wiley.

Blank, R. M. (1994). The employment strategy: Public policies to increase work and earnings. In S. H. Danziger, G. D. Sandefur, & D. H. Weinberg (Eds.), *Confronting poverty.* Cambridge, MA: Harvard University Press.

Block, J. H. (no date). *The child-rearing practices report (CRPR): A set of Q items for the description of parental socialization attitudes and values.* Berkeley, CA: University of California.

Brayfield, A. A., Deich, S. G., & Hofferth, S. L. (1993). *Caring for children in low-income families: A substudy of the National Child Care Survey, 1990.* Washington, DC: The Urban Institute Press.

Bryant, J., & Anderson, D. R. (Eds.). (1983). *Children's understanding of television: Research on attention and comprehension.* New York: Academic Press.

Chall, J., Snow, C., Barnes, W., Chandler, J., Goodman, I., Hemphill, L., & Jacobs, V. (1982). *Families and literacy: The contribution of out-of-school experiences to children's acquisition of literacy.* Harvard Graduate School of Education, final report to the National Institute of Education.

Chapin Hall Center for Children. (1992). *Community resources for students: A new look at their role and importance and a preliminary investigation of their distribution across communities.* Chicago: Author.

Clark, R. M. (1983). *Family life and school achievement: Why poor Black children succeed or fail.* Chicago: The University of Chicago Press.

Clark, R. M. (1987). Family organization, communication styles, and children's competence development. *Equity and Choice, 4,* 27–34.

Clark, R. M. (1990, Spring). Why disadvantaged students succeed: What happens outside school is critical. *Public Welfare,* 17–23.

Cline, V. B., Croft, R. G., & Courrier, S. (1973). Desensitization of children to television violence. *Journal of Personality and Social Psychology, 27,* 360–365.

Coates, B., Pusser, H. E., & Goodman, I. (1976). The influence of "Sesame Street" and "Mister Rogers' Neighborhood" on children's social behavior in the preschool. *Child Development, 47*, 138–144.

Comstock, G. (1980). New emphases in research on the effects of television and film violence. In E. L. Palmer & A. Dorr (Eds.), *Children and the faces of television: Teaching, violence, selling* (pp. 129–147). New York: Academic Press.

Condry, J. (1993). Thief of time, unfaithful servant: Television and the American child. *Daedalus, 122*, 259–278.

Dickinson, D. K., & Tabors, P. O. (1991). Early literacy: Linkages between home, school and literacy achievement at age five. *Journal of Research in Childhood Education, 6*, 30–46.

Dornbusch, S., Ritter, P., Leiderman, H. P., Roberts, D. F., & Fraleigh, M. (1987). The relation of parenting style to adolescent school performance. *Child Development, 58*, 1244–1257.

Dorr, A. (1986). *Television and children: A special medium for a special audience* (vol. 14). Beverly Hills, CA: Sage Publications.

Drabman, R. S., & Thomas, M. H. (1974). Does media violence increase children's toleration of real-life aggression? *Developmental Psychology, 10*, 418–421.

Dwyer, K. M., Richardson, J. L., Danley, K. L., Hansen, W. B., Sussman, S. Y., Brannon, B., Dent, C. W., Johnson, C. A., & Flay, B. R. (1990). Characteristics of eighth-grade students who initiate self-care in elementary and junior high school. *Pediatrics, 86*, 448–454.

Entwisle, B. (1975). *Evaluating Baltimore City's school-age day care program: Results of a pilot study*. Providence, RI: Brown University (unpublished paper).

Fetler, M. (1984). Media effects on the young: Television viewing and school achievement. *Journal of Communication, 34*, 104–118.

Fuller, B., & Liang, X. (1993). *The unfair search for child care: Working moms, poverty, and the unequal supply of preschools across America*. Cambridge, MA: Harvard University.

Galinsky, E., Howes, C., Kontos, S., & Shinn, M. (1994). *The study of children in family child care. Highlights of findings*. New York: Families and Work Institute.

Gerbner, G., & Gross, L. (1980). The violent face of television and its lessons. In E. L. Palmer & A. Dorr (Eds.), *Children and the faces of television: Teaching, violence, selling* (pp. 149–161). New York: Academic Press.

Gravett, M., Rogers, C. S., & Thompson, L. (1987). Child care decision among female heads of households with school-age children. *Early Childhood Research Quarterly, 2,* 67–81.

Hargreaves, M. B., Werner, A., & Joshi, P. (1994). *The evaluation of to strengthen Michigan families. Process report: Draft.* Cambridge, MA: Abt Associates.

Hartup, W. W., & Moore, S. G. (1990). Early peer relations: Developmental significance and prognostic implications. *Early Childhood Research Quarterly, 5,* 1–17.

Hofferth, S. (1994). Personal communication. Memorandum regarding estimates of the number of latchkey children from SIPP, Fall 1991.

Hofferth, S. L., Brayfield, A., Diech, S., & Holcomb, P. (1991). *The National Child Care Survey 1990.* Washington, DC: The Urban Institute Press.

Howes, C., Olenick, M., & Der-Kiureghian, T. (1987). After-school care in an elementary school: Social development and continuity and complementarity of programs. *The Elementary School Journal, 88,* 93–103.

Lefkowitz, M. M., Eron, L. D., Walder, L. O., & Huesmann, L. R. (1977). *Growing up to be violent: A longitudinal study of the development of aggression* (vol. PGPS–66). New York: Pergamon Press.

Lein, L. (1979). Parental evaluation of child care alternatives. *Urban and Social Change Review, 12,* 11–16.

Liebert, R. M., & Sprafkin, J. (1988). *The early window: Effects of television on children and youth* (3rd ed.). New York: Pergamon Press.

Long, T. J., & Long, L. (1983). Latchkey children. *ERIC Document Reproduction Services, ED 226 836,* 1–37.

Manley-Casimir, M. E., & Luke, C. (Eds.). (1987). *Children and television: A challenge for education.* New York: Praeger.

Marazon, R. A. (1994). Mister Rogers' Neighborhood as affective staff development for teachers of young children: A story of conflict, conversion, conviction, and celebration. *Young Children, 49,* 34–37.

Marshall, N. L., McCartney, K., Garcia Coll, C., & Marx, F. (1994). Project summary: Boston after-school experiences study. Wellesley, MA: Center for Research on Women, Wellesley College.

Mayesky, M. E. (1980, December). A study of academic effectiveness in a public school day care program. *Phi Delta Kappan*, 284–285.

Medrich, E. A., Roizen, J., Rubin, V., & Buckley, S. (1982). *The serious business of growing up: A study of children's lives outside school*. Berkeley, CA: University of California Press.

Messer, S. C., Wuensch, K. L., & Diamond, J. M. (1988). Former latchkey children: Personality and academic correlates. *Journal of Genetic Psychology, 150*, 301–309.

Meyers, M. K., & van Leuwen, K. (1992). Child care preferences and choices: Are AFDC recipients unique? In S.M. Butterick (Ed.), *Research on children* (pp. 34–43). Washington, DC: National Association of Social Workers.

Milavsky, J. R., Kessler, R., Stipp, H., & Rubens, W. S. (1982). Television and aggression: Results of a panel study. In D. Pearl, L. Bouthilet, & J. Lazar (Eds.), *Television and behavior: Ten years of scientific progress and implications for the eighties* (vol. 2) (pp. 138–157). Washington, DC: U.S. Government Printing Office.

Miller, B. (1994). Memo to data collection group (unpublished).

Mitchell, A., Cooperstein, E., & Larner, M. (1992). *Child care choices, consumer education, and low-income families*. New York: National Center for Children in Poverty.

Murphy, S. (1995, June 27). Critics assail bill requiring care for children under 14. *The Boston Globe*, pp. 1, 21.

Nimon, M. (1992). Children's reading: A research report. *ERIC Reports, ED 355 496*, 1–25.

Palmer, E. L. (1988). *Television and America's children: A crisis of neglect*. New York: Oxford University Press.

Palmer, E. L., & Dorr, A. (Eds.). (1980). *Children and the faces of television*. New York: Academic Press.

Patterson, C. J., Vaden, N. A., Griesler, P. C., & Kupersmidt, J. B. (1991). Income level, gender, ethnicity, and household composition as predictors of children's peer companionship outside of school. *Journal of Applied Developmental Psychology, 12*, 447–465.

Pence, A. R., & Goelman, H. (1987). Silent partners: Parents of children in three types of day care. *Early Childhood Research Quarterly, 2*, 103–118.

Peterson, J. L., & Zill, N. (1980). *Parent estimates of time use by U.S. children of grammar school age* (draft).

Posner, J. K., & Vandell, D. L. (1994). Low-income children's after-school care: Are there beneficial effects of after-school programs? *Child Development, 65,* 440–456.

Presser, H. B. (1988). Shift work and child care among young dual-earner American parents. *Journal of Marriage and the Family, 50,* 133–148.

Rodman, H., & Pratto, D. J. (1987). Child's age and mother's employment in relation to greater use of self-care arrangements for children. *Journal of Marriage and the Family, 49,* 573–578.

Seppanen, P. S., Love, J. M., deVries, D. K., Bernstein, L., Seligson, M., Marx, F., & Kisker, E. E. (1993). *National study of before & after school programs* (final report to the Office of Policy and Planning, U.S. Department of Education). Portsmouth, NH: RMC Research Corporation.

Sheley, J. (1984). Evaluation of the centralized, structured, after-school tutorial. *Journal of Educational Research, 77,* 213–217.

Singer, J. L., & Singer, D. G. (1981). *Television, imagination, and aggression: A study of preschoolers.* Hillsdale, NJ: Lawrence Erlbaum Associates.

Snow, C. E. (1993). Families as social contexts for literacy development. *New directions for child development, 61,* 11–24.

Snow, C. E., Barnes, W. S., Chandler, J., Goodman, I. F., & Hemphill, L. (1991). *Unfulfilled expectations: Home and school influences on literacy.* Cambridge, MA: Harvard University Press.

Sonenstein, F. L., & Wolf, D. A. (1991). Satisfaction with child care: Perspectives of welfare mothers. *Journal of Social Issues, 47,* 15–32.

Thomas, M. H., Horton, R. W., Lippincott, E. C., & Drabman, R. S. (1977). Desensitization to portrayals of real-life aggression as a function of exposure to television violence. *Journal of Personality and Social Psychology, 35,* 450–458.

Timmer, S. G., Eccles, J., & O'Brien, K. (1985). How children use time. In F.T. Juster & F.P. Stafford (Eds.), *Time, goods, and well-being* (pp. 353–382). Lansing, MI: Institute for Social Research, University of Michigan.

Turner, C. W., Hesse, B. W., & Peterson-Lewis, S. (1986). Naturalistic studies of the long-term effects of television violence. *Journal of Social Issues, 42,* 51–73.

U.S. Bureau of the Census. (1994). Personal communication on historical estimates of latchkey kids, 1958–1991.

Vandell, D. L., & Corasaniti, M. A. (1985). *After school care: Choices and outcomes for third graders*. Paper presented at the annual meeting of the American Association for the Advancement of Science, Los Angeles, CA, May 27, 1985.

West, J., Hausken, E. G., & Collins, M. (1993). National Center for Education Statistics: Profile of preschool children's child care and early education program participation. *ERIC Document Reproduction Service, ED 355 046*, 3–44.

Whitebook, M., Howes, C., & Phillips, D. A. (1989). *Who cares? Child care teachers and the quality of care in America* (executive summary, National Child Care Staffing Study ed.). Oakland, CA: Child Care Employee Project.

Wiegman, O., Kuttshcreuter, M., & Baarda, B. (1992). A longitudinal study of the effects of television viewing on aggressive and prosocial behaviors. *British Journal of Social Psychology, 31*, 147–164.

Williams, P., Haertel, E. H., Haertel, G. D., & Walberg, H. J. (1982). The impact of leisure-time television on school learning: A research synthesis. *American Educational Research Journal, 19*, 19–50.

Woods, M. B. (1972). The unsupervised child of the working mother. *Developmental Psychology, 6*, 14–25.

Zill, N., Gruvaeus, G., & Woyshner, K. (1977). *Kids, parents and interviewers: Three points of view on a national sample of children*. New York: Foundation for Child Development.

12

Innovations in Toddler Day Care and Family Support Services: An International Overview

Sheila B. Kamerman and Alfred J. Kahn

This article focuses on policy and program innovations in toddler day care and family support services in Europe, where child day care for children age three to compulsory school age is largely universal. Infant day care is increasingly provided at home by the child's own employed parent, on a paid and job-protected leave. Public debate is now centering on toddler day care—that is, care for one- and two-year-old children. Recognition is growing that these very young children also need a group experience, regardless of their parents' employment status. Implications for child day care policy, program development, and practice are presented.

Sheila B. Kamerman, D.S.W., is Professor of Social Policy and Planning; and Alfred J. Kahn, D.S.W., is Professor Emeritus of Social Policy and Planning, Columbia University School of Social Work, New York, NY. The authors co-direct the Cross-National Studies Research Program.

In Europe, day care for children age three to compulsory
school age is largely universal, covering almost all children
regardless of their parents' employment status. Infant day
care increasingly is taking the form of care provided at home by
the child's own employed parent, on a paid and job-protected
leave, designed to ensure the child a good start in life. The arena
over which public debate is occuring now, and where creative
programming is emerging, is toddler day care—care of one- and
two-year-olds—and family support services targeting families
with infants and toddlers. In the toddler day care arena, there are
diversity, creativity, and experimentation, as well as a growing
recognition that very young children have need of a group experience regardless of their parents' employment status.

What this means for child day care policy, program development, and practice—the objectives and their acheivement, the
"curricula," the quality, and the costs and who pays them—are
the focus of this article,[1] which draws on a recently completed
three-year study of infant and toddler day care and family support services in Europe. The European experience can provide
fresh insights and alternative models that those in the U.S. might
consider.

Background

U.S. Context

Infant and toddler day care services, as distinct from child day
care generally and care of three- to five-year-olds in particular,
was not a significant issue in the U.S. until the 1980s. Prior to that
time, child day care policies were thought of largely in relation to
three- to five-year-olds. It was assumed that children younger
than that were cared for by their mothers at home. The small
number with employed mothers were assumed to be taken care
of by relatives, or perhaps domestic servants or nonrelatives, but
in the children's own homes. Low-income single mothers with
very young children were assumed to be supported by AFDC

and their children not seen as in need of nonparental care. Head Start, the major child care/compensatory education program established in the 1960s, focused on three- to five-year-olds. The original debate about the never-to-be implemented Federal Interagency Day Care Regulations (FIDCR) did not even involve the care of children under three; indeed, it was only in 1975 that standards for infant and toddler day care were included [Nelson 1982].

Child day care for children under age three emerged as a significant issue largely in response to the growing trend among married women with children of this age to be in the labor force. By the late 1980s, half the children under age three had "working mothers," and by the mid-1990s, the figure rose to 60% [U.S. Department of Labor, 1985, 1986, 1987].[2]

A new and growing interest in providing supportive services to families with very young children has been paralleling the developments in toddler day care. These new, community-based, so-called "family support" programs provide information and referral services to parents, parent education classes, and drop-in child day care services. They sometimes operate under the auspices of education, social welfare, child day care, or freestanding services. National recognition of these developments first took place in 1983, at a Yale University conference held under the auspices of the Bush Center. Federal recognition of these developments emerged in legislation enacted in 1993 [Kamerman & Kahn 1995: 152–153].

The major difference between the infant and toddler day care services and family support services in the U.S. is that the former target children, in particular children of working parents, and the latter families, in particular, vulnerable and high-risk families with children, or those with identified problems (usually without an employed parent, or headed by a very young and inexperienced mother, a single mother, or a parent considered at risk of neglecting or abusing the child). It is in this context of the growing interest in infant/toddler day care and family support services (and the considerable concern about the quality of center-based child day care and family child care for very young children in the U.S.) that we describe innovative developments in Europe.

The European Context

Advanced industrialized countries have almost unanimously elected universal but voluntary preschool for children from the age of two, two and one-half, or three until age five, six, or seven, varying with a country's age of compulsory schooling. Developments in infant/toddler day care need to be understood in this context.

These preschool programs are variously justified as preparing children for school, enhancing child socialization and development, and, somewhat less frequently, as offering good quality child day care while parents work. So important are the school-readiness concerns and so highly valued are the socialization and developmental opportunities that participation is, in most places, unrelated to parental employment status, family income, cultural background, or judgments about parental capacities. Indeed, just about *all* children ages three to five attend in some countries (France, Belgium, Italy), and *almost all* in others (Germany, Denmark, Finland, Sweden). These programs are heavily subsidized, operate largely in the public sector (or with extensive public subsidy) and cover at least the normal schoolday (in the Nordic countries the full workday is covered).[3] Countries have various arrangements for supplementary care to match parental work hours. Where the preschool and school day are short (Germany), there are problems.

In contrast to the universal child day care for children ages three to five in Europe, care for those from birth to age two remains, as in the U.S., an essential response to female labor force participation. Yet there is also increasingly an affirmation of the importance of offering even the youngest children an experience that provides cognitive stimulation and socialization with peers and other adults, even if there is a parent at home during the day.

For context we note that only about two-thirds of three- to five-year-olds in the U.S. were in some form of out-of-home child day care in 1990 (largely part-day), as were about one-quarter of those under age three. This compares with almost complete coverage for three- to five-year-olds in Europe, and coverage of about 60% of those under three in Denmark, almost 50% in Finland and Sweden, and 30% in France and northern Italy. Some western European countries offer far less coverage than the U.S., however: United Kingdom (2%), Germany (5%), and Italy (6%). The U.S. has no national policy providing a paid parental leave after childbirth, in contrast to the long leaves (four months to three years) available throughout Europe.

Denmark. Denmark has the highest provision of child day care for those under age three in all of the West, combining center-based child day care and family child care of high quality. Of particular interest for our purposes, infant/toddler day care is delivered under social services auspices, with programs including children from the age of six months (when the basic Danish paid parental leave ends, although it now can be supplemented by another six months) through six years, when compulsory schooling begins. Some programs are age segregated, but a growing number are integrated. Active parent involvement is emphasized.

France. France has the highest preschool coverage for three- to five-year-olds internationally and the highest proportion of children under three in care after Denmark, Sweden, and Finland. Its services for children under age three are under health auspices; its preschool programs serving children ages two to five are under education auspices. Two-year-olds may be served in either system but most of those in out-of-home child day care are in the preschool. Like the Italian programs (see below), family support services emerging in France are arising out of a child care (or health care) base, as a universal program, sometimes targeted to deprived, disadvantaged, immigrant children and their families, but also meant for other French children and parents.

Italy. Italy has almost all its three- to five-year-olds enrolled in preschool, but has only limited coverage for those under three. Program creativity in north-central Italy with regard to the three- to five-year-olds has inspired many countries. These regions have also experienced recent and significant expansion in programs serving children under three (largely age nine months and older, when the Italian maternity leaves end). All child care programs in several regions in north-central Italy are under education auspices and the programs for children under three include both full work day child day care and a variety of family support services.

Finland and Sweden. In systems covering all children to age seven, Finland and Sweden have pioneered in offering parental at-home options for infant day care, while also legislating a right to a guaranteed child day care place (in the Finnish case, for those under age three, in the Swedish case, for those ages eighteen months and older). Like those in Denmark, child day care services in these two countries are all under social service auspices, in a separate, special system.

England. Along with Germany, England has the smallest proportion of very young children in child day care, perhaps in part because of its low (but recently rising) labor force participation rates for women with very young children. Coverage for those under age three, and especially those under two, is almost nonexistent, apart from informal family child care. England's experience is of special interest, however, because several local jurisdictions are now attempting to integrate their education and social service programs into one child day care system, under education auspices. Furthermore, in contrast to Italy and France, where family support services have emerged out of the child day care system, services in England are currently emerging out of the social service/social welfare system. They are targeted to high-risk families.

Program Innovations

Toddler and infant day care is in greater supply in some European countries than in the U.S., but in smaller supply elsewhere. Also, the U.S. and Europe have experienced new developments in family support services. It is useful to ask, therefore, what are the programs like, what is their quality, how are they paid for, and what kind of financial burden do the parents carry? We begin by noting the diversity of program models, describing, as well, the most innovative family support service programs. While other countries are also of interest and are mentioned briefly, this article features exemplary programs in Denmark as a whole and leading regions in Italy. This selectivity highlights outstanding innovative programs and permits a reasonable amount of detail.

Program Models[4]

Danish toddlers (most infants are cared for by their parents at home on leave) may be cared for in centers serving children under age three, in centers serving children under age six, or in supervised family child care homes. Danish child day care programs and the early childhood educational philosophy in Denmark stress age integration and sibling-like groups, the absence of a formal curriculum, and an emphasis on child-initiated activities in a relatively unstructured environment. Recognizing that many children spend long days in care most of the week, while their parents spend a full day at work, the program staff members realize that they are part of a dual socialization experience for children. Yet they also agree that they should not and do not wish to replace the family or take over the child's socialization. As a result, they have developed a program philosophy that emphasizes psychological and social development, rather than formal instruction.

The lack of a formal curriculum, however, does not mean disorganization. The programs have a basic structure with regard to opening and closing times; times for breakfast, lunch, and snacks; and nap times. Children engage in interaction with adults as well as with other children, using a variety of activities and materials. The settings are warm, safe, attractive, and stimulating, and no one is lost in a crowd. In any comparative context, or on its own terms, this is splendid child day care.

The child day care staff members, in the child development tradition, are called *pedagogues*, not teachers. They work with children without preparing specific curricula or programs, day by day. The children are offered activity choices; the pedagogues are trained to respond to the children's leads and to encourage success and development of skills. Each child is treated as an individual. Indeed, the recognition of the long day of care and the tight midweek family schedules supports the effort to create a family-like environment for center care. Put somewhat differently, the feeling is that children with two working parents often have all of their daytime activities organized and that what they really miss is time to just "hang out." The Danes appear to have institutionalized this concept by making it possible for children to hang out in their child day care programs; to be with siblings, if possible; and to have the span of opportunities for interaction provided by participation in a program with children of a range of ages.

Age integration is a concept currently being worked out. One sees different versions in action in different cities and in different program forms. It is said that young children benefit from play with slightly older children, and that the age range permits the organization of activity groups that correspond to children's interests and development. These arrangements also make it easier for authorities to çope with changes in demand for child day care, as birth cohort sizes fluctuate. Of some interest, as Denmark shifts from age-grouped programs to age-integrated programs, Sweden, which pioneered the latter ("sibling groups") has become more concerned with cognitive impact and is increasingly grouping children by age. Regardless, its child day care quality matches that of Denmark.

Family child care is not regarded in Denmark as secondary to group child day care programs, despite the less formal staff training providers receive. The large public family child care system began as a temporary measure, developed to cope with serious shortages in the supply of center-based care and the unsatisfactory nature of the informal child day care system that was filling the gap. Now it is a public service with salaried personnel, who receive job-related benefits and who are selected, guided, supervised, and helped to become ever-more qualified by assigned and qualified supervisors. By now, family child care, the most commonly used resource for children under age three, is a firmly established alternative, to which authorities give the same status as center-based care; many parents of young children consider it preferable to the institutional facilities. Many centers have linkages with family child care providers in the community and there are also community facilities that regularly bring family child care providers and the children they care for together, while assuring as well a firm backup system for emergencies.

Finally, we note that parents play an active role in all types of child day care in Denmark, either on policymaking boards or in various family-oriented special activities.

Like the Danish programs, the Italian infant and toddler day care centers stress socialization, developmental, and cognitive objectives. In contrast to the deliberately unstructured Danish model, however, the Italian program has groups that are age-based (three to 12 months, 12 to 24 months, 24 to 36 months) and a much more deliberate curriculum than its Danish counterparts. Despite a great emphasis on creativity and individualism, Italian infant and toddler programs are clearly and deliberately "structured." They provide an educational and socialization service appropriate for all very young children but now limited largely to the children of working parents. In contrast to the country's universal preschool program, quantity and quality of programs for children under age three vary widely across regions, with north-central Italy having a leadership role in coverage and quality.

A range of part-day to full-day child day care programs and a close relationship to a diversity of child-day-care-related family support programs (see below) suggest the innovative quality of these programs. Family child care, however, either formal or informal, does not exist, although there is some discussion about developing some experimental initiatives.

Centers begin each year in September with a new entering class of infants. Few children enter at an age younger than nine months. (The Italian maternity leave ends at this point.) The first week is just for the staff to prepare for the year. From then to mid-October the new children are phased in, about two or three each week. The children who will attend the preschool in the fall spend one day a week from the previous January to July in the first group at the preschool, to facilitate their transition.

Centers are largely in specially built low-rise buildings. They are designed so that there is a large open area off the entrance (a "piazza" or village square) where all the children and staff members gather at the beginning and end of the day, and to which all children have access in the course of the day for more active play. Each group has its own room located off the central piazza, and each of these, equipped with tables and chairs, is subdivided into a colorful and spacious area for play, a second area for quiet play and eating, and a third area for sleeping. Some centers also have an office for a pediatrician who holds a health clinic at the center once a week for the children in the center.

Each group has its own menu posted at the entrance to the group room, allowing parents to see what their child has eaten that day. The children are deliberately introduced to different types of food, including those not served at home. At the same time, staff members are very sensitive to cultural differences in regard to food and special diets. Moslem, Indian, and Turkish children are in these centers, and diversity is accepted and supported.

Whenever feasible, centers are located near a preschool and near several part-day child day care centers and family support centers as well (see below). In Italy, close links are emphasized between and among the centers, the preschools, the family support programs, and the health and social service programs, and between the preschools and the primary schools.

Although the care coverage of children under age three is modest even in this region, quality is high and there is conviction about the need for a universal program (albeit not necessarily for hours equal to a full workday). The family support (family center) programs (see below) that were established in the 1980s are designed to satisfy the objective of part-day coverage and to meet the needs both of very young children and of their mothers and caregivers for socialization/development/education experiences.

The Danish and Italian infant and toddler day care programs offer contrasting illustrations of high quality, affordable, exemplary, and innovative programs. With very different philosophies, both strive to respond to the needs of children in their societies. The children may have different family lives and daily experiences, and the countries may emphasize different social values, yet clearly these children are experiencing intellectual, social, and physical stimulation and enhanced development while being cared for outside of their own homes, and parents are an important component of the programs, albeit in different ways.

The most extensive and innovative developments in family support services are in these same north-central parts of Italy. These regions have a new concept of a diversified system of child and family services for children under age three and their families that includes child day care centers as one component but adds to them a variety of other types of group experiences for children with different needs. The target group includes children whose parents are not in the labor force, children with part-time working parents, children cared for by grandparents and other relatives, and children cared for by nonrelatives. The new programs are designed to be used part-day or part-week. The whole initiative is directed toward, first, meeting the needs of children; second, meeting the needs of mothers or parents; and third, helping parents exchange experiences and concerns with other parents and obtain expert guidance from professionals if they wish, including information, help, and support in their parenting role. Ultimately, the program contributes to parents' socialization and education, as well as that of their children, through peer interaction and interaction with the staff.

Included among these new types of programs are part-day centers, part-week centers, mother-toddler groups, and a variety of other flexible forms of child day care and child and parent groups. None of these are proposed as alternatives to or substitutes for existing traditional centers, but rather as a supplement to and extension of the latter.

The leading French and Italian child development researchers strongly believe that, given small family size and the paucity of children in neighborhoods, the social isolation of many of these mothers and their children can be devastating. Supplementary and supportive group experiences are essential and will lead to better adaptation in preschool. These experiences should provide opportunities for children to interact with other children and to separate from their mothers, and for mothers, parents, and caregivers to interact with one another and their children and staff members. The theory is that these mothers will learn more from exposure to other mothers than they will from the professional staff; even these very young children will learn from other children and from their mothers' enhanced parenting skills as well. Wherever these new types of centers are opened, mothers and grandmothers are enormously enthusiastic. The goal is sufficient expansion to allow complete coverage of all children under age three whose families wish to use the facilities.

Parents (usually mothers) or caregivers are expected to come with their child at least twice a week; coming less often makes it more difficult for children to adjust to the group. Most come three or four times a week; some, under special circumstances, come every day. A maximum of about 20 to 25 mothers with their children participate in each morning and afternoon session. In general, women whose children are under age 18 months tend to come out of their own needs, while those with children 18 months and older come in response to their perception of their child's needs.

Unfortunately, these developments are too recent for there to be any outcome data. No longitudinal studies are planned, nor any rigorous evaluations. There are some studies of the impacts of preschools, however, that strongly suggest positive results [Anolli & Mantovani, n.d.].

Nonetheless, government officials and the public generally are becoming increasingly aware of the potential for learning that very young children have and how this needs to be nurtured. Local governments are recognizing that child day care services enhance the social fabric and strengthen the civil society. Resources are limited and the proposed strategy is sensitive to this constraint, but there is growing recognition of the value of such an investment. Fifteen percent of the costs come from the regional government, 15% from parent fees (which are income-related), and the remainder from the local government.

Program exemplars in Milan, called Family Time Centers, are located in a wide range of communities, middle class as well as working class and low-income. Given the limited number of child day care places available, priority is given to children or families with special needs (handicapped, immigrant, lone mothers) but the goal is to have a universal program. The problems that tend to receive priority are more likely to be social or physical handicaps rather than family pathology (e.g., child abuse). Cases of children who are neglected or at risk for maltreatment are more likely to be served in a full-day child day care center. It is generally assumed that no more than 10% to 20% of enrollment in any of the Family Time Centers will be problem cases; as this figure is approached, the pressure for establishing a new center becomes intense.

Toddler Day Care Quality and Staffing

Quality, as a function of group size, staff:child ratios, staff qualifications, and center size, ranges across and within the countries. Denmark, like Sweden, has the highest quality child day care. Danish infant and toddler centers typically have 30 to 40 places, with three or four groups of ten children each, and with two staff members for each group. For purposes of staff:child ratios, each child under age three counts the same as two children age three and older. Family child care providers may care for a maximum of five children.

About half the center staff members have special postsecondary school training; family child care mothers are required to have between two and six weeks of special training, depending on the locality, before beginning to care for children.

Salaries of the professional early childhood educators are relatively high, equal to the average wage for females. Since, in addition, wages in Denmark for women are much closer to wages for men than is true in the U.S., child day care staff members earn much better wages than comparable U.S. staff members. One result may be the much lower staff turnover rate in Denmark—about 10% a year—in contrast to 25% or higher in the U.S.

Italy's Emilia Romagna, a region with an extensive supply of high quality infant/toddler day care, has a policy supporting a three-group center of 60 children in attendance, staffed by 11 teachers, four auxiliary staff, and two cooks; there may be 15 infants (ages nine to 12 months old) among the 60. A smaller center with 42 children and no infants would have six teachers, two auxiliary staff members, and one cook. Staff members are all public employees and salaries are pegged at a civil service middle level (about the same level as for preschool and primary school teachers). Here, too, staff turnover is low. In the past, most staff members have been secondary-school trained. The trend now is to use college graduates but not necessarily those with a child development specialization; however, in-service training is strongly emphasized.

Thus, staff:child ratios are high in these programs in Denmark, Finland, Sweden, and Italy, and staff members are relatively well paid. Turnover is therefore low and children are assured of stable caring relationships.

Costs, Financing, and Affordability

Child day care for children under age three is an expensive service everywhere. In many countries, however, society views such care as a worthwhile investment and shares in the costs to a much greater extent than in the U.S.

In Denmark, where the quality of care is uniformly high, operating costs are also high. The cost of a place in an infant/toddler center in 1991 was $12,324 a year ($6,708 for a family child care place). These costs are substantially higher than the costs generally ascribed to "high quality" programs in the U.S., and more than five times as high as the funds allocated to such care for beneficiary children of this age under AFDC rules—$200 a month. Even the cost of family child care in Denmark is almost three times as high as that allowed under AFDC.

Despite such high costs, however, infant/toddler day care services are far more affordable for parents in the continental European countries than in the U.S. The U.S. Bureau of the Census reports that of all families paying for child day care for a child under age three in 1988 (the latest date for which there are such data), the average expenditure was 8% of family income; for families with incomes below the poverty threshold, expenditures accounted for 21% of family income; for those with moderate incomes (below half of median income), expenditures took 18% of income [U.S. Bureau of the Census 1992]. A 1990 survey [Willer et al. 1991] found child day care fees accounting for still higher proportions of family income—10% generally, and 23% for poor and modest-income families.

Child day care services receive far more extensive public subsidies in the European countries than in the U.S. European parents pay income-related fees, but these fees are not expected to cover all or even most of the operating costs.

In Denmark, an average fee for a child age three or under equaled about 5% of median family income (about $50,000 a year) in 1991, and less than that for family child care. No poor families pay fees and only at about two-thirds of median-income would families pay a full fee. Even the maximum fee is only about $2,900 a year for a ten-hour day, all-year, high-quality program whose costs amount to more than four times that amount; this is in contrast to a comparable fee for U.S. parents of about $8,000 a year or more.

For purposes of comparison, parent fees accounted for 22% of operating child day care center costs in Denmark in 1990; 26% in France (and 38% of family child care costs), between 20% and 25% in Italy; and an astonishing 11% in Finland. The remaining costs are picked up by government—the local government in Denmark and Finland, a combination of local and regional government in Italy, and a combination of local government and the family allowance fund in France. In contrast, parent fees constituted 76% of operating costs of child day care centers in the U.S. (up from 70% in the mid-1970s) while government subsidies declined during those years to 19% (from 29% earlier). Capital costs in Europe are carried either by the local government (Denmark and Finland), the regional government (Italy), or by the local government and the family allowance fund (France).

Two-thirds of the child day care centers and nursery schools in Denmark are public. The remainder are publicly funded and subject to the same regulations and standards as the public programs, although they operate under contract with voluntary (private nonprofit) agencies. All child day care programs are public in Finland, and almost all the programs for children under age three are public in Italy; the French pattern, like the Danish, is a mixed picture, but largely public. Except in Britain, which in any case has publicly-funded places for only about 2% of those under age three, there are no for-profit centers in any of the other countries.

In effect, these are expensive programs, but as a matter of public policy, parent fees are kept at an affordable level for all, and quality is not sacrificed to achieve affordability.

Conclusion

Preschools and other types of child day care centers are universal in Europe and currently serve almost all the children age three to five regardless of their mother's employment status. Despite economic pressures, there is no evidence that the western European countries are curtailing support for these programs. Infant and toddler day care services are expanding in almost all of the western European countries, albeit modestly in most. In times of economic recession and high unemployment prevalent in recent years, demand pressures ease; nonetheless, a large gap exists between supply and demand, and shortages exist in all countries, even Denmark, which has places for almost 60% of children under age three. As in the U.S., supply, quality, financing, costs and parents' share of them, staffing, and curriculum are all being discussed and sometimes debated, and the results could inform the U.S. debate. Of particular interest are the different and innovative program models and the implications they have for quality and costs.

School readiness, an important issue in the U.S., is equally important in these countries. All stress the value of preschool in achieving this objective and the negative consequences for children in primary school when the earlier experience is not available. Of particular interest, however, is the growing concern with "preschool readiness" in those countries with universal preschools (France, Italy, Denmark), and the importance of providing a still earlier group experience for the very young children. As part of this concern, the cognitive and socialization aspects of these programs are receiving growing emphasis, as well as programmatic emphasis being placed on helping children and parents adjust to transitions as an important factor in a successful preschool and primary school experience.

Program auspice, another important issue in the U.S., varies significantly across the countries, with interesting implications for the U.S. Except for the Nordic countries, there is a clear consensus that preschool programs for three- to five-year-olds should be under education auspices. Even the British are moving in this direction. Where infant/toddler day care is concerned, auspice is more varied: social services in Denmark, Finland, and Sweden; social services but a beginning move toward education in England; health care in France, but with half the two-year-olds in an education-based program and more likely to be so over time; health care in part of Italy and education in the rest; and education completely in some other countries, such as Spain.

Of some interest, the highest quality programs in these countries are those in Denmark (and Sweden), and Italy, under two completely different types of auspice (social services and education), and then France and Finland, with still different auspices (health). Thus, it certainly seems that auspice by itself does not make much difference.

Child day care costs and who pays the costs are also critical matters. Child day care services are expensive in all these countries—indeed, far more expensive than in the U.S., for far better quality, but the costs are apparently an accepted and acceptable expense for the society. Services are paid for by some combination of government expenditure (national and/or local) and parent fees. The latter cover a maximum of one-quarter to one-third of operating service costs, depending on the country, and far less in some jurisdictions (and far, far less than in the U.S.). Yet parent fees for child day care constitute a far lighter burden on family income than in the U.S. (and programs for the threes and over are completely free in several countries). Most of the costs, by far, are picked up by the government; these programs are viewed as an investment in children and their future and supported as such by the society.

To conclude: the care of very young children and support for their parents are both receiving growing attention in Europe. Several countries have a more extensive supply of infant and toddler day care services than we do in the U.S., and these countries all have far more extensively subsidized services that are more readily afforded by parents than in the U.S. At least as important, in a few countries there is conviction about what very young children and their parents need that goes beyond child day care for the children of working parents. The goal is to respond to a broader set of needs—cognitive, social, physical, psychological—and so to move toward a more holistic child and family service. In this context, child day care, early childhood education, maternal and child health care, and family support services are emerging as a comprehensive and integrated young child and family service system. ◆

Notes

1. The study on which this report is based was carried out between 1991 and 1993 in six European countries—Denmark, Finland, France, Germany, Italy, and Britain—and sponsored by the Carnegie Corporation and the Spencer Foundation. It focused on the full range of social policies directed toward very young children (under age three), and their families, including financial support, health care, employment-related policies, child day care, and family support services. The full study is reported in S. B. Kamerman and A. J. Kahn, *Starting right: How America neglects its youngest children and what we can do about it* (New York: Oxford University Press, 1995). Here, however, we concentrate on the last two—the infant/toddler day care services and the supportive services provided to the children and their parents from infancy on. We choose our illustrations from among those countries whose experiences were

found to be most relevant for answering our questions. Detailed country case studies and extensive program descriptions are contained in A. J. Kahn and S. B. Kamerman, *Social policy and the under 3s: Six country case studies* (New York: Columbia University School of Social Work, 1994).

2.   1990s data supplied directly by BLS.

3.   S. B. Kamerman and A. J. Kahn (Eds.), *Child care, parental leave, and the under-3s: Policy innovation in Europe* (Westport, CT: Auburn House, 1991). *See* also Note 1.

4.   For a more extensive description of infant and toddler day care in Europe, see S. B. Kamerman and A. J. Kahn, *A welcome for every child: Care, education, and family support for infants and toddlers in Europe* (Washington, DC: Zero to Three, 1994).

References

Anolli, L., & Mantovani, S. (undated). *Tempo per la familigie* (Family Time Centers). Reports prepared for the Bernard Van Leer Foundation, Milan, Italy.

Kamerman, S. B., & Kahn, A. J. (1995). *Starting right: How America neglects its youngest children and what we can do about it.* New York: Oxford University Press.

Kamerman, S. B., & Kahn, A. J. (1994). *A welcome for every child: Care, education, and family support for infants and toddlers in Europe.* Washington, DC: Zero to Three.

Kahn, A. J., & Kamerman, S. B. (1994). *Social policy and the under 3s: Six country case studies.* New York: Columbia University School of Social Work.

Nelson, J., Jr. (1982). The politics of federal day care regulation. In E. F. Zigler & E. W. Gordon (Eds.), *Day care: Scientific and social policy issues* (pp. 277–291). Boston: Auburn House Publishing Company.

U.S. Bureau of the Census. (1992). *Who's minding the kids? Child care arrangements: Fall 1988.* Current Population Reports, P70–30. (Data from the Survey of Income and Program Participation). Washington, DC: U.S. Government Printing Office.

U.S. Department of Labor. (September 19, 1985, August 20, 1986, August 12, 1987). *Bureau of Labor Statistics News.*

Willer, B., Hofferth, S. L., Kisker, E. E., Divine-Hawkins, P., Farquhar, E., & Glantz, F. B. (1991). *The demand and supply of child care in 1990.* Washington, DC: National Association for the Education of Young Children.

13

Child Day Care in the Schools: The School of the 21st Century

*Edward F. Zigler, Matia Finn-Stevenson, and
Katherine W. Marsland*

The development and education of children in the
United States is being increasingly compromised by a
lack of coordinated high-quality services that accord
with the changing needs of families. The School of the
21st Century is a school-based/school-linked program
that promotes the optimal development of all children
by providing high-quality services from the birth of
the child through age 12. The model has been
implemented in over 300 schools. This article discusses
the rationale of the program, the use of the school in
the delivery of support services, the model as it has
been implemented in various communities, and the
benefits as well as challenges associated with the
expansion of the traditional mission of the school.
Preliminary results of a three-year outcome evaluation
are included.

*Edward F. Zigler, Ph.D., is Director; Matia Finn-Stevenson, Ph.D., is Associate
Director; and Katherine W. Marsland, B.A., is Implementation-Coordinator, Bush
Center in Child Development and Social Policy, Yale University, New Haven, CT. The
authors gratefully acknowledge that the support of Kraft Foods has enabled the development of The School of the 21st Century and the writing of this article.*

257

The School of the 21st Century is a school-based/school-linked family support program designed to promote children's optimal development by providing high-quality child day care and support services to children from birth through age 12. At its core are two child care components: before- and after-school and vacation care for school-age children and full-day child day care for three- to five-year-old children. The child day care components operate year-round, including holidays, snow days, school vacations, and inservice days when the schools are not in session. Schools of the 21st Century also include several outreach components: home visiting by trained parent educators to parents of children from birth to age three; information and referral services; networking and professional development for family child care providers; and health and nutrition services. In addition, as figure 1 illustrates, many Schools of the 21st Century have expanded their core services to include partnerships with community-based child day care providers and additional services that may be needed in the community. Together, the components establish an infrastructure for the coordination of four interrelated social systems that have the largest impact on children's development: the family, the child day care environment, the school, and health care services.

All components of The School of the 21st Century are designed to be flexible and adaptable to the needs and resources of a given community. Thus, The School of the 21st Century is not a program per se but a constellation of services delivered and coordinated under the auspices of schools that facilitate interaction among these four systems in behalf of families and children.

Implemented in over 300 schools in 14 states, The School of the 21st Century was conceptualized in 1987 in response to the pressing need for a system of high-quality services that meet the needs of contemporary American families [Zigler 1987]. Implementation, research, and ongoing conceptual development of the model are coordinated by the Yale University Bush Center in Child Development and Social Policy.

FIGURE 1

The School of the 21st Century

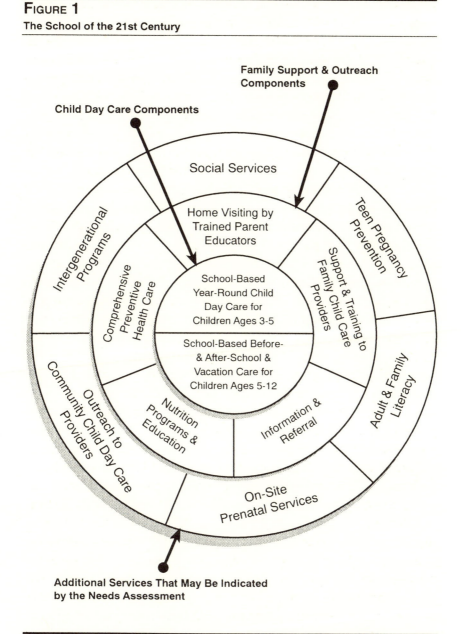

Child Day Care Components

Family Support & Outreach Components

Social Services

Home Visiting by Trained Parent Educators

Intergenerational Programs

Teen Pregnancy Prevention

Comprehensive Preventive Health Care

Support & Training to Family Child Care Providers

School-Based Year-Round Child Day Care for Children Ages 3-5

School-Based Before- & After-School & Vacation Care for Children Ages 5-12

Outreach to Community Child Day Care Providers

Nutrition Programs & Education

Information & Referral

Adult & Family Literacy

On-Site Prenatal Services

Additional Services That May Be Indicated by the Needs Assessment

The theory underlying the model is that child day care, like the other three social systems noted above, is an environment the child experiences that helps determine the child's development. If the quality of the environment is high, the child is able to learn and acquire the skills necessary for later success in school. If the quality is low, the child's development is compromised. The four social systems are interdependent, with factors in each one influencing the others. Of concern is the reality that many of America's children are in child day care settings where the quality is so poor that their developmental needs are not met.

The School of the 21st Century is providing the means for increasing the availability and accessibility of high-quality child day care. In this article, The School of the 21st Century is described as it has been implemented in several communities, including the benefits and challenges inherent in the use of the school for the provision of child care and support services. The role of the Yale Bush Center and preliminary results of a three-year outcome evaluation conducted in one of the sites are also presented.

Background

Over the last three decades, rising rates of divorce, teen pregnancy, single parenthood, and dual-income families, along with increasing mobility, have challenged the traditional definition of the American family. Although a detailed description of these changes in family life is beyond the scope of this article, one of the most striking changes has been the growth in the number of women with young children who are in the out-of-home workforce. Currently, 55.4% of mothers with children under six and 51% of mothers with infants are employed outside of the home [U.S. Department of Labor 1993]. The number of mothers with older children who are working is even higher [U.S. Department of Labor 1993].

The stress associated with these changes has profoundly affected the nature of family life. Parents must juggle both work and family responsibilities without the benefit of support systems such as assistance from relatives. Consequently, the need for some form of external support—whether it be information about child-rearing and child development or full-day child day care—is now virtually universal. Despite a variety of efforts, however, existing services are fragmented and hard to access, constituting, in effect, a nonsystem. The healthy development of a growing number of children is thus threatened by the lack of a coordinated system of comprehensive family support.

Affordable, high-quality child day care is the most pressing need in this regard. Though this need has been the focus of national attention for over three decades, studies indicate that the demand for child day care, particularly for infants and school-age children, continues to exceed the current supply [Hayes et al. 1990; Kisker & Maynard 1991; Fuller & Liang 1995]. Further, because child day care is a major expense for many families and the quality of care is directly related to cost, high-quality care is beyond the means of many middle- and low-income families [Hofferth & Wissoker 1992]. Consequently, children are often placed in care that is either custodial (neither growth-enhancing nor growth-inhibiting) or of poor quality (growth-inhibiting). In a national study of child day care centers serving primarily pre-school-age children, it was found that staff wages and turnover were central indicators of quality [Whitebook et al. 1989]. Only 43% of the child care staff sampled, however, earned more than five dollars per hour, despite having levels of education higher than those of the average American worker. Further, annual staff turnover among these workers was 41%, and was directly related to low salaries. Even more disturbing, follow-up calls indicated that 37% of child care workers left over a six-month period.

The quality of care for infants is also an issue. Parents often choose family child care settings because they believe that the small group size and homelike atmosphere is conducive to the development of infants and toddlers. Although this is the case with good-quality family child care, a national study of family child care and relative care found that only 9% of the homes sampled were of high quality, whereas 56% were rated as custodial and 35% were rated as poor [Galinsky et al. 1994].

A related issue concerns the availability of good-quality, affordable school-age child day care. In the absence of child day care programs that accommodate parents' work schedules, many school-age children are left alone at home and have come to be referred to as children in self-care. Although some contend that such arrangements may be appropriate for school-age children, the effects of self-care are controversial [Rodman et al. 1985]. Some studies note that children who are in self-care often report feeling lonely and afraid and are at high risk for injury [Long & Long 1982; Garbarino & Stocking 1980]. Additionally, in a nationwide study, Richardson et al. [1989] found that among children and young adolescents who are in self-care, delinquency and drug and alcohol abuse are more prevalent than among those who are in supervised care. These findings hold regardless of such variables as family income and ethnic background.

Lack of affordable, good-quality child day care is a source of great concern for parents and creates stress that permeates the entire family system [Freidman 1987]. The child-care problem touches the lives of all families, regardless of their income. Legislative attempts to deal with the need for good-quality, affordable child day care failed until 1990, when the Child Care and Development Block Grant was enacted. In terms of better meeting the need for child day care, however, the law's impact is negligible. For example, the law targets 75% of the block grant to serve low-income families. In California, before the enactment of the law, child day care centers in that state served 25% of the eligible families. Studies also point out that not only in California but in other states as well, the money for subsidizing child day care has increased but is hardly sufficient [Stoney 1994]. Moreover, the Child Care and Development Block Grant has not confronted the need for good quality, affordable child day care for working families.

The School of the 21st Century

The need for a coordinated, accessible child day care and family support system led to the conceptualization of The School of the 21st Century. The model calls for implementing a child day care system within the already existing educational system, making use, where possible, of available school buildings. The components of The School of the 21st Century, noted above, not only ensure a comprehensive array of services for children and families, but also make possible continuity of care and support for children—the foundation necessary for subsequent learning to occur.

The strength and ultimate potential of The School of the 21st Century stem from its comprehensive nature and its integration with the education system. By eliminating the distinction between child day care and education, the model actualizes the notion that learning begins at birth and continues in all settings, not just within the classroom [Zigler & Finn-Stevenson 1994].

In The School of the 21st Century, the school is no longer seen as a building in which formal schooling is delivered during limited hours. Instead, the school becomes a place where formal schooling, child day care, and family support occur together. The traditional school operates, for example, from eight in the morning to three in the afternoon, nine months of the year. In The School of the 21st Century, however, the building is open from six or seven in the morning to six in the evening, 12 months a year, to provide core child day care and family support services, and other services as may be needed. Existing school and community programs, such as Head Start, other preschool or after-school services, programs serving children with special needs, and so forth, become a part of The School of the 21st Century, enabling coordination of services, activities, and resource sharing.

Implementation

A distinguishing feature of the program is the flexibility with which it can be adapted to a range of different communities.

While all Schools of the 21st Century share a common philosophy and overall goal, implementation of the program components is driven by the needs and resources of each community.
Therefore, it is important to stress at the outset that each School
of the 21st Century differs in the extent to which its components
are school-based or school-linked, the scope of services it provides, and its organizational structure. For example, whereas the
majority of Schools of the 21st Century provide child day care
services in the elementary schools, in Leadville, Colorado, a rural
community located in the heights of the Rocky Mountains, The
Center (as The School of the 21st Century in Leadville is known)
is operated by the school district in a former elementary school
building. A high percentage of Leadville families are of low
socioeconomic status, and The Center was initiated with the in-
tention of improving the developmental and educational prospects of children in these families. All families in the district,
however, are eligible for The Center's services, regardless of their
income level. Because most parents in Leadville commute long
distances to work in the tourism industry, The Center provides
services from 5:30 A.M. to 6:30 P.M. each day (additional family
support services are provided until 10 P.M.). The Center is open
every day, including weekends and all national holidays, and has
not closed since its opening in 1988. Transportation for school-
age children to and from the local elementary school is provided
by the school district. In addition to child care, The Center provides home visits by trained parent educators, referrals, and
health and nutrition services. The Center also coordinates a range
of other services geared to the needs of Leadville families, including a fully inclusive Head Start program, infant care, on-site
prenatal screening, an intergenerational program for at-risk
youths, Graduate Equivalency and English as a Second Language classes, and a year-round food program available to all
adults in the community.

   In contrast, Schools of the 21st Century in Independence,
Missouri, are based in all of the district's 13 elementary schools,

each one of which provides child day care for children ages three to 12. Independence, the first School of the 21st Century site, is a suburban working class community where the most pressing need was for high-quality affordable child day care. Both information and referral services for children with special needs and a home visiting program (Parents As Teachers) were in place before the district initiated The School of the 21st Century. These services were brought under The School of the 21st Century umbrella, and the information and referral service was expanded to include referrals for child day care. In addition, the district developed both a successful Family Day Care Provider Network and a comprehensive nutrition program, and became an authorized Medicaid case manager. All residents are eligible for services, and the district reimburses child day care providers for training expenses in order to promote professional development and enhance the quality of child day care in the community.

Guiding Principles

Though each program is unique, all Schools of the 21st Century adopt a uniform set of principles that guide implementation from planning through stabilization and evaluation. These principles are derived from research in child development and are based on the belief that all families and all children must be able to obtain the services they need. Further, each child must be viewed as a member of a unique family system whose needs influence the child's ability to realize his or her potential. Because these needs vary as children grow and develop, support services should be available throughout the childhood years.

The first guiding principle calls for universal access to high-quality child day care. Toward this end, School of the 21st Century child day care is based on parental fee for services, with a sliding scale and subsidies built in to ensure access by middle- and low-income families.

Second, to enable children's optimal development, child day care must focus on all aspects of development: social, cognitive, physical, and emotional. Therefore, the components of The School of the 21st Century are geared toward the different needs of children at various stages of development, with child day care services placing a particular emphasis on socioemotional development. Preschool child day care, for example, emphasizes play and social interaction. School-age child day care, though, provides children with experiences that are qualitatively different from the academic day, such as physical activities, organized recreation, or quiet time to relax.

The third principle emphasizes the importance of professional development for child day care providers. Stability of care, as evident in consistency of staff over a period of time, and the educational and training background of the care provider are important indicators of quality [Phillips & Howes 1987]. Historically, however, staff turnover in the field has been twice that of other occupations and child care workers often lack opportunities for professional development [Johnson 1987]. Schools of the 21st Century work in partnership with child day care providers to make training opportunities available and to establish a supportive and professional environment for child day care workers, thereby enhancing the quality of child day care throughout their communities. For example, some Schools of the 21st Century have made benefit programs available to child day care providers in the community. Others have developed training opportunities and career ladders that are available to both on-site and community-based providers. Finally, many sites operate resource lending libraries from which local providers may borrow toys, books, and other curriculum materials.

Fourth, Schools of the 21st Century promote and encourage parental participation. Research indicates that parental involvement is a key factor in the success of programs such as Head Start [Zigler & Valentine 1979] and that parental participation enhances both children's development and learning [e.g., U.S. Department of Education 1994]. Each School of the 21st Century addresses the expressed needs of families in the school community, and parents are encouraged to participate in the planning process.

Fifth, The School of the 21st Century is noncompulsory. Programs and services are available on a voluntary basis, and families make their own decisions about which, if any, they use.

Finally, an effective system of good-quality child day care and family support must be integrated with the political and economic structure of society. Schools of the 21st Century establish the framework for such integration by tying the provision of child day care and family support services to a recognized and easily accessible institution—the public schools.

Establishing a School of the 21st Century

Procedural Guidelines

Schools interested in implementing The School of the 21st Century model contact the Yale Bush Center and must commit themselves to the program's guiding principles before beginning implementation. This generally takes the form of a letter of commitment from the district superintendent and the building principal. Subsequently, members of the Bush Center staff meet with representatives from the district to assess the school's organizational capacity to implement the program. This audit includes consideration of factors such as the support of central office personnel, the availability of an individual with a background in child development who can devote at least 50% of his or her time to program coordination, the district's previous experience in program planning and coordination, and the district's commitment to making available or raising the funds necessary to cover start-up and, in part, operational costs. In addition, administrators at both the district and school level are required to attend the Bush Center's Training Institute, which provides an orientation to the program and its philosophy along with workshops regarding each component. Thereafter, the school receives ongoing advisory support and technical assistance from the Bush Center. Generally, technical assistance is most intensive during the planning period.

Needs Assessment

As a first step toward implementation, schools conduct a needs assessment on two main areas: the characteristics and needs of the population to be served by the program, and the scope of existing child day care and family support services in the community. This information is essential to effective planning for several reasons. First, it enables schools to prioritize the implementation order of the program components. Though many schools, particularly those in urban areas, find a need for all of the components and often additional support services, implementation of the entire program at one time is not recommended. Instead, most schools adopt a phase-in implementation strategy whereby services are initiated over time (generally a three- to five-year period). Second, information about existing programs and support services is needed to prevent duplication of efforts. The School of the 21st Century does not seek to replace or supplant existing programs. Rather, schools implementing the program work in partnership with existing agencies and providers to enhance the quality and accessibility of services. For example, in Pine Bluffs, Wyoming, sufficient community-based child day care for preschoolers made additional school-based services for this population unnecessary.* Therefore, rather than creating competing services, the district offered training and educational opportunities to child day care providers and referred families in need of care to the existing programs. Interaction between the

---

*Recently, the district hired both a new superintendent and an elementary school principal. Because, as we will discuss later, leadership is critical to any program's long-term success, it is unclear how these administrative changes will impact Pine Bluff's School of the 21st Century.

child day care centers and the school is considerable. Since the community lacked school-age child day care, home visiting, and information and referral, these services are all delivered by the school.

The needs assessment information is also useful in identifying potential areas of collaboration. Research indicates that collaboration is vital to the long-term stability of family support programs [e.g., U.S. Department of Education 1993]. Toward this end, schools are encouraged to establish an advisory committee comprising school personnel, parents, school board members, administrators, business and community leaders, and representatives from collaborating agencies. An effective advisory committee enables the program to establish unified goals and builds on the expertise and resources of its members. Further, collaboration among key stakeholders from both the community and the school enhances the programs' compliance with each of The School of the 21st Century principles. Collaboration with community-based agencies is not an easy task, however. It has been achieved in different ways depending on local circumstances, ranging from informal arrangements for purposes of information-gathering and referrals to formal partnerships. In this regard, Schools of the 21st Century have had much in common with collaboration activities of other family support programs as described by Kraemer [1993].

Schools of the 21st Century have selected a variety of methodologies in conducting their needs assessments, including surveys, door-to-door canvassing, focus groups, and the use of existing data bases. Many schools have combined two or more methods to ensure that the results are complete and accurate. Though some districts have the capacity to conduct and interpret the assessment data independently, technical assistance from the Bush Center staff is often requested. In addition, schools are encouraged to draw on the experience of other Schools of the 21st Century with similar demographics and resources.

Planning

The results of the needs assessment are used in two ways: as the baseline for future evaluation that the schools are encouraged to conduct, and as the basis for planning. The data enable the schools not only to establish implementation priorities, but also to establish a time line for doing so, to deal with management and governance matters, and to create a financial plan. Again, assistance from Bush Center staff and consultation with similar schools within The School of the 21st Century network is often helpful during this process.

In many cases, some of the components of the program already exist in the community and are incorporated into The School of the 21st Century during the planning process. In Independence, Missouri, for example, Parents As Teachers (PAT) had already been established as part of a statewide initiative. In Paragould, Arkansas, the Home Instruction Program for Preschool Youngsters (HIPPY), another home-visiting program, was already operating in the district. In both of these cases, The School of the 21st Century became the hub for both the provision of services and coordination with other program components. In yet another example, many school districts already sponsor school-age child day care programs. The goal in these cases is to maximize both quality and accessibility through effective integration and coordination of services.

Though the time frame varies, most schools find that the needs assessment and planning process require from six to nine months. Planning does not end with the implementation of the first component, however. Rather, it is a dynamic and ongoing process throughout the life of the program and is constantly informed by the changing needs of participating children and families; The School of the 21st Century provides the mechanism for establishing a framework for the addition of other services, including adult education and prenatal care.

Funding

Funding is one of the biggest concerns that schools have regarding implementation of the program. The program was designed to be self-supporting through parental fees for child day care. Most schools, however, particularly those in poor urban areas, require start-up funds and additional funding for program expansion and subsidies for lower-income families. Start-up costs generally include renovation of space, acquisition of materials, and money for staff salaries for the first six to 12 months of operation. Schools have financed these costs in a variety of ways, including grants from community foundations, local corporations, and state and federal sources [Giles 1994]. In both Connecticut and Kentucky, where state legislation enabled the creation of Family Resource Centers that are based on The School of the 21st Century model, schools interested in implementing the program were invited to apply for start-up grants. In most cases, however, it is necessary to pursue a combination of funding sources. For instance, both Leadville and Independence financed start-up expenses by a combination of support from local foundations and state grants.

Operational costs include expenses such as staff salaries and training, supplies, rent, and utilities. In most cases these costs are offset by in-kind donations from the local district. For example, in Leadville, The Center occupies a former elementary school building that is maintained by the district. In addition, many schools have successfully applied federal funds, such as Chapter 1, drug prevention, and Title IV-E and IV-B, to School of the 21st Century services. One recent trend of particular interest has been the use of Medicaid case management funds. This approach has been used most extensively in the Independence school district, where the application of Medicaid funds to services such as nursing has enabled the district to apply savings to School of the 21st Century programs, namely health and nutrition services. In all cases, successful financing depends largely on the entrepreneurial skills of the program coordinator, building principal, and district superintendent.

Administrative Support

In addition to assisting with funding, the principal and superintendent provide leadership critical to the acceptance of the program by school personnel, the local school board, and the community at large. This is particularly true during the early stages of implementation, which require at least 5% of the principal's time and at least 10% when preschool child day care is introduced [Finn-Stevenson et al. 1989]. At the district level, The School of the 21st Century is coordinated out of the central office, but at the building level, each principal is responsible for overseeing the program's operation and supervising the site coordinator. Because of the importance of the principal and superintendent in this respect, their commitment to implementing the program is prerequisite to becoming a School of the 21st Century site.

Staffing

Related implementation concerns for most schools are staffing and organizational structure. All sites are required to hire a program coordinator who can devote at least 50% of his or her time to The School of the 21st Century. The coordinator is responsible for all aspects of program administration—staffing, management of the budget, fund raising, and coordination with partnership organizations. The coordinator also works closely with the building principal to ensure that School of the 21st Century components are incorporated into the overall school community and that all school personnel are kept informed of services available to students and their families. In addition to these administrative responsibilities, the coordinator works closely with parents and is responsible for staff development. Therefore, it is important that this person have both a background in early childhood development and strong interpersonal skills.

Staff development is particularly important. Schools of the 21st Century are committed to both quality programming and staffing. As discussed above, education and training of child care providers is a vital feature of high-quality child care programs. Therefore, Schools of the 21st Century strive to hire staff members with training and/or education in early childhood development. If, however, a school is unable to hire early childhood educators, it hires staff members with training in child development and actively promotes their professional development through in-service workshops and other training or educational opportunities. Further, schools refer to staffing standards set forth by both the Child Welfare League of America (CWLA) and the National Association for the Education of Young Children (NAEYC). Schools also offer *ongoing* opportunities for training and professional development to *all* staff members in the school building; these training opportunities are also made available to providers in the community. This is particularly important for family child care providers, who are often isolated and lack access to the training necessary for licensing and to information about operating a successful small business. Toward this end, some schools have established relationships with local community colleges for the provision of education and training in early childhood development and developmentally appropriate curricula. In addition, Schools of the 21st Century are encouraged to promote career development by establishing career ladders that encourage providers to seek ongoing training. Finally, schools are strongly encouraged to seek accreditation as soon as possible from organizations such as the National Council on Accreditation and NAEYC.

Space

Lack of sufficient space is also a frequent implementation problem. Given the increase in elementary school enrollments during recent years, obtaining adequate space can be one of the most difficult problems that schools confront. This challenge, however, can be met in a number of ways. For example, The School of the 21st Century in Norfolk, Virginia, rented portable units. In this instance, the entire school made the decision to have fourth and fifth graders in those units so that the entire first floor of the school building could become an early childhood wing. Likewise, in West Hartford, Connecticut, a kindergarten teacher voluntarily relocated her classroom to create space for a family/early childhood center. Some schools have space but must renovate it to make it appropriate for preschoolers. In a very few cases, schools have had to rent additional space in the school neighborhood. Most schools are able to renovate or modify multipurpose areas by adding carpeting, room dividers, and portable furnishings that create a comfortable and stimulating atmosphere for school-age child care. In West Hartford, both an atrium and a classroom are modified daily for child day care before and after school.

Challenges and Benefits

The School of the 21st Century has paved the way for a growing number of programs that see the school as accessible to children and thus essential for the delivery and/or coordination of services. This point is made by Dryfoos [1994], who describes full service schools that focus on the provision of social services. Other programs such as New Beginnings in San Diego, California, have linked family support services to the school through referrals by school personnel rather than basing the delivery of services at the school site [Payzant 1992]. Yet another variation of school-linked services is exemplified by Cities in Schools, a national program designed to cope with the needs of economically disadvantaged students by introducing early intervention and family support services. In this model, existing health and social services are repositioned into the schools to streamline service delivery and increase access. The central role of the school in the coordination of services is a common feature in each of these approaches.

Concerns

The appropriateness of the school's assumption of such a role, however, has been the topic of considerable debate, particularly with respect to child day care. In particular, some child day care professionals [e.g., Chaskin & Richman 1992] and national organizations [e.g., National Black Child Development Institute 1987] express concern that school-linked services tend to reflect the institutional needs of schools rather than the developmental needs of the children they serve. For example, some fear that rather than emphasizing play and social interaction, school-based preschool programs might establish academically oriented curricula. Some are also concerned that school-age child day care programs might result in an extension of the academic day or require children to participate in organized activities without allowing time for relaxation and play at the end of the school day.

These concerns are valid, and present an important issue with respect to implementation of The School of the 21st Century. The potential for academically oriented programs exists, however, regardless of whether the program is school- or community-based (Mitchell & Modigliani 1989). To address this concern, Schools of the 21st Century child day care programs are required to use developmentally appropriate curricula (such as High Scope). In addition, Schools of the 21st Century must provide staff members with training in child development and developmentally appropriate practices. Further, programs are expected to adhere to quality criteria set forth by NAEYC or CWLA. This commitment to quality is reflected in high staff:child ratios, small group sizes, and staffing practices that demonstrate committment to the overall professional development of all child care providers.

In addition, some child day care providers fear that School of the 21st Century child day care programs will compete unfairly for staff and enrollment. Because implementation is based on need, however, schools do not duplicate services in cases where sufficient child day care services already exist. Rather, schools in such communities establish relationships with the existing providers to promote high-quality services and coordinate service delivery within The School of the 21st Century framework, as was the case in Wyoming. Schools can also attenuate potential opposition by establishing nonthreatening fee structures, by inviting child day care providers to attend School of the 21st Century orientation and training sessions, and by encouraging provider participation in the planning process. In addition, the Family Day Care Provider Network establishes the opportunity for schools to develop mutually beneficial relationships with many providers. Providers who participate in these networks benefit from referrals, training opportunities, support groups, small business seminars, toy-lending libraries, and other activities in which they have an interest. Some programs have also established informal drop-in sessions for family child care providers and their children; others have created back-up systems to assist providers in managing emergencies or illnesses.

Finally, whereas some of the opposition stems from outside of the school, there is, at times, concern among the teaching staff that the program will drain already scarce educational resources. Our experience, however, has been otherwise. The School of the 21st Century child care components are designed to be self-supporting, primarily through fees for their services. When needed, additional funds are procured from federal and state government and/or corporate and community foundations. Very often, schools and local nonprofit organizations may collaborate on grant proposals to reduce potential competition. Further, Schools of the 21st Century generally receive in-kind donations in the form, for example, of rent-free space, but they have not relied on school resources to pay for the program. Rather, such in-kind donations actually increase the district's return on investments in existing structures by maximizing their use. Schools also realize qualitative benefits from increased parental participation and community support. Furthermore, schools benefit from the enhanced school readiness of children who have received the stable, nurturing, and stimulating care necessary for optimal learning, and whose need for preventive services has been met early in life.

Benefits

School districts that implement The School of the 21st Century can realize an array of benefits for children, parents, schools, and the community in general. Some of these potential benefits result from circumstances unique to individual school districts; other, more general benefits are realized by most School of the 21st Century programs. These benefits include:

- Reductions in the number of hours children remain unsupervised;
- Increased consistency of care;
- Reductions in the number of different child day care arrangements that children must tolerate;
- Reductions in children's risk of developing behavioral problems;
- Reduced absenteeism;
- Reduced risk, over time, in the need for special services;
- Enhanced school readiness;
- Reduced parental guilt and stress;
- Increased parental satisfaction with the public school;
- Increased availability of affordable child day care; and
- Improved family child care.

The Role of the Yale Bush Center

Implementation of The School of the 21st Century is coordinated by the Yale Bush Center, and technical assistance is individualized to meet the needs of each school or district. Initially, these functions were carried out by a small core staff, who worked closely with individual sites. As The School of the 21st Century network has grown, however, the Bush Center has established a Peer Training Network that capitalizes on the expertise of personnel from more mature sites. Additionally, the Bush Center is piloting the use of implementation associates to work directly with sites in their region of the country, coordinating peer training, and brokering relationships with outside consultants. Each year, the Bush Center also selects The School of the 21st Century demonstation sites at various stages of implementation. These schools host site visits and workshops and provide peer training to others within the national network. Further, the Bush Center is working at the state level in several states toward the enactment of legislation enabling statewide implementation. Eventually, the Bush Center's emphasis will shift from direct technical assistance to the sites to the role of training both regional and national trainers.

Since 1989, the Bush Center has also hosted an annual Training Institute that orients new sites to The School of the 21st Century components and principles; it provides advanced workshops regarding implementation of the individual components as well. Renamed the National Academy and redesigned in 1995, the annual conference also provides administrators with an important opportunity to network with peers from other programs and exchange information relating to key implementation matters.

In addition to providing and coordinating technical assistance, the Bush Center is engaged in both process and outcome evaluation projects. Currently, the Bush Center is completing a three-year outcome evaluation of the pilot program in Independence, Missouri [Finn-Stevenson & Chung, in press]. Preliminary results of this evaluation suggest the following:

- The program enjoys significant support from both parents and school personnel.
- Mothers of preschool-age children reported spending additional time with their children.

- The percentage of parents using just one child day care arrangement, rather than several over the course of a week, increased across the three years.
- Children who participated in School of the 21st Century child care achieved higher academic outcomes than did children in the matched comparison group.

Schools are also encouraged to conduct their own evaluations, with assistance from the Bush Center as needed. Results from these evaluations indicate that :

- In urban areas, in particular, school vandalism decreased significantly after implementation of the School of the 21st Century program.
- Parents experienced a great deal less stress.
- Community support for the public schools increased significantly.

With respect to implementation, reports from principals and site coordinators have indicated that the majority of initial training activities focused on staff development and orientation to The School of the 21st Century design and philosophy. In particular, both principals and site coordinators have emphasized the importance of the relationship between the two professions that The School of the 21st Century unites: child day care providers and elementary/primary school teachers. Toward this end, principals and site coordinators can be strong role models by demonstrating mutual respect through their interactions both with one another and with their staff members. Further, they establish organizational and procedural guidelines that are respectful, inclusive, and supportive of all adults in the building. For example, most Schools of the 21st Century do not differentiate between the traditional teaching staff and the child day care staff when planning staff meetings or school events. Such examples concur with an earlier process evaluation [Finn-Stevenson et al. 1989] and underscore the importance of the principal's leadership to the program's overall success and to The School of the 21st Century's commitment to strengthening and unifying *all* early childhood professionals.

Conclusion

The School of the 21st Century creates the infrastructure for the coordination of a continuum of child day care and support services that modern families need in order to effectively rear their children. By integrating these services with the school, the program enhances the availability, quality, and affordability of services, and improves children's developmental and educational prospects. Further, schools implementing the program become a valued community resource to which parents turn for support and where families as a whole are welcome. Moreover, The School of the 21st Century is consistent with the federal "Goals 2000: Educate America Act," particularly the first and eighth goals that call for increased school readiness and parental involvement, respectively. Our nation's future and our ability to compete in an increasingly competitive international economy depend largely upon our children's ability to realize their educational potential. The School of the 21st Century and programs like it represent viable strategies for creating a comprehensive system that enables ongoing family support and focuses on the optimal development of all children. ♦

References

Chaskin, R. J., & Richman, H. A. (1992). Concerns about school-linked services: Institution-based versus community-based models. *Future of Children*, 2(1), 101–117.

Dryfoos, J. G. (1994). *Full-service schools: A revolution in health and social services for children, youth, and families.* San Francisco, CA: Jossey-Bass.

Finn-Stevenson, M., Chung, A. M., & Zigler, E. F. (in press). *The School of the 21st Century: Results of a three-year outcome evaluation.* Manuscript submitted for publication.

Finn-Stevenson, M., Ward, B. A., Young, A., & Raver, C. C. (1989). *Schools of the 21st Century in Independence and Platte County, Missouri: An interim progress report.* Working paper. New Haven, CT: Bush Center in Child Development and Social Policy.

Freidman, D. (1987). *Family supportive policies: The corporate decision making process.* New York: Conference Board.

Fuller, B., & Liang, X. (1995). *Can poor families find child care? Persisting inequality nationwide and in Massachusetts.* Cambridge, MA: Harvard Child Care and Family Policy Project.

Galinsky, E., Howes, C., Kontos, S., & Shinn, M. B. (1994). *The study of children in family child care and relative care.* New York: Families and Work Institute.

Garbarino, J., & Stocking, S. H. (Eds.). (1980). *Protecting children from abuse and neglect: Developing and maintaining effective support systems for families.* San Francisco: Jossey-Bass.

Giles, D. (1994). *Financing alternatives for Schools of the 21st Century.* Working paper. New Haven, CT: Bush Center in Child Development and Social Policy.

Hayes, C. D., Palmer, D. A., & Zaslow, M. (Eds.). (1990). *Who cares for America's children?* Washington, DC: National Academy Press.

Hofferth, S. L., & Wissoker, D. A. (1992). Price, quality, and income in child care choice. *Journal of Human Resources, 27*(1), 70–111.

Johnson, W. (1987). *Workforce 2000: Work and workers for the 21st Century.* Indianapolis, IN: Hudson Institute.

Kisker, E., & Maynard, R. (1991). Quality, cost, and parental choice of child care. In D.M. Blau (Ed.), *The economics of child care.* New York: Russell Sage Foundation.

Kraemer, J. (1993). *Building villages to raise our children: Collaboration.* Cambridge, MA: Harvard Family Research Project.

Long, L., & Long, T. (1982). *Latchkey children.* Washington, DC: National Institute of Education.

Mitchell, A., & Modigliani, K. (1989). Young children in public schools? The "only ifs" reconsidered. *Young Children, 44*(6), 55–61.

National Black Child Development Institute. (1987). *Child care in the public schools: Incubator for inequality?* Washington, DC: Author.

Payzant, T. W. (1992). New beginnings in San Diego: Developing a strategy for interagency collaboration. *Phi Delta Kappan, 74,* 139–146.

Phillips, D.A., & Howes, C. (1987). Indicators of quality in child care: Review of the research. In D. A. Phillips (Ed.), *Quality in child care: What does research tell us?* Research Monograph of the National Association for the Education of Young Children, 1. Washington, DC: NAEYC.

Richardson, J., Dwyer, K., McGuin, K., Hansen, W., Dent C., Johnson, C. A., Sussman, S. Y., Brannon, B., & Flay, B. (1989). Drug and alcohol use among eighth grade children who look after themselves after school. *Pediatrics, 84,* 556–566.

Rodman, H., Pratto, D., & Nelson, R. (1985). Child care arrangements and children's functioning: A comparison of self-care and adult care children. *Developmental Psychology, 21,* 413–418.

Stoney, L. (1994). *Promoting access to quality child care: Critical steps in conducting market role surveys and establishing rate policies.* Washington, DC: Children's Defense Fund.

U.S. Department of Education. (1993). *Together we can: A guide for crafting a profamily system of education and human services.* Washington, DC: Author.

U.S. Department of Education. (1994). *Strong families, strong schools: Building community partnerships for learning.* Washington, DC: Author.

U.S. Department of Labor. (1993). *1993 handbook on women workers: Trends and issues.* Washington, DC: Author.

Whitebook, M., Phillips, D., & Howes, C. (1989). *Who cares? Child care teachers and the quality of care in America.* (*National Child Care Staffing Study*), pp. 10–13. Oakland, CA: Child Care Employee Project.

Zigler, E. F. (1987, September). *A solution to the nation's child care problem: The School of the 21st Century.* Address presented at the National Health Policy Forum, Washington, DC.

Zigler, E. F., & Finn-Stevenson, M. (1994). School's role in the provision of support services for children and families: A critical aspect of program equity. *Educational Policy, 8*(4), 591–606.

Zigler, E. F., & Valentine, J. (Eds.). (1979). *Project Head Start: A legacy of the War on Poverty.* New York: Free Press.

14

Collaborative Models of Service Integration

Gwen Morgan

Collaborative models of service integration embedded in a policy perspective will have a positive impact on all children from birth to the start of kindergarten, a group for which there is no single recognized system for delivery of early childhood care and education. Further, child day care resource and referral agencies have the potential to be the mediating structures that render collaboration possible, and should be strengthened and supported. Preconditions for successful collaboration, differences between programmatic and policy collaborative models, and the "eagle-eye" versus the "organization-centric" view of integration are discussed.

Gwen Morgan, M.S., is Founding Director, Center for Career Development in Early Care and Education, Wheelock College, Boston, MA.

Speakers and writers frequently quote an African proverb, "It takes a whole village to raise a child," when seeking to persuade us that caring communities, with a commitment to necessary services and a focus on the family, are essential to the support of families with children. But at a conference on the Carnegie report, *Starting Points: Meeting the Needs of Our Youngest Children*, in April 1994, several speakers invoked the village image to make the point that communities themselves are endangered, with Shorr stating that "The village has disintegrated" [Schorr 1994].

Strong interest currently exists in creating new models for helping in communities that would restore the values of the village [Carter 1994; Goodlad 1992; Jackson et al. 1994; Kirst 1992]. One model of service integration [Lawson 1993] even refers to its work as "family support villages." Some models of service delivery focus holistically on needs identified by the individuals or families served, try to break down artificial walls between disciplines and bureaucracies, bring professionals from different systems into collaborative relationships, and involve the families themselves (the users) in planning solutions. These programmatic models frequently target low-income populations.

At the same time, interest is also growing in improving the systems that affect the quality and cost of service delivery, particularly those systems affecting families with young children. The interest in improving programmatic models and the interest in improving systems are not necessarily the same interest, however, although they overlap. One seeks to improve programs and their relationships with those they serve; the other seeks to improve overall policy for program funding, supportive infrastructure, and quality assurance.

Collaborative Models for Service Integration

Both the federal government and private foundations are expressing interest in community-based models for focusing services on the family. Lawson and Hooper-Briar [1994] classify these models into four types: home- and neighborhood-based service centers or family resource centers (often in public housing); community-based service centers or family resource centers (one-stop shopping); school-linked delivery of services to families; and school-based comprehensive services to families.

These models might be based in a housing project (often centering on child day care), a health/social service complex, a local school, a shopping center, a community health center, or some other community base that families find to be a comfortable and natural setting to go to for services. A few child care resource and referral agencies (CCR&Rs) are broadening their scope and transforming themselves into family resource centers.

Regardless of the setting, the same collaborators need to work together: the health system, including mental health; the welfare/social service system; law enforcement agencies; the school system; recreation and cultural agencies; and the early childhood system, including Head Start, the schools, and a wide diversity of homes and centers from which government and parents purchase child day care/early childhood education.

Any of the community-based models might be conceptualized as hubs of family support villages, the attractive image used by Lawson and Hooper-Briar [1994] to characterize a school-based model. One model might create a hub in the community by co-location of services, counting on proximity to bring about increased collaboration among providers of service and increased convenience for consumers of service. Another model might create a hub by becoming the funding agent of the different service systems targeting a certain population, with collaborative agreements and waived bureaucratic rules leading to increased integration. Presumably, a model might create a hub by changing the systems themselves, actually replacing the different agencies that serve families.

For families with school-age children, schools are often chosen as an appropriate hub. They are a universal service for this population of children and their families, although even they do not encompass children younger than kindergarten age. Most models of service integration, however, are not generally created for universally serving all families; they are usually targeted to low-income families or families with problems and limited access to services.

On the one hand, these models may bring some needed order to a fragmented service system, at least from the perspective of those needing and using direct services. On the other hand, they may overlap one another and add to, rather than solve, the problem of service fragmentation and complexity in the community. The real challenge for those working toward collaboration is making sure that efforts to improve the community fit together, and that those efforts support the resources in place in the community.

Policy Perspectives vs. Program Perspectives

Models of service integration may be viewed from a programmatic perspective or from a policy perspective. The two are not the same. In fact, the programmatic perspective that has predominated since the 1960s is in part responsible for the large number of categorical funding sources, the turf battles, and the fragmentation among funded programs. Esterline wrote [1976: 1–4] that "Policy is an official agreement among people that we will act in predictable ways because to do so is in the public interest. Program, on the other hand is a specific action targeted to a specific group designed to solve a specific problem."

Program, Esterline said, is the enemy of true policy. It creates gaps and overlaps, and encourages covert and overt competition, stalemating, and turf guarding. Fragmentation is not solved by the creation of another competing program. The overly narrow professional disciplines created by higher education, professionalism, and credentialing systems also inhibit holistic service. Models of service integration designed from a programmatic perspective use collaborative and interprofessional service efforts to correct the fragmentation, overspecialization, and lack of focus on the consumer's view of needs. The program approach itself, however, may be a part of the problem, and not necessarily a solution.

The policy perspective, in contrast, focuses not on the agency delivering a service but on the systems of the community, the reduction of duplication, the establishment of accountability through consolidation or coordination of funds, and the creation of linkages. The policy perspective becomes especially important for the critical years between birth and the start of kindergarten, because there is no single recognized system for delivery of child day care to families with children of this age, and no commitment to universalizing access to such programs.

Programmatic models of service integration differ from policy models in two aspects.

1.   Programmatic models are targeted to certain population groups.

In general, the new collaborative models are seldom intended to replace the way that helping services are delivered to the middle class in the community. They focus on impoverished families who lack access to the existing services. The report *All Our Children: The American Family Under Pressure* by Keniston and the Carnegie Council on Children [1977] contrasted the way in which the general population gets services and the stigmatizing way in which the poor are provided with similar services. Service integration models in general do not propose changes in the system used by the middle class. Although destigmatization may be a priority for these models, universalization is not usually a goal.

2.   Programmatic models proffer a comprehensive approach by concentrating a number of services in one place.

This might imply that comprehensive service and one-stop concentration is better in *all* cases. That assumption, reminiscent of the assumption that a big, comprehensive high school is better than a small one, may be a fallacy. The comprehensive service model, however, does not necessarily make this assumption on a policy level. The model is a program, not a policy. It makes no effort to persuade us that all services for all people are better if they are large enough to incorporate a full range of services on the premises.

Three major systems exist for funding and delivering early childhood services: Head Start, the schools, and purchase-of-service. Of these, purchase-of-service is by far the largest and the oldest. Some of the best quality programs—as well as some of the worst—can be found in this system. The country cannot afford to lose the best of the resources and knowledge that have accumulated in this system for more than 100 years.

Fragmentation, however, has resulted in mediocre to low quality in too high a percentage of this system, as well as in Head Start and the schools. For child day care, the policy perspective requires the creation of a system that plans for and delivers high quality services to all children—both fee-paying and subsidized—and not just to a targeted population of low-income families.

It is important not to confuse program with policy. Some excellent programs take place in quite small but rather autonomous facilities. For example, the Dandelion School, which received an award last year from *Working Mother* magazine for the high quality of its child care/education program, has just 17 children enrolled. Its only "comprehensiveness" lies in the breadth of approach of its tiny staff, and in the community linkages it has.

Care must be taken to preserve such small but excellent programs. From a service perspective, big is not automatically better. Bureaucratic systems are not automatically better than diverse small services. A governmental system of services in which small programs lose much of their autonomy would not be a policy improvement.

For example, the public school systems are striving for excellence by restoring some degree of autonomy to individual schools so that they can pursue and achieve excellence unencumbered by needless bureaucratic rules and policies stemming from the larger system. School-based management has been a goal for this system, and charter schools assert the same need for autonomy. Without school-based management or some means for greater autonomy, the schools cannot pursue excellence, and they cannot become effective community collaborators.

At the same time, the purchase-of-service system, which already has agency-based management, is thought by some to be in need of a more highly managed approach than it currently has. Others disagree. This desire to preserve diversity of auspices, choices for parents, and a degree of autonomy for the pursuit of excellence at the program level has led to the creation of a national infrastructure network of resource and referral agencies to support child day care programs.

Collaboration

Most models of collaboration have a program perspective. Head Start and the schools are beginning to collaborate with a programmatic approach, but neither system has made much progress in collaborating with the purchase-of-service system, or even in locating it. In fact, many of the models of service integration have failed to incorporate centers, nursery schools, and family child care homes—often because the leadership in schools and social services are not aware of how to access leadership in this nonsystem.

In general, even the largest child day care center is smaller than the smallest of schools. Because child day care services are small, with a high degree of autonomy, the number of child day care centers is large. Community collaboration and funding of this system are possible only through some central intermediate structure. A nationwide system of CCR&Rs fulfills this function, although their strength varies from one community to the next.

In some communities, CCR&Rs are supported by state and federal funds, United Way contributions, and business dollars, and effectively link parents to programs in schools, Head Start, and the purchase-of-service system. They provide access for potential funders and service delivery collaborators to reach the many programs. In other communities, CCR&Rs are weak and underfunded. CCR&Rs are in place as a network across the country, however, and have an effective national organization: the National Association for Child Care Resource and Referral Agencies (NACCRRA).

The CCR & R system constitutes the major link for child care community programs to funding sources and collaborating services. Curiously the planners of school-linked services seldom reach child day care through this system. It may be that the CCR&R system itself lacks awareness of its important mediating role of accessing the child day care system in behalf of those who wish to collaborate with them.

Vantage Points for Integration

Integration models can be seen from an agency perspective, from an eagle-eyed vantage point above the entire community, or from both. Those looking from the perspective of the school or other agency in the community may reasonably ask, "How can my service, my organization, my system, be more effective in behalf of families in this community?" Even though this is a reasonable question, it is important that this organizational perspective not be the only vantage point. Organization-centricism is a barrier to collaboration.

A view from the agency window can be contrasted with the eagle-eye view of the community that asks, "What are the service systems used by families in this community that should be linked to achieve greater effectiveness?" The eagle-eye view requires a better understanding of the culture of the community than most leaders have been trained to have, and may represent a future direction for professional training of community leaders. The understanding of the culture of the community is a necessity for school principals, as well as leaders in health, social service, and resource and referral agencies.

Kagan [1991] identified four related kinds of service integration, based on their source, which have been expanded by Lawson and Hooper-Briar [1994] to five, as follows:

- **Client-Centered Integration:** Persons served constitute the source (e.g., consumer-guided work).
- **Provider-Centered Integration:** Parameters of professional specialization and interprofessional relations constitute the source (e.g., integrated staffing, role change).
- **Program-Centered Integration:** Delivery systems for services and goods constitute the source (e.g., co-location, fiscal linkages, shared information systems).
- **Organization-Centered Integration:** Organizational structures and cultures constitute the source (e.g., new umbrella organization, new authority systems).
- **Policy-Centered Integration:** Local, regional, state, and national policies constitute the source (e.g., eligibility and access criteria, funding streams, accountability criteria and procedures).

These classifications represent planning perspectives. Lawson and Hooper-Briar [1994] point out that a synergy ideally exists among the five kinds leading to a broad agenda for systemic change, rather than an overly narrow view from only one perspective.

Visions

Overlapping visions can lead to covert conflict and stalemating. Those planning for collaboration must be aware of the visions of others. To succeed, efforts must combine the following three compatible visions:

- Family-centered service integration at the community
  level (a programmatic vision);
- Child-focused, family-centered programs for young
  children (another programmatic vision); and
- Redesigned funding for high quality child day care
  programs, including Head Start, the schools, and the
  purchase-of-service system (a policy vision).

The present fragmented system is clearly dysfunctional and
is reminiscent of the categorical funding streams of the 1960s.
Collaboration as a theme was frequently discussed during that
earlier period, and the holy grail of service integration was ener-
getically pursued. Lessons learned from that period should be
applicable today.

The Community Coordinated Child Care (4–C) concept,
abandoned by the federal government, has persisted at state and
local levels and has had more effect on current communities than
may be generally recognized. 4–C brought divergently funded
groups in child day care and education together around the same
community table, including funding decision makers, service
providers, and parents. Some communities used the 4–C mechanism to coordinate all children's services; others focused only on
child day care. Many current leaders in child day care found out
through 4–C how hard it is to collaborate, particularly in urban
areas [Morgan 1971].

The 4–C concept was implemented in one of two ways by
various communities. Some communities implemented it from a
policy perspective and made sure that funding streams were
coordinated and family focused. These policy models worked
well and actually changed the system for child day care delivery
in some areas where categorical funding had not created strong
vested interests and turf battles. Other communities viewed 4–C
as a program that captured many funding streams for one multi-
funded program, which coexisted with other programs rather
than changing the system. These outcomes are indicative of the
differences between a policy and a program perspective.

Preconditions for Successful Collaboration

During the 1960s and early 1970s, Esterline [1976] and others identified the following elements as preconditions for successful coordination at the community level:

- knowledge of the different systems/agencies;
- shared perceptions of the shortage of resources;
- consonance of values;
- shared vision;
- autonomy to act and lack of rigidity of rules; and
- responsiveness of funding sources (bottom-up met by top-down).

These elements appear to be as valid today as they were 20 years ago. If we are serious about achieving community collaboration, knowledge of the different agencies in the community is an essential strand in professional education. A leader cannot collaborate without knowledge of the community and its system of services. The eagle-eye view must be taught.

Consonance of values may be achieved by focusing on families and validating their own views of their needs and solutions, just as a focus on the customer has corrected many of the problems of quality faced by businesses, schools, and other types of organizations affected by the Total Quality Management movement. The other elements serve as a reminder that a local community will not be able to deliver integrated services or make effective use of funding streams without policy change, responsiveness, and leadership at the state and federal levels [Morgan 1971].

Trends in Disciplinary Frameworks

There may be one more precondition for collaboration—helping professionals must be able to communicate with one another across their conceptual frameworks. If overspecialization has impeded the ability of helping professionals to work together with a holistic focus on the family, then the academic community bears some responsibility for change. Fortunately, the academic preparation of professionals in the helping fields, particularly health, social work, and education, has begun to be affected by the strong movement toward a holistic and family-centered philosophy. Those who prepare professionals are aware of the Tower of Babel effect of separate professional disciplines, which have made collaboration more difficult, and are rising to the challenge.

Lawson [1993] identifies three disciplinary frameworks for collaboration across disciplines: interdisciplinary or multidisciplinary, cross-disciplinary, and transdisciplinary. The first brings together a group of specialists from different fields to give different perspectives in turn. This model was a goal in the child care field in the 1950s and was seldom realized because of its cost. It may have inspired Head Start's goal of comprehensiveness.

The cross-disciplinary framework brings specialists from closely allied fields together to restructure the assumptions and ideas of their traditional disciplines. It occurs naturally when a person trained in one discipline enters roles commonly held by a second discipline. The child day care field has benefited from some cross-disciplinary effects when social workers fill roles in the early childhood field, and vice versa.

The interdisciplinary and crossdisciplinary frameworks build from the strengths of the traditional disciplines. Transdisciplinary work, in contrast, assumes that task completion is being limited by traditional frameworks and assumptions of individual disciplines. New intellectual frameworks and critical thinking are applied in order to transcend these limitations.

Conclusion

Models of service integration, whether based in schools, in family resource centers, or in other settings, are not incompatible with policy efforts to create a child day care infrastructure. They may be perceived, however, as competing approaches, and this perception may impede support for one or the other. In addition, while school-based models as well as other models may improve service delivery—and are therefore worthy of enthusiastic support as programs—they are not adequate as policy solutions for the fragmentation of funding for child day care.

Infrastructure models that support a diverse system of child day care, on the other hand, may improve child day care policy, and are worthy of enthusiastic support for that reason. CCR&Rs are the strongest model at present, and should be strengthened further so that every community has an infrastructure agency, devoid of turf biases, that helps parents make choices by providing them with information about available options, information on quality and how to choose the best quality care, and family supportive telephone counseling. These same community-based agencies provide other infrastructure support such as training, supply building, community planning, data collection, policy reports, and assistance to employers. In many communities, these will be the mediating structures that make collaboration possible. ◆

References

Carnegie Corporation of New York. (1994). *Starting points: Meeting the needs of our youngest children.* New York: Author.

Carter, J. L. (1994). Moving from principles to practice: Implementing a family-focused approach in schools and community services. *Equity and Choice, 10*(3), 4–9.

Esterline, B. (1976). *Coordination: A conceptual model and practical consideration.* Paper presented to the Education Commission of the States National Seminar on State Capacity Building, Boston, MA.

Goodlad, J. (1992). *Toward educational communities.* Cincinnati, OH: Education Commission of the States National Seminar on State Capacity Building.

Jackson, B., Krasnow, J., & Seeley, D. (1994). *The league of schools reaching out: New York City cluster building family-school-community partnership report, 1990–93.* Boston: Institute for Responsive Education.

Kagan, S. L. (1991). *United we stand: Collaboration for child care and early education services.* New York: Teachers College Press.

Keniston, K., & The Carnegie Council on Children. (1977). *All our children: The American family under pressure.* New York: Harcourt, Brace, & Jovanovich.

Kirst, M. J. (1992). Changing the system for children's services: Building linkages with schools. In Council of Chief State School Officers (Ed.), *Ensuring success through collaboration.* Washington, DC: Council of Chief State School Officers.

Lawson, H. A., & Hooper-Briar, K. (1994, April). *Informational and technical assistance materials for interprofessional collaboration and service integration initiatives.* Paper presented at a meeting of Wheelock College faculty. Oxford, OH: Miami University School of Education and Allied Professions.

Lawson, H. A. (1993) *Toward healthy learners, schools, and communities: Footprints on a continuing journey* (Work in Progress Series No. 3). Seattle, WA: Institute for Social Enquiry.

Morgan, G. G. (1971). *Evaluation of the 4–C concept.* Washington, DC: Day Care and Child Development Council of America.

Schorr, L. B. (1994, April 13–14). Presentation at Carnegie Corporation of New York Starting Points Conference.